The Poor in the Ecclesiology
of Juan Luis Segundo

American University Studies

Series VII
Theology and Religion
Vol. 113

PETER LANG
New York • San Francisco • Bern
Frankfurt am Main • Paris • London

Mary Kaye Nealen

The Poor in the Ecclesiology of Juan Luis Segundo

PETER LANG
New York • San Francisco • Bern
Frankfurt am Main • Paris • London

Library of Congress Cataloging-in-Publication Data

Nealen, Mary Kaye
    The poor in the ecclesiology of Juan Luis
Segundo / Mary Kaye Nealen.
      p. cm. — (American university studies. Series
VII, Theology and religion ; v. 113)
    Includes bibliographical references.
    1. Segundo, Juan Luis.   2. Church—History of
doctrines—20th century.   3. Liberation theology.
4. Poverty—Religious aspects—Catholic Church.
5. Catholic Church—Doctrines—History—20th century.
I. Title.   II. Series.
BX1746.N46 1991   261.8′34569′092—dc20   91-3910
ISBN 0-8204-1595-2   CIP
ISSN 0740-0446

Die Deutsche Bibliothek-CIP-Einheitsaufnahme

Nealen, Mary Kaye:
The poor in the ecclesiology of Juan Luis Segundo /
Mary Kaye Nealen.—New York; Berlin; Bern;
Frankfurt/M.; Paris; Wien: Lang, 1991
   (American university studies : Ser. 7, Theology and
religion ; Vol. 113)
   ISBN 0-8204-1595-2
NE: American university studies / 07

The paper in this book meets the guidelines for permanence and
durability of the Committee on Production Guidelines for
Book Longevity of the Council on Library Resources.

© Peter Lang Publishing, Inc., New York 1991

Printed in the United States of America.

Dedicated to
Vincent,
Emilie,
Ignace,
and Esther,
whose hearts have been with the poor.

ACKNOWLEDGMENTS

The author gratefully acknowledges Orbis Books for permission to reprint from the following works of Juan Luis Segundo, translated by John Drury: *The Community Called Church*, 1973; *Grace and the Human Condition*, 1973; *Our Idea of God*, 1973; *The Sacraments Today*, 1974; *Evolution of Guilt*, 1974; *The Hidden Motives of Pastoral Action*, 1974; *The Liberation of Theology*, 1979; *Faith and Ideologies*, 1984; *The Historical Jesus of the Synoptics*, 1985; *The Humanist Christology of Paul*, 1986; *The Christ of the Ignatian Exercises*, 1987; *An Evolutionary Approach to Jesus of Nazareth*, 1988. Also reprinted by permission: Clodovis Boff and Leonardo Boff, *Introducing Liberation Theology*, translated by Paul Burns, New York: Orbis Books, 1986; John Eagleson and Philip Scharper, eds., *Puebla and Beyond: Documentation and Commentary*, New York: Orbis Books, 1979; Gustavo Gutierrez, *We Drink from Our Own Wells*, translated by Matthew J. O'Connell, New York: Orbis Books, 1984; and Latin American Episcopate, *Evangelization in Latin America's Present and Future* in *Puebla and Beyond*. Finally the author thanks Fr. Juan Luis Segundo for permission to reprint passages from *Teología abierta III: Reflexiones críticas*.

TABLE OF CONTENTS

PREFACE

As conventional wisdom maintains, a good question is worth a book. A question—many questions, in fact, which focus into one—has given rise to the book which follows. In the effort to explore in Juan Luis Segundo's thought what the situation of poor people means for the church, I owe much gratitude to those who first of all helped generate the questions and then encouraged the pursuit of answers.

To my family, especially my parents, I express thanks first. For the genesis of the questions lay in their compassionate and self-sacrificing love, and the inquiry has progressed with their persevering encouragement.

To my religious congregation, the Sisters of Providence, my debt of gratitude is many-faceted. During the preparation of this work, the leaders and members of St. Ignatius Province have given unstintingly of the financial and, particularly, the spiritual and emotional resources necessary to succeed. In addition, the Sisters of Providence of Bernarda Morin province, Chile, welcomed me into their homes and ministries for several months in 1986 to assist my research in every way they could.

To my many other hosts and hostesses in South America I extend heartfelt appreciation. Father Juan Luis Segundo made time in his extremely busy schedule to talk with me about issues related to his writings. Women and men in Chile, Brazil, Uruguay, Argentina, and Peru provided hospitality and facilitated a wide variety of experiences—theological, pastoral, social, and cultural—related to the church and the poor.

To my professors and classmates at the Catholic University of America, particularly Drs. Patrick Grantfield and Elizabeth Johnson, I voice deep gratitude. Their guidance and the breadth and integrative power of their knowledge have been of immense value. Many members of the faculty, staff, and administration at the College of Great Falls have encouraged and assisted the completion of this volume. The help of Ms. Susan Lee, reference librarian, in obtaining materials has been invaluable. James and Robin Dodds have expertly prepared the manuscript for publication.

To each of these persons and to all my companion searchers I say, "Thank you for the questions as well as for the outcome." The inquiry continues.

Great Falls. Montana
August 1991

INTRODUCTION

In the late 1970's, Juan Luis Segundo wrote in the preface of *Theologies in Conflict: The Challenge of Juan Luis Segundo* by a fellow Jesuit, Alfred Hennelly: ". . . having probed more deeply into this book, which is largely devoted to my own thinking, I think I have every right to expect that it will not join the ranks of the consumer theology that now overwhelms us even more than we may think."[1] What Juan Luis Segundo desired—if the author felt compelled to write a book about him at all—was that the writing represent a genuine dialogue for the sake of vital concerns in that author's own setting.

For Segundo himself is vigorously engaged with his setting. His environment is marked by vast, dehumanizing poverty and by profound political and religious change. Segundo, like his contemporary Latin American theologians, has formulated a theology which relates the Christian concept of salvation to the process of full humanization already begun in history. God's reign, which comes to transform the miserable situation of the poor, is at work within a single order of history and grace.

Proclaimed and inaugurated by Jesus, God's reign becomes manifest in the church as a faithful, prophetic community of Christian disciples at the service of the poor in the world.

The engagement with reality and desire for the full humanity of all people are essential values for Segundo in his theology. They also orient this study, which it is to be hoped, will be more than "another book about Segundo." It is an attempt to join the practical and interpretative movement for change which Segundo calls the "hermeneutic circle."[2] "And the circular nature of this interpretation stems from the fact that each new reality obliges us to interpret the word of God afresh, to change reality accordingly, and then to go back and reinterpret the word of God again. . . ."[3]

Within this wider purpose, then, of the most effective action possible on behalf of one's human sisters and brothers, the specific objective of the following volume emerges. It is to investigate systematically the theological meaning of the poor in the works of Segundo, to analyze the role of the poor in his ecclesiology, and to evaluate his position. This will be done in six chapters.

Chapter One will explore the historical context and theological method of Segundo's ecclesiology. The first part will survey his Latin American, Uruguayan, and postconciliar setting. It will highlight aspects of history which relate to the church's mission of service to the world, especially to the poor. It will point up as well those elements of history which help to explain his minority concept of the church. The second part will provide an overview of Segundo's theological method.[4] It will give particular attention to the hermeneutic circle and to existentialist, Marxist, and evolutionary influences on his thought.

Chapter Two will examine the identity and role of the poor in Segundo's project. It will first address the question: Who are "the poor" in Segundo's thought? It will summarize and characterize his general or implicit references to them. It will then investigate specific usage of "the poor" in regard to the Old Testament, the time of Jesus, and contemporary society. Following this identification, the chapter will analyze the role of the poor as Segundo presents it in relation to history, to scripture, and to Christian praxis.

Chapter Three will be the first of three central chapters on the significance of the poor for the church. These three will each develop one part of a synthetic statement made by Segundo in *Reflexiones críticas*, "The church, if it wants to be faithful to the gospel, can only be a prophetic community at the service of the poor, marginalized, and dehumanized people of the earth."[5] Chapter Three will develop "to be faithful to the gospel." It will explore the gospel foundation for this ecclesial vocation, the nature of the faith response, and the possibility that this response can be that of a majority.

Chapter Four will take up the "prophetic community" of the definition. It will focus first on the community formed by Jesus' disciples. It will then investigate the demands which such a prophetic function places upon them.

Chapter Five will concentrate on the third part of the definition, "the service of the poor, marginalized, and dehumanized people of the earth." It will respond to two questions: Are the poor subjects or objects of the church's mission? What are the implications for the nature, sacramental life, and morality of the church defined in terms of its service to the poor of the world?

Chapter Six will then offer critical reflections on eight prominent aspects of Segundo's thought related to the place of the poor in his ecclesiology. These aspects are: (i) his method in general; (ii) the identity of the poor; (iii) popular religion; (iv) the political dimension; (v) the interpretation of scripture; (vi) the nature and mission of the church; (vii) response to the teaching authority of the church; and (viii) the relationship of the poor and the church. A conclusion will follow this assessment.

It is hoped that the value of this study will be threefold: First, to encourage an appreciation of Juan Luis Segundo's contribution to contemporary ecclesiology as an act of collaboration in God's work of transforming the inhuman lot of the poor; second, to foster theological work from the side of the poor in the church of North America as well as of Latin America; and third, to assist the critical consciousness of North American Christians who desire to commit themselves more deeply to the church's mission with and for the poor.

NOTES

1. (Maryknoll, N.Y.: Orbis Books, 1979), xviii.

2. *The Liberation of Theology*, trans. John Drury (Maryknoll, N.Y.: Orbis Books, 1979), 7-38; henceforth *LT*.

3. *LT*, 8.

4. Note may be made here of the language which Segundo uses to refer to human beings. Throughout his work, he ordinarily uses such terms as "el hombre" ("man"), "el laico" ("lay man"), and "los pobres" ("the poor [men]") without adverting to their connotations of male exclusivity. An example appears in his 1984 volume, *Reflexiones críticas* where Segundo speaks on p. 11 about "the most human solutions to the problems of men" ("las soluciones más humanas a los problemas de los hombres"). (*Teología abierta* III [Madrid: Ediciones Cristiandad, 1984], henceforth referred to as *RC*. It is the yet untranslated portion of a new edition of Segundo's early series, *Teología abierta para un laico adulto*, A Theology for Artisans of a New Humanity [Maryknoll, N.Y.: Orbis Books, 1973-74]).

   In the following study this is my practice: When I use my own translations, I employ the more inclusive forms such as "person" or "humanity." When I utilize published translations I quote Segundo as translated. A difference exists between the publications by Orbis Press of Segundo's earlier works in English and his later ones. In the series *A Theology for Artisans of a New Humanity* (1973-74), non-inclusive language is customary. In the later series *Jesus of Nazareth Yesterday and Today* (1984-88), inclusive language for both God and human beings prevails. This fact suggests that language which refers more equitably to both women and men is an editorial decision of Orbis Press and not of Segundo himself.

5. ". . . la Iglesia, si quiere ser fiel al evanglio, sólo puede ser una comunidad profética al servicio de los pobres, marginados y deshumanizados de la tierra" (*RC*, 159).

1

JUAN LUIS SEGUNDO'S
CONTEXT AND METHOD

Ours is a new age of history with critical and swift upheavals spread-
ing gradually to all corners of the earth. . . . It is a situation that
challenges [people] to reply; they cannot escape.[1]

Thus *Gaudium et spes* pointed out the crucial nature of the events in
which the church of the late twentieth century finds itself. The challenge of
the events lies in the call to respond to the "hope and anxiety and wonder" of
the people they affect. And the people so affected are often those outside the
centers of power in the world, the poor and dehumanized. Well before the
Second Vatican Council published these words, Juan Luis Segundo accepted the challenge to reply to the urgent questions which faced, and
continue to face, the church in the world.

Therefore, the first chapter of this study of the poor in the ecclesiology
of J. L. Segundo will survey the history which has given rise to the questions
and shaped his reply. The survey will give attention to elements of history
related to the church's mission of service to the world, especially to the
marginalized. It will note as well within this history the minority-majority
dynamic so central to Segundo's ecclesiology regarding the poor. The
chapter will then examine Segundo's theological method grounded on this
history. It will demonstrate how the experience of poverty and dehumanization formed the basis of his entire theology and specifically of his
ecclesiology.

HISTORICAL CONTEXT

Three particular aspects of history strongly influenced Segundo's theology. He is a Latin American ecclesiologist, whose particular experience of the poor and of the church was influenced but not determined by the four hundred years of Christian history on his continent. He is an Uruguayan theologian shaped by the history and culture of the Plate River region, a history little emphasized in North America and a culture distinctive in South America. He is a postconciliar thinker, who has not only drawn from but contributed to the renewed, inculturated faith which the triple event of Vatican II, Medellín, and Puebla epitomize. Part One of this chapter will explore these three aspects in turn.

LATIN AMERICAN THEOLOGIAN

The world in which the colonial church existed was to a large extent an imperial world. On May 4, 1493, Pope Alexander VI granted to the Catholic kings of Spain and Portugal dominion over the Indies and the exclusive privilege of Christianizing the natives. This *real patronato* or royal patronage of the church resulted in virtually absolute jurisdiction by the kings over ecclesiastical affairs in Latin America.[2] Offspring of medieval Christendom, this church-state unity embodied a belief that the finality of the church and that of the state were identical: to effect the salvation of the world.[3] While such a unique degree of control afforded benefits to both church and crown, it produced a church that was at once powerful in money and influence and weak in evangelizing mission.

Within the largely hierarchical and triumphal outlook of the colonial church, certain minority perspectives were nevertheless evident. Persons such as Antonio de Montesinos, O.P. (d. 1545), Bartolomé de Las Casas, O.P. (1474-1566), José de Acosta, S.J. (1539-1600), and Bernadino de Sahagún, O.F.M. (d. 1510) reflected on the reality of conquest and evangelization from the side of persons outside the centers of power, and they challenged the prevailing view. Contemporary Latin American theologies of liberation look with pride to their roots in the theology generated by the efforts of Las Casas, defender of the Indian people, and of other likeminded prophets.[4]

The nineteenth century brought the European wars of independence, the force of the Inquisition employed against revolutionary movements in the

Spanish colonies, and the growing wealth of the Latin American church. Following the emergence of the new Latin American republics, it became clear that the institutional church would not soon regain its temporal power in league with the state. Desiring to reinvigorate church life and improve communications, however, Pope Leo XIII convened a Plenary Council of Latin American Prelates in Rome in 1899.[5] The bishops addressed at the council such problems as religious ignorance, superstition, socialism, Masonry, and the press. It is true that the council emphasized the defense of the faith more than active evangelization. Nevertheless, it succeeded in generating a "collegial consciousness" among the Latin American bishops that held important implications for the future.[6]

Cultural life also fostered a new ecclesial vitality. Latin American intellectuals were increasingly disenchanted with the positivist and materialist values of the liberals. Among the former, the humanistic Arielists[7] stimulated a renewed look at religious and theological principles.[8] A Catholic intellectual renewal took place as well. The first Catholic universities were founded in Santiago and Lima, and a strong neothomist intellectual current developed in the early part of the twentieth century.[9]

In this more positive atmosphere, the Latin American bishops began to form the laity in Catholic Action groups. The new Catholic Action movement, which became officially established throughout the continent in the 1930's, in effect expanded upon the ministry of Catholic associations and workers' clubs already active for more than sixty years. In a society increasingly marked by alienated masses of working class people, the church under the impetus of the social encyclical of Pope Leo XIII in 1891, *Rerum novarum*, showed an enhanced comprehension of its role in contemporary society. As a result, by 1910 the church's advocacy of the workers was meeting open opposition from political conservatives.[10]

Students as well as workers participated extensively in Catholic Action.[11] While they worked primarily to relate the message of the gospel to their milieu, their movements exerted great political influence as well in both Catholic and secular universities. The Second Inter-American Study Week (1953) of student Catholic Actionists in Chimbote, Peru, was highly significant. It pointed clearly to a new emerging theological and ecclesial reality which explicitly addressed the social, cultural, economic, and political setting for Christian apostolic efforts.[12]

Influential as Catholic Action was in the life of the Latin American church, especially through its emphasis on a distinct role for the laity and its engagement with the concrete situation (which also relieved the pressure for revolutionary change), it was a basically conservative and elitist movement within a "new Christendom"[13] model of church. It aimed "to win back the masses to the faith and to quicken the social conscience of the upper classes so as to induce them, under the hierarchy's supervision, to take paternalistic measures to mitigate the suffering and isolation of the masses."[14] Within a few years of the students' 1953 meeting in Chimbote, it was clear that the theology of Catholic Action needed a different base.

The middle of the twentieth century also saw the emergence of socialist and national security states,[15] both of which challenged the "new Christendom" form of church-state relationship. As the Latin American nations struggled to gain the benefits of a capitalist economy,[16] great pressures built up, governments adopted repressive methods to maintain order, and the church looked for new means to carry on its evangelizing work. As one vehicle for this effort, the Latin American Episcopal Conference (CELAM) formed in 1955 at the conclusion of the International Eucharistic Congress in Rio de Janeiro.[17] Of great importance was the gradual development of the *communidades eclesiales de base* or basic Christian communities after 1950.[18] The next milestone in the relationship of the church and the world was the Second Vatican Council (1962-65), which will be examined later.

URUGUAYAN THEOLOGIAN

The Church of Uruguay

The church in Uruguay dated from the arrival of Jesuit and Franciscan missionaries in 1616 and the Indian Christians who lived in the first colonial settlement of 1620.[19] The country was at first subject to the bishop of Buenos Aires. In 1819, however, the last legal bishop of Argentina died, and King Ferdinand refused to nominate bishops for the Republic of Uruguay.[20] Uruguay lacked any service by a bishop for a time after 1819,[21] and waited for its own prelate until 1856.

Contemporary Uruguayan church history began with the first presidential term of José Batlle y Ordóñez in 1903.[22] Under Batlle, a strong advocate of Comtian positivism who viewed the church as extraneous to public life, separation of church and state occurred in 1916. Strong anticlericalism accompanied the prevailing secularization.[23] Paradoxically, while the Arielist reaction against materialism and utilitarianism contributed to a resurgence of Catholicism in Latin America generally, it did not overcome the strong spirit of laicism and agnosticism in Uruguay, where active Catholicism remained largely an elite lay endeavor.[24]

As a nation, Uruguayans enjoyed a high degree of social advancement and prosperity in the early part of the twentieth century. Nevertheless, the economic means to sustain it began to deteriorate. By the end of the 1950's, the violence and reactive government repression prevalent elsewhere in Latin America marked Uruguay as well. A group of urban guerrillas in Montevideo called the *Tupamaros* contributed to the unaccustomed culture of violence which faced the people and the church of Uruguay.[25]

Justifying their action by the terrorist activities of the *Tupamaros*, the military took over the government in 1973. In the twelve years of militia rule, 1,500 persons were taken political prisoners and 15,000 deprived of their political rights. A return to civilian government began under the patronage of the armed forces in 1981 with the presidency of Gen. Conrado Alvarez Armelino and the restoration of an enlarged Council of State.[26] In 1986, Julio María Sanguinetti Cairolo, leader of the then governing Colorado Party, was elected President of the republic and began his term by declaring amnesty for the nation's political prisoners. Following months of controversy, a law granting amnesty to members of the military charged with human rights violations from 1973-86 took effect in December 1986.[27]

During this time of turmoil, the offical church in Uruguay maintained a largely low-profile, conservative stance. While pastoral leaders spoke out in defense of human rights during the years of military rule, the practice of the Catholic faith, and particularly a prophetic practice, continued to be that of a minority. As recently as the visit of Pope John Paul II to Uruguay in May 1988, the London *Tablet* described church life in the country thus:

> . . . In terms of the Catholic faith Uruguay has been lost to the Church for most of this century. The anti-clerical tradition inherited from the beginning of this century has persisted, anti-religious legislation remains, and secularism is an important part of the political scene.[28]

The Theological Ministry of Segundo

Juan Luis Segundo's theology originated and matured in the midst of this political, social, cultural, and ecclesial environment. Born in Montevideo in 1925, he pursued his philosophy studies as a young Jesuit in Argentina and was ordained to the priesthood in 1955. After obtaining a licentiate in theology from the University of Louvain in 1956, he continued studies at the University of Paris. For the Doctorate in Letters granted there in 1963 he presented two dissertations. The first was entitled *Berdiaeff: Une réflexion chrétienne sur la personne*,[29] and the second a two-volume work on ecclesiology, *La cristiandad ¿una utopía?*[30]

After Segundo's return to Uruguay he founded the Peter Faber Center in March 1965. This center in Montevideo brought together specialists in theology and the social sciences[31] for study of the faith within the Uruguayan culture,[32] publishing *Perspectivas de Diálogo* as its official organ.[33] In 1975 the government suppressed the review and confiscated the publication materials; the following January in the face of the political hostility the Jesuit order closed the center itself.

The seminars which Segundo conducted for lay people and religious during the 1960's and early 1970's were important vehicles for his theological leadership. They generated his first series, *A Theology for Artisans of a New Humanity*,[34] and, less directly but truly, much of his subsequent writing. Yet because the theological reflection practiced during these short, intensive workshops also at times stimulated criticism of current church attitudes and practices, and encouraged commitment to persons outside the church, including dialogue with Marxists and other non-Christians, the seminars met opposition from diocesan authorities. When asked in the mid-1970's to cease the seminars, Segundo complied.

Segundo, nonetheless, continued to teach about faith and the church in their cultural context. His many courses included those at Cuernavaca, Mexico; postgraduate offerings in theology of liberation at the Jesuit house of studies in Belo Horizonte, Brazil; and instruction at the Instituto de Hombre in Montevideo and in Buenos Aires, Argentina.[35]

A further important aspect of Segundo's theological ministry, which has likewise been a part of his method, was his leadership of reflection groups. He formed the first group of adults inquiring about the meaning of their faith in 1963 upon the completion of his studies in Paris. The original group is still in existence, and has given rise to others. Some groups in Montevideo meet weekly; a large group there gathers each September for a yearly course, whose themes have often presaged the content of later books.[36] Other groups in more distant locations, such as Brazil and Canada, meet with him on occasion. All the reflection groups have the option for the poor as a necessary condition for belonging, although not all members work directly with the poor. Two groups in Montevideo, once a single group, comprise almost entirely younger, middle-class persons who work with the marginalized.[37]

POSTCONCILIAR THEOLOGIAN

On October 1, 1962, the Second Vatican Council convened in Rome. While this is not the place for a full discussion of the import of the Council, several points related to this study may be made. In all, 601 Latin American bishops participated in the Council;[38] the delegations from Latin America, Asia, and Africa constituted approximately forty percent of the episcopal membership.[39] Yet the Council documents do not reflect proportionately the character of this presence. Although the bishops early in the Council highlighted the urgent issues of peace and social justice,[40] numerous intra-church questions soon gained the floor. Important though they were, topics such as the vernacular in the liturgy, ecumenical openness, and religious freedom represented primarily northern hemispheric concerns which over-shadowed the socio-political priorities of southern Christians.[41]

Segundo acknowledged the support that Vatican II gave to the founda-tions of the faith renewal which had been developing in Latin America shortly before and during the time of the Council. Yet he maintained that only one document, *Gaudium et spes*, adopted at the end of the four years, stimulated a spirit of marked "enthusiasm, hope and renewal."[42] He per-ceived a close relationship in both content and method between this council document and the proceedings of the Medellín conference three years later. Yet he noted that "the Latin American bishops gained from Vatican II more a 'spirit' or a 'mentality' — if one wishes, an 'attitude' — than a strictly theological orientation."[43] In the Medellín documents, for example, little reference was made to the "more explosive and innovative" passages of *Gaudium et spes*. In contrast, "a generic spirit of 'service to humanity,' and this within human history, flows through all or almost all the documents of Medellín."[44]

A short three years after the close of the Vatican Council, the Latin American bishops in 1968 convoked their second general conference in Medellín, Colombia, to address the question of ecclesial and social transfor-mation. Segundo called the conference "a geographically situated version of Vatican II."[45] Of the sixteen documents they produced on the theme "The Church in the Present-Day Transformation of Latin America in the Light of the Council," three are particularly relevant to this study: "Justice," "Peace," and "Poverty of the Church."[46]

The ten years following Medellín were trying ones. Strong opposition to this new ecclesial direction and to the liberation theology[47] which arti-culated it arose in Europe and in Latin America.[48] The conservative members of

CELAM drew up under the leadership of the Secretary General, Archbishop Alfonso Lopéz Trujillo, a consultative document in November 1977 for a general conference to override the decisions of 1968.

The deaths of Popes Paul VI and John Paul I in 1978, and the election of Pope John Paul II delayed the beginning of the Third General Conference of CELAM. Yet when they convened in 1979 in Puebla, Mexico, the bishops confessed that in spite of Medellín, the 1971 Synod document on justice in the world (*Convenientes ex universo*), and Paul VI's *Evangelii nuntiandi*, the continent was in a more serious state than it had been ten years earlier. The social situation of the people was worse, the distance between rich and poor greater, and the oppressive structures stronger and more complex.[49]

By the end of the conference, after facing strong reactionary influences on the one hand and the mediating presence of Pope John Paul II on the other,[50] the bishops defined their evangelizing task in highly prophetic terms. It is true that the doctrinal portions of the final document possessed a more traditional character than the descriptions of the reality.[51] Yet in the document, which drew heavily upon *Evangelii nuntiandi*, the delegates described evangelization as a liberating process which upholds human rights, confirmed the importance of basic ecclesial communities, introduced new implementing themes, and reaffirmed the priority of the poor for the church.[52] By affirming the preferential option for the poor, the bishops vindicated Medellín and rejected charges that it represented approval of a Marxist class struggle. They situated it within the evangelizing mission of the church:

> With renewed hope in the vivifying power of the Spirit, we are going to take up once again the position of the Second General Conference of the Latin American episcopate in Medellín, which adopted a clear and prophetic option expressing preference for, and solidarity with, the poor. . . . We affirm the need for conversion on the part of the whole Church to a preferential option for the poor, an option aimed at their integral liberation.

> The vast majority of our fellow humans continue to live in a situation of poverty and even wretchedness that has grown more acute. We wish to take note of all that the Church in Latin America has done, or has failed to do, for the poor since the Medellín Conference. This will serve as a starting point for seeking out effective channels to implement our option in our evangelizing work in Latin America's present and future.[53]

SUMMARY

The historical context of Juan Luis Segundo's work has shown three major influences upon his ecclesiology: the history of the Latin American church since its colonial beginnings, the history and contemporary reality of the Uruguayan church, and the experience of Vatican Council II as implemented in Latin America through the episcopal conferences at Medellín and Puebla. This history has directly contributed to several aspects of Segundo's thought on the poor and the church: a church for the world, a minority church, and a church which mediates God's transforming action on behalf of the poor. The second part of the chapter will now present an overview of the method by which Segundo developed his thought on the church and the poor.

THEOLOGICAL METHOD

In *The Liberation of Theology*, originally published in 1975, Segundo articulated the theological method he had been using up to that point and which he has continued to employ. The core of the method is his hermeneutic circle,[54] for which he spelled out its necessary preconditions:

> . . . First I think it would be wise for me to reiterate the two preconditions for such a circle. They are: (1) profound and enriching questions and suspicions about our real situation; (2) a new interpretation of the bible that is equally profound and enriching.[55]

He went on to summarize the four essential stages of the circle:

> **Firstly** there is our way of experiencing reality, which leads us to ideological suspicion. **Secondly** there is the application of our ideological suspicion to the whole ideological superstructure in general and to theology in particular. **Thirdly** there comes a new way of experiencing theological reality that leads us to exegetical suspicion, that is, to the suspicion that the prevailing interpretation of the bible has not taken important pieces of data into account. **Fourthly** we have our new hermeneutic, that is, our new way of interpreting the fountainhead of our faith (i.e., Scripture) with the new elements at our disposal.[56]

This section will treat first the preconditions of Segundo's hermeneutical circle and then each of its stages by turn.

PRECONDITIONS OF THE HERMENEUTIC CIRCLE

The first precondition to which Segundo referred was "profound and enriching questions and suspicions." In an early work he had told of a striking question posed to him by an African delegate to a Young Catholic Worker conference in Rio de Janeiro. " 'On this continent which has been, practically speaking, Christian for four centuries, Christians have allowed these *favelas* [slums] to arise, and can live for days, months and years with this misery. What meaning then does the word Christianity have for you?' "[57] Segundo had discovered in that observation a lifelong source of stimulation for his theological and exegetical reflection.

Questions are powerful; instruments of understanding, they serve also as tools for change. In the preface of *From Society to Theology* Segundo asserted: "When domination turns from anonymous to open repression, the imperial center is attacked by questions. And the hour for us to speak arrives. Because all weapons rebound upon those who use them."[58] Not lightly did Segundo make profound questions a basis for his interpretive method.

The second precondition of the hermeneutic circle presumes an assent to both the possibility and the worth of new ways of understanding the bible. The young African worker's question above undoubtedly sends the serious Christian back to the scriptures with different ears and eyes. And in turn an altered grasp of the biblical message affects concrete actions toward improving a situation. New problems and questions continually arise throughout history, and "if our interpretation of Scripture does not change along with the problems" — Segundo held — "then the latter will go unanswered; or worse, they will receive old, conservative, unserviceable answers."[59]

In the author's view, this principle applies to Christian and non-Christian alike. The person committed to changing reality first needs to acknowledge that a given theology has an inherent bias. A liberating theology professes a dedication to the humanization of the world.[60] Thus for non-Christians and followers of Jesus alike a prejudice for humanization becomes the criterion for the rightness and meaning of life, and for a grasp of God's word. Segundo discovered the universal criterion at work in Jesus' Samaritan parable:

> A heart sensitive to others, a loving heart, finds **neighbors** wherever it gets a chance to approach a needy person with love. And only those who start from **pre**-judice in favor of the human being — even though

they may be pagans or atheists — understand the law and the will of Jesus' God.[61]

In short, the ability to enter into the hermeneutical circle as Segundo described it presumes two things: questions which penetrate the surface impressions of life and the willingness to allow new meanings of the bible to emerge from an interaction of the scriptures with a commitment to fuller human life for all.

STAGES OF THE HERMENEUTIC CIRCLE

Based on the questions which poverty and oppression provoke, Segundo's method comprises four stages. Springing from a professed partiality to fuller humanness for all people, it spirals through experience, suspicion, critique, and revision. These four moments encompass both theology and biblical interpretation.

Starting Point in Reality

In the first stage of Segundo's circle of interpretation one experiences reality in ways which generate ideological suspicion of what lies beneath appearances. This section will explore this first stage and two supporting convictions: the reality is historical, and it can be understood better through the insights of existentialist, Marxist, and evolutionary thinkers.

Reality is Historical

A renewed, liberating theology accepts thoroughly its own historical character: everything it deals with is shaped by history and has an impact on history. In regard to decision-making based on only one isolated aspect of a situation (for example, the decision to support a government because it is non-Marxist) Segundo noted:

> Ordinarily a religious — and Christian — evaluation made prior to, and outside of, an historical process presupposes that a reading and understanding of the gospel message provides one with absolute certainties. Thus, instead of relativizing the religious aspect of the process, one relativizes the process in the name of a gospel message that one supposedly has come to know and interpret correctly. No attempt is made, for example, to balance such things as people's

> suffering, humiliation, and death against the results — limited and
> human of course — that can be hoped for from the process.[62]

Further, Segundo judges that only when an absolute becomes concretized in history, with all the volition and creativity necessary for that to
happen, can it be a genuine absolute and not a false god:

> It is that we must recognize that every absolute must be pondered and
> realized anew over and over again amid the relativity of history. If we
> do not do that, if we give in to convenience, routine, or conservatism,
> then the absolute in which we say we believe will imperceptibly turn
> into an idol.[63]

If Segundo emphasizes that theology is historical, he also stresses that
history is theological. As will be seen shortly, he presents biblical history as
the process by which God educates human beings. A theology of history,
expressed in its essentials in *Gaudium et spes* and *Lumen gentium*, integrates
the unique role of Christ, the responsibility of human persons, and the
reciprocal service of church and society. Although it has not yet arrived at its
goal, history is already moving toward its completeness in Christ. " . . .The
progressive recapitulation of humanity in the Body of Christ . . . is effected
in the Church, not only when she loses her boundary-limits but also when,
within those limits, she takes cognizance of what is being fulfilled in history
and serves it."[64]

The notion of praxis is an important aspect of the theology of history.
Segundo subscribes to the definition of theology held by most liberation
theologians as "critical reflection on praxis."[65] Yet in his volume on Paul, he
made some important distinctions. Defining "praxis" as "practice grounded
in a theory [which is] in turn . . . nurtured and revised by new elements
discovered in experiential practice,"[66] he rejected oversimplifications of
praxis as a theological starting point:

> But it is not a simple matter to carry that precedence [of praxis prior to
> reflection] over to theology or any group discussion of the signifi-
> cance of Jesus of Nazareth.
>
> It is true that **reflection** is always a second act. But it is also true that
> experiences preceding us in time take on a certain **precedence** insofar
> as they constitute a totality with its own intrinsic unity that is indepen-
> dent of our own practice here and now. . . . We must put aside our own
> pragmatic urgencies for the time it takes to grasp the overall sig-
> nificance and importance of that historical complex by examining its
> various elements.[67]

Thus in granting the importance of praxis, he worked to maintain as well the coherence of the larger historical situation, past and present, beyond an immediate pragmatism.

In conclusion, Segundo has stressed the historical nature of existence itself. He frames history, and the role of the church in it, as a process where God is already working to bring all humanity to its fullness in Christ. Finally, he situates theological reflection in praxis in the sense of committed historical action.

Reality Understood in an Existentialist, Marxist, and Evolutionary Context

Existentialist Thought   Educated in Belgium and France in the 1950's and early 1960's, Segundo acquired an extensive knowledge of existentialist thinkers, among whom the Russian philosopher Berdyaev uniquely influenced his own thought. In the Introduction to *Berdiaeff*, Segundo noted the centrality of the person: "Whether in the content of the message or in the philosophical task, the person proves henceforth to be the keystone of the prophetic philosophy of Berdyaev."[68] Even the original title of his christological series, "The Person Today Before Jesus of Nazareth,"[69] symbolized the focus on the human person which he expressed in the first pages of *The Historical Jesus in the Synoptics*: "On the basis of the two human dimensions (**faith** and **ideology**) . . . , we will now try to determine methodically what contribution, if any, Jesus of Nazareth and the tradition stemming from him makes to the process of humanization."[70] Uruguayan and Russian shared the same central value.

Also highly significant for a theologian of liberation are the complementary emphases on liberty, love, and creativity which he discerned in the philosopher. In *Berdiaeff*, Segundo depicted the Russian "illuminating a whole sector of human experience, and certainly the most positive: that of love, of creation, of ecstasy; in short, those moments of fullness where the human being grasps the fundamental harmony between liberty and being."[71] Notice the similarity and continuity of Segundo's idea of liberty in "Concepción cristiana del hombre" ("A Christian Conception of the Human Being"): "Christianity sees in the liberty of each human person an irreducible value. God is love, and to love is always to begin by wanting to be free to be loved."[72]

While both Berdyaev and Segundo saw liberty and love closely related, the latter gave the linkage more prominence overall. Berdyaev perceived in the latter gave the linkage more prominence overall. Berdyaev perceived in love a manifestation of freedom (versus necessity); Segundo, the foundation of revelation, of Christianity, in fact, of all truth: ". . . God is love and . . . all effective love is converted into absolute value, in the only true absolute value of human existence."[73] In *A Community Called Church* Segundo spoke in similar terms: ". . . We have not been liberated by [the law] to live any way we choose; we have been liberated to follow a **new law**, one which is not hanging over us but is rather the very embodiment of our free being: the law of love."[74]

Liberty and love in turn engender creativity. That "heroic combat of the creative consciousness" of Berdyaev's *The Meaning of Creation*, opposed to necessity and obligation,[75] is prominent throughout Segundo's work as well. Transformed into a creator, the person acts out of a freedom which transcends legalism and forms a new basis for moral action.[76] This freedom results in a **"true and definitive** efficacy, which neither promises victories nor promotes triumphalism, [and] is rooted in creativity placed in the service of love and humanization."[77]

Briefly, these three themes related to the person — liberty, creativity, and love — represent a notable inheritance from the philosopher of religious experience, Nicholas Berdyaev.

Marxist Thought   Segundo employed Marxist ideas in a complex and highly nuanced way. Out of extensive study and dialogue with Marxists and other non-Christians — at whose service he believed the church to be — he retrieved the concept of ideology which he refashioned for his own theological purpose. From the work of such thinkers as Karl Marx, Friedrich Engels, Milan Machovec, and George Lúkacs he drew questions and insights which helped him articulate in the public arena his basic conviction that Christians are here on earth to make love effective by helping all people come to their full humanness.[78]

"Ideology," a term well-known for its use by Karl Marx and his disciples, played a prominent role in Segundo's system. He first gave extended treatment to the crucial pair of terms, "ideology" and "faith," in *The Liberation of Theology*. There he explained faith as the "ideal that one presumes will be satisfying" which gives direction to a person's choices, and ideology as the "means and ends used to attain" this ideal.[79] He made a further clarification, using the same complementarity of concepts to explain biblical revelation. "One element is permanent and unique: **faith**. The other is changing and bound up with different historical circumstances: **ideologies**."[80]

In *Faith and Ideologies,* where he articulated the foundation for his whole christological series, Segundo presented faith as the act of credence and the perception based on it which grounds every person's life:

> "Faith," conceived as a meaning-structure and a valuational structure, does not simply inform us about what we ought to do; in the life of the adult at least, it is also a crucial factor in deciding how that adult perceives reality. Faith, in other words, is not simply the way in which we endow our perception with some value; it is also a cognitive principle which enables us to see certain things rather than other equally obvious things.[81]

This fundamental human faith becomes religious faith as well when the person accepts "transcendent data," such as the message of Jesus, and the testimony of persons who witness to the values expressed in that transcendent data.[82]

Segundo then explained ideology, the anthropological counterpart to faith, in this way:

> I shall use the term "ideology" for all systems of means, be they natural or artificial, that are used to attain some end or goal. I could also say . . . that ideology is the systematic aggregate of all that we wish for in a **hypothetical** rather than an absolute way. In other words, it is every system of means.[83]

While, by the concept of ideology, the author referred to the production of an effect, he included in this concern for efficacy the elements of consciousness, theory, and science. He linked ideology to both aspects: doing something and being aware of what one is doing. He continued:

> I am going to use the word **ideology** for all human knowledge about **efficacy** (or **effectiveness**). The human knowledge in question deals with what will happen in the face of certain conditions or circumstances, or with the conditions one must satisfy if one wants certain results. . . . This type of knowledge always arises in subordination to values, or to satisfactions.[84]

In the light of the clarification which has been made of these two fundamental concepts, it will be easier to understand how Segundo drew upon Marxist philosophy. First of all, he rejected the tendency simply to designate Christianity a "faith" and Marxism an "ideology":

> To be sure, Christianity is not the only faith and Marxism is not the only ideology. In the cultural panorama of Western history Christian

faith has clashed with many ideologies. . . . Taking faith in a broader
anthropological sense, we also know that Marxism has engaged in
polemics against psychoanalytic thought and existentialist thought. . .
[and] against behaviorist sociology and its claims to be a values-free
science.[85]

Such polemic to the point of "anathematizing each other as a whole"[86]
works to the benefit of neither system. Rather, Segundo credited Marx with
a humanistic faith which, "even though depending in the last instance on the
mode of production of his age, enabled him in the first instance to place
himself in the service of the more human cause while so many others were
adapting themselves to the existing ideologies."[87]

In addition, the claim of Marxism to be a method of scientific criticism
provides Christianity with a useful tool.[88] Segundo recognized this by
saying:

What historical materialism does, to the extent that it avoids relapsing
into coarse determinism . . . is establish in a richer and more realistic
way the often unnoticed relationship between the values one professes
and the realizations one accepts. . . .

Nothing would seem more obvious than the fact that Christians need
that sort of **suspicion**, if Christianity is concerned about reality rather
than fiction.[89]

In other words, when he reflected on historical materialism in relation to
efficacy, Segundo found it valuable to the degree that it represents a scientific method, an ideology in the sense of a system of means. Equally, he
called it misleading insofar as it claims a scientific precision which it cannot
possess.

Segundo has presented a far more comprehensive examination of Marxist thought than these remarks represent. He showed a willingness to listen
to ideas and questions of many who espouse Marxism. Yet conversely he
judged that "the latter does not expect or value any doctrinal contribution
from faith as a corrective or complement to its own thought."[90] Furthermore,
if Christianity can profit from historical criticism in the order of ideology,
then (even apart from the issue of atheism[91]) Marxism lacks an appreciation
of the ways that values are transmitted culturally.

Evolutionary Thought   Some of the same values which were prominent in
the thinking of existentialist Nicholas Berdyaev appeared also in that of

anthropologist Pierre Teilhard de Chardin. Segundo recognizes the latter's regard for the person, in whom liberty, love, and creativity form an integral part of the human history which moves toward its culmination. Throughout Segundo's entire corpus, Teilhard's concept of evolutionary history has exerted a great influence.

In the early *Grace and the Human Condition* Segundo presented Teilhard de Chardin as a significant contributor to the new theology of history in *Gaudium et spes*, a unified history which takes human liberty and commitment seriously.[92] The French scientist-theologian emphasized positive, effective action within an evolution toward the Omega Point:

> . . . Teilhard censures those who are carried away by a disembodied idealism and who rest content with right intention alone. More than anyone else the Christian "knows" what the Christification of the world signifies. More than anyone else he knows that the definitive body of the Risen One is fashioned through human actions. So he, more than anyone, should show greater lucidity and responsibility in his activities.[93]

As he spoke of the ultimately positive movement of history toward the triumph of love, Segundo stressed the remarkable and minority character of this triumph. Basing his conclusions on the passage in Matthew and its parallel in Luke, "If you greet only your brothers, what is there extraordinary about that?,"[94] he commented on the extraordinariness, necessarily of a minority character, demanded of Christians

> because the triumph of love throughout the evolutionary process is never a quantitative one. It is a minority affair without being an elitist one. It is a minority affair because it wells up from the entropy-ridden base that continues to dominate quantitatively even on the human level. It is not elitist because the love which thus comes to life is at the service of negentropy in the universe. It structures the universe for syntheses that are richer, more human, more redemptive.[95]

In the final volume of *El hombre de hoy ante Jesús de Nazaret*, Segundo developed a contemporary evolutionary reading of Jesus' significance. While still influenced by Teilhard de Chardin,[96] he also incorporated the research of biologist-anthropologist Gregory Bateson.[97] He portrayed the circuit (as opposed to linear) movement of the universe toward its ultimate future.[98] He demonstrated that the flexibility needed for evolutionary movement depends upon the interplay of both entropy (change, adaptation) and negentropy (order, continuity). While such responsiveness or flexibility marked the life of Jesus, he argued, it often does not characterize Jesus' historical community. Only the reciprocal action of realistic historical commitment and the mystery of death and resurrection produces such flexibility.[99]

To summarize, Segundo expressed a conviction which underlies the first stage of the hermeneutical circle when he said "that a theology worthy of the attention of the whole human being . . . stems from a pretheological human commitment to change and improve the world."[100]   Such a commitment begins from the reality with a conscious partiality in favor of the human being which, it will be seen, is expressed particularly in an option for the poor. This section has surveyed three currents of thought which have influenced Segundo's theological project, and specifically   his hermeneutical task: existentialism, Marxism, and evolutionary thought. One notes that he said of the first stage, "there is our way of experiencing reality, which leads us to ideological suspicion." To what point of suspicion has this section led?

It has led to questions like the following. If existentialist thinkers represented by Nicholas Berdyaev have stressed the liberty, love, and creativity which are proper to the human person, then what prevents so many people in the world from living lives which manifest these values? If Marxist thinkers have proposed systematic criticism of social, political, and religious superstructures which do not correspond to people's need to make a decent living, then how has historical Christianity served this need in the light of Jesus' proclamation of good news for the poor? And if evolutionary thinkers such as Pierre Teilhard de Chardin and Gregory Bateson have envisioned the corporate fullness of human life toward which history moves, then to what extent has Christian theology assisted the integration of potentialities and limits — physical, mental, spiritual, and societal — which enables this fullness to come about? Stage two will help to deepen this questioning process.

Application of Ideological Suspicion

Stage two in the hermeneutic circle applies the ideological suspicion aroused in stage one to the systematized values or "ideological superstructure" of society in general and of theology in particular. Through it the theologian and reflective Christian continue to develop sensitivity toward other human beings by recognizing where their own motivations lie. They can more easily uncover the inconsistency of their values, and the incongruity of their actions with their values.

The gospels showed Jesus continually bringing to light hardness of heart and 'bad faith' where they existed in his listeners.[101] He did this in his confrontations with the Jewish authorities and through his "hermeneutical parables," such as that of the good Samaritan.[102] "Jesus' line of argument . . . points up the exact nature of the faith or the system of values underlying their religious interpretations (i.e., their ideology)."[103]

At the same time Jesus invited a conversion of thinking in the leaders and in the poor people themselves:

> It should be apparent that the polemical parables and these theological debates converge to form the overall strategy of Jesus in favor of the poor. He will dismantle the ideological mechanism wherewith the poor themselves turn the popular religion they practice into an instrument of oppression that benefits those with power in Israel.[104]

Yet because Jesus' situation was not identical to today's nor his manner of carrying out the criticism of distorted systems directly translatable to the present, disciplines appropriate to contemporary society are needed. This necessity flows from the "suspicion. . .that anything and everything involving ideas, including theology, is intimately bound up with the existing social situation in at least an unconscious way."[105] In light of this suspicion it needs to be asked, Where and to what extent has theology itself succumbed to the deviations of an unjust order?[106] Once the question is asked, the Christian can employ theories which enable people to study the **causes** of oppression.[107]

Segundo looks to the social sciences for help with this task. Cautiously assessing sociology's value to theology, he acknowledges that efforts to date have "certainly not solved the problem of the proper relationship and the possibility of collaboration between sociology and theology."[108] This said, Segundo declares politics to be the most valuable, in fact the essential, field to critique the systems which include theology. As a liberation theologian he sums up the close link that exists between faith or theology and politics:

> Liberation theology consciously and explicitly accepts its relationship with politics. First of all, it incorporates into its own methodology the task of ideological analysis that is situated on the boundary line between sociology and politics. And insofar as direct politics is concerned, it is more concerned about avoiding the (false) impartiality

of academic theology than it is about taking sides and consequently
giving ammunition to those who accuse it of partisanship.[109]

Segundo demonstrated a politically oriented ideological critique most
comprehensively in *Faith and Ideologies*. He did not try to single out "an
ideology," Marxist or otherwise, which interferes with a network of values
such as Christianity. Rather, he identified faith and ideology as two central
and interrelated dimensions of all human life, including the religious and the
political. He fashioned them conjointly into an analytical tool to "liberate
both the ideology and the faith from their one-sided, superficial, and self-
sufficient aspects."[110]

Using faith and ideology, Segundo examined Marxism "to salvage the
imperishable nucleus of the Marxist ideology insofar as it does relate
precisely to faith."[111] He found Marxist thought retrievable to the extent that
its humanistic values are recognized as the orientation of its (scientific)
historical criticism.[112] At the same time, Segundo challenged the church to
distinguish genuine Christian values from a purely cultural tradition. He
pointed out the twofold importance of such a distinction. If the church
engages in such criticism of its own faith and ideologies, it can "unlock
mental mechanisms, liberate thinking, and thus gradually transform tradition itself and return it to the people in the form of richer energy equa-
tions."[113] If it fails to do so, it risks that its committed, thinking members
will reject the elements which it needs to transmit its values adequately
through the culture, such as the scriptures, the sacraments, the creeds, and
the forms of piety.[114]

What does this inquiry into Segundo's method show about the
hermeneutic circle and its potential value for the topic of the poor and the
church? Segundo set forth in *The Liberation of Theology* and employed in
Faith and Ideologies an ideological critique. His analytical method does not
identify **an** ideology. Rather, it examines the **ideological dimension**, in
relation to the embodied values, of systematic forms which tend to create or
maintain dehumanizing conditions in any sphere (including the ecclesial) of
human life. When the analysis uncovers ideological aspects or systems of
means which contribute to justice and freedom for people, then they are to be
used. At times these systems of means may be nontraditional for the
Christian, such as Marxian "suspicion," directed toward discrepancies between the values professed and the way these values are realized,[115] or
historical materialism which can offer a certain "concreteness" and "sci-
entificness" of method.[116] At other times these systems of means may be
quite unsophisticated. Segundo comments that

> ... A "theology of the people" would seem to lead us towards a hermeneutic circle that could very well enrich such a [liberative] theology and keep it vital. For one of the most fruitful suspicions from the methodological standpoint results from comparing a culture that is logically and conceptually structured in a tight-knit way with the wisdom of the common people, the content of their rituals and imaginative creations, and the internal logic of their strangest attitudes.[117]

Segundo synthesizes the basic thrust of the second stage of the hermeneutic circle in this way,

> that we must understand and appreciate the ideological mechanisms of established society if theology is to take the word of God and convert it from a vague outline to a clearly worked out message. Otherwise theology will become and remain the unwitting spokesman of the experiences and ideas of the ruling factions and classes.[118]

New Experience of Theological Reality

Stage three in the hermeneutic circle represents a variation on stage one: a revised theological perspective which in turn provokes suspicion of the customary way that scripture is interpreted. As in stage one, the first requirement is a commitment to change; the commitment to change theology entails two things. First, a theology that **is** liberative is more important than one which **talks about** liberation. "In other words," Segundo explains, "liberation deals not so much with content as with the method used to theologize in the face of our real-life situation."[119]

As a result, when theology actually becomes liberative in history, people do not view God the same way they did before. Not surprisingly, " ... God shows up in a different light when his people find themselves in different historical situations."[120] Segundo describes the perception of God by those who commit their lives to and for the poor:

> ... This God is like a political figure who comes newly to power — this is the image Jesus used to speak of the Father — and whose first concern is not to judge people, to determine who is good and who is evil. Rather, God goes immediately to those who suffer most, to those who are most marginalized, most prevented from being truly human.[121]

With this altered way of understanding God and other theological realities, one is ready to read the bible in new ways. Clearly, the theoretical frameworks or ideological mechanisms brought to light in the previous stage of the hermeneutical circle affect the way one hears scripture. In the measure that systems oppress, they produce a deformed reading of the gospel. By corollary, the church's gospel-inspired mission in the world is distorted as well.

To summarize this third stage of the circle, Segundo reasserts that the initial commitment to concretize one's belief is indispensable, and

> that without a keen sensitivity and a determination to turn theology into a serviceable tool for orthopraxis, for a social praxis that is liberative, a false and quasi-magical concept of orthodoxy will dissolve theology into universal, ahistorical concepts.[122]

And now this newly honed theological tool brings its sharp edge to the understanding of the scriptures.

Reinterpretation of the Bible

Stage four of the hermeneutical circle effectively recapitulates the principles already formulated in stages one through three.[123] In its turn, this final stage generates a new experience of reality in the hearer/reader, who is propelled to a further level of the circle.

The Process of Learning to Learn

In keeping with an evolutionary approach to the history of the universe and of God's saving action, Segundo has since his earliest publications conceived of the scriptures as expressions of an educational process. "Etapas precristianas de la fe" ("Prechristian Stages of the Faith") presented the Hebrew scriptures as the result of a four-stage initiation into the mystery of salvation:

> Stage I: The Absolute of the Land of Israel
> Stage II: The God of the Covenant with Israel
> Stage III: The Transcendent God and Creator
> Stage IV: God, the Legislator of the Universe[124]

Segundo likewise argues that the religious development inherent in biblical history prior to Christ continues after Christ as well:

> But in reality what Jesus does, during these three years of living with his disciples, is to bring them to reenact rapidly the religious stages through which Israel passed during ten centuries, in order to become capable of understanding the Good News. He certainly communicated this as well, but he left it as a seed, a seed which the ecclesial community would develop with its immense extension and would expand with its preaching.[125]

Sacred scripture is therefore essentially "a sacred history revealed by God to different writers"[126] and "the education, accomplished by God, of the faith of the chosen people, in the different stages of this same education."[127] From this conception of the biblical process, Segundo draws important ecclesial and pastoral implications. Pastoral activity must take into account "in an evolutionary and creative way" the distinct situations and needs of the given ecclesial situation.[128]

The later works of Segundo resumed and added to this understanding of the scriptures. In *The Liberation of Theology* he interpreted the process of "learning to learn" with the help of Gregory Bateson's principle of "deutero-learning."[129] By it he linked his biblical theology with the sciences and with communications theory.

Similarly in *The Humanist Christology of Paul* Segundo reflected on equating the interpretation of Scripture with deutero-learning. He spelled out two elements to be kept in balance in this process. The first is that "the enrichment and maturity we expect to gain as a result [of the learning process] depend on our going through **multiple** experiences that will broaden our horizon beyond what we can reach by our own individual experience."[130] Iconic language, which is the more symbolic and artistic form of language, is needed for this broadening so that "we thus can experience as our own the crises faced by other human beings, and truly feel the impact of solutions that were liberating and humanizing in very different circumstances."[131]

The second element is the practical, concrete connection with one's own experience: "The anthropological faith stirred in us by the chain of witnesses must somehow open a concrete way out for us, an opening to a more mature and happy human life for us in our present situation."[132] Segundo considered that Latin American theology tended, at the expense of the first element, to overemphasize "the undeniable importance of fashioning a theology that is meaningful for **praxis**."[133] The learning process itself liberates through its broadening, critical aspects.

A final point concerning the biblical educational process is the importance of community on both the secular and the faith levels:

On the secular level it is obvious that this deutero-learning process requires some sort of community. This is even more true of the faith. The use of a specific tradition of faith, which is bound up with the interpretation of a privileged nucleus of the historical experiences, requires a community. We call this community of faith "the Church."[134]

The Importance of Shared Values

Segundo examined the behavior of the historical Jesus and concluded that Jesus' primary consideration was a matter of values: the human heart. Here, he said, "human beings make their most critical and decisive options."[135] And the options fundamentally concerned human suffering. Thus "the ultimate criterion in Jesus' theology is the remedy brought to some sort of human suffering, however temporary and provisional that remedy may be."[136] What was commonly seen to be of absolute value, such as religious practices, Jesus treated as simply a means, an instrument, an ideology. In Mark's narrative of the disciples picking grain on the sabbath, for instance, "Jesus' conclusion is a radical one. It is the sabbath that is relative, human welfare that is absolute: 'The sabbath was made for man, not man for the sabbath' (Mk. 2:27)."[137]

In the same way, in the kingdom of Satan dispute (Mk. 3:22-30 and parallels), Jesus shrugged off a debate about whose authority was at work in an exorcism and healing. "If someone is cured, says Jesus, God always comes off the winner. The welfare of human beings is always God's cause and God's work. Once again the more human criterion, the less 'religious' criterion, is the more divine one."[138]

It follows, then, that the way to understand the scriptures is according to God's values manifested in Jesus' values. As the earlier discussion of the hermeneutic circle and especially of stage four has shown, God's preference revealed in Jesus is for the poor of the earth. "Indeed Jesus seems to go so far as to suggest that one cannot recognize Christ, and therefore come to know God, unless he or she is willing to start with a personal commitment to the oppressed."[139] In his arguments with the Pharisees and his interpretative parables Jesus raised the questions which penetrate to the heart both of the listening and of the message.[140]

The Option for the Poor as a Hermeneutic Principle

When in *The Liberation of Theology* he credited James Cone with carrying out a complete hermeneutic circle in *A Black Theology of Liberation*, Segundo also agreed with Cone's assertion that

> ... orthodoxy possesses no ultimate criterion in itself because being
> orthodox does not mean possessing the final truth. We only arrive at
> the latter by orthopraxis. It is the latter that is the ultimate criterion of
> the former, both in theology and in biblical interpretation. The truth is
> truth only when it serves as the basis for truly human attitudes.[141]

A little later in the same book he further specified the interpretative criterion of orthopraxis. "A real, effective option on behalf of the oppressed can de-ideologize our minds and free our thinking for the gospel message."[142]

Then in a recent article, Segundo became even more explicit. This foundational commitment to bringing about a more just and human society is the unique way to understand the gospel as spirit and life:

> I am not going to approach the option for the poor as a result of the
> theology of liberation nor as one of its favorite themes, but as the
> hermeneutical key. In other words, it is something prior in order to
> understand the gospel and prevent its letter from killing. In this sense,
> I propose this response as something universal which has worth not
> only for Latin America but for the whole world.[143]

Far from being a casual opinion or an intellectual construct, this key involves the hearer of the Gospel totally, as a risk and a wager of both faith and life.[144]

The option for the poor is simultaneously preevangelical and evangelical. The conversion which it entails prepares the heart to receive God's word, and the word makes explicit what the hearer or reader has already grasped in a preliminary way.[145] This decision also provides the epistemological basis for understanding the word of God. The choice made, even at the risk of conditioning the reading of the word, gives a certain shape to the reading for the very purpose of understanding it.[146] Recall Segundo's observation that a reading of the gospel from the basis of this option is of the spirit and therefore lifegiving.[147]

Yet the Christian who reads the bible in such a manner is not content solely to **receive** God's word with converted ears and eyes. She or he faces the challenge and "the healthy risk of interpreting Jesus anew in the face of equally new problems."[148] A liberative interpretation of Scripture is for Segundo a creative hermeneutic:

> So we must keep going back and writing gospels. That does not take
> any of the wonder or exclusivity away from the moment when the first
> canonical Gospels were written. Today, centuries later, the Spirit of

Jesus can see to it that the new gospels are spiritually as faithful to
Jesus as the first ones were.[149]

Now, to use Segundo's own words to summarize this fourth stage of the
hermeneutical circle, the stage that is the end and again a beginning, it is
evident "that we must salvage the sovereign liberty of the word of God if we
are to be able to say something that is really creative and liberative in any
given situation."[150]

In short, the hermeneutic circle culminates — and initiates a new
stage — with the interpretation of scripture qualified by the practical
commitment to a more human life for the poor and by the ideological
critique based on this commitment.

SUMMARY

This chapter has prepared the way to take a close look, in Chapter Two,
at the identity and role of the poor and, in Chapters Three through Five, at
the significance of the poor for the church. It has surveyed the historical
setting out of which Juan Luis Segundo has produced his theology of the
poor and the church. It has likewise summarized his theological method,
including certain prominent currents of thought which have influenced him
in carrying out this task.

Historically, Segundo's theology manifested the painful efforts of the
Latin American continent and church to move out of a centuries-long
multiform colonialism. It reflected the highly intellectual, articulate, secular, lay character of Uruguayan culture. It revealed as well the continuing
transformation in a church newly engaged, under the influence of the Second
Vatican Council, Medellín, and Puebla, with the society at whose service it
exists.

Methodologically, the Uruguayan theologian's work drew widely from
the poetry, philosophy, and natural and social sciences articulated by the
persons of past and present with whom Segundo has conversed. In particular, it integrated existentialist, Marxist, and evolutionary insights into an
historical, political theology. It grew out of the conviction that a reality
characterized by such poverty, injustice, and oppression as that of Latin
America demands questioning. Thus Segundo's theology followed a spiral
of experience, suspicion, critique, and revision which encompassed both

theology and the interpretation of scripture out of a professed partiality to fuller humanness for all people. It has now led to the specific questions of this study.

NOTES

1. *Pastoral Constitution on the Church in the Modern World* (*Gaudium et spes*, 1965), art. 4, in *Vatican II: The Conciliar and Post Conciliar Documents*, ed. Austin Flannery (Northport, N.Y.: Costello Publishing Company, 1975).

2. J. Lloyd Mecham, *The Church and State in Latin America* (Chapel Hill, N.C.: University of North Carolina Press, 1966), 14ff.

3. Enrique Dussel, *A History of the Church in Latin America: Colonialism to Liberation (1492-1979)*, trans. and rev. Alan Neely (Grand Rapids, Michigan: William B. Eerdmans Publishing Company, 1981), 37-8.

4. Dussel, *A History of the Church*, 314-17.

5. Frederick B. Pike, "Catholicism in Latin America," *The Church in a Secularized Society* by Roger Aubert et al, Vol. V, *The Christian Centuries*. (London: Darton, Longman and Todd, 1978), 344-5.

6. Dussel, *A History of the Church*, 106.

7. Their name derived from the book Ariel by the Uruguayan José Enrique Rodó, published in 1900. In it, Rodó "depicted Ariel as the creature of intellectual and spiritual pursuits, concerned with art, beauty and moral development as ends in themselves, rather than with material progress" (Frederick B. Pike, *Spanish America 1900-1970: Tradition and Social Innovation* [New York: W. W. Norton and Company, 1973], 20).

8. Pike, 345-6.

9. See Dussel, *A History of the Church*, 107. Concerning the foundation of the Catholic universities in Santiago and Lima, Frederick B. Pike noted that "both these universities were primarily concerned with forming an élite that could appreciate, guard, and nourish the most exalted of human values" ("Catholicism," 346).

10. Note Dussel's summary of Catholic Action in *A History of the Church*, 108-9. It began officially in Uruguay in 1934. See also Pike, "Catholicism in Latin America," 348-9, on the church's increasing involvement in social issues in the early 1900's.

11. Latin Americans tended to favor the student model, *Juventud Universitaria Católica* (JUC). See Dussel, *A History of the Church*, 109; and Edward A. Cleary, *Crisis and Change: The Church in Latin America Today* (Maryknoll, N.Y.: Orbis Books, 1985), 3-6.

    Student movements were significant for J. L. Segundo's theology. Refer especially to *Teología abierta*, Vol. III: *Reflexiones críticas* (Madrid: Ediciones Cristiandad,

1984; will be referred to as *RC*), an untranslated volume in a new edition of the
series *A Theology for the Artisans of a New Humanity*, trans. John Drury
(Maryknoll, N.Y.: Orbis Books, 1973-4).

In *RC* Segundo replied to the criticism of his theology as "elitist" in contrast to
Gustavo Gutierrez' "popular" theology. He qualified these descriptions in relation
to their common origins within a middle class, university environment (footnote, p.
28). At a later point in the book (ch. V) and in more than one article Segundo spoke
of these origins when he discussed the two theologies of liberation he saw operating
today, one primarily "for" the people, the other mainly "of" the people.

12. Cleary, 4-5.

13. The Christendom-Christianity tension is a theme throughout Segundo's work. He
    equates Christendom, the cultural phenomenon of the post-Constantinian centuries,
    with religious practice which emphasized minimal participation of the maximum
    number of persons. Civil institutions carried out and supported Catholic practice.
    Christianity, on the other hand, he identifies with the living of the gospel message
    through personal conviction, with the conversion and practical demands which this
    living entails. Thus Christendom-Christianity is another dimension of masses-
    minorities. See *The Liberation of Theology*, trans. John Drury (Maryknoll, N.Y.:
    Orbis Books, 1976), 211-16.

    Among Segundo's earlier works, see for example *Función de la Iglesia en la
    realidad rioplatense* (Montevideo: Barreiro y Ramos, 1962), 8-9, 34-35, 47; *La
    cristiandad: ¿una utopía?*, I, *Los hechos* (Montevideo: Cursos de Com-
    plementación Cristiana, 1964), especially Ch. I; and *Masas y minorías en la
    dialéctica divina de la liberación*, Cuadernos de Contestación Polémica (Buenos
    Aires: Editorial La Aurora, 1973, Ch. 2 and passim).

14. Pike, *Spanish America*, 25. The issue of elites and masses in Latin American social-
    cultural life is part of the context for Segundo's concept of the church as a minority
    at the service of the masses. See, for one, Enrique Dussel's *A History of the Church*
    where he discusses elites in relation to the intellectual renewal, Catholic Action, and
    the social struggle on pp. 106-10, and "catholicism" and "Catholic church" in terms
    of **minorities/ elites and masses** on pp. 117-21.

    Elites in Latin America, eds. Seymour Martin Lipset and Aldo Solari (New York:
    Oxford University Press, 1967), resulted from a Seminar on Elites and Development
    in Latin America held at the University of Montevideo in June 1965. See Ivan
    Vallier's paper, "Religious Elites: Differentiations and Developments in Roman
    Catholicism," 190-232, and Lipset and Solari on elite analysis in the preface.

    Elites, Masses, and Modernization in Latin America, 1850-1930, ed. Virginia
    Bernhard (Austin: University of Texas Press, 1979) is the published lectures by E.
    Bradford Burns and Thomas E. Skidmore on cultural and labor history.

    Also significant is the Second General Conference of the Latin American Episco-
    pate at Medellín, Colombia. Vol. I, *Position Papers*, of *The Church in the Present-*

Day Transformation of Latin America in the Light of the Council, ed. Louis M. Colonesse (Washington, D.C.: United States Catholic Conference, 1968), includes the position paper by Most Rev. Luis E. Henríquez of Caracas, "Pastoral Care of the Masses and the Elites." Vol. II, Conclusions, contains the final documents "Pastoral Care of the Masses," 89-96, and "Pastoral Concern for the Elites," 97-106.

15. Joseph Comblin explored this reality extensively in *The Church and the National Security State* (Maryknoll, N.Y.: Orbis Books, 1979). In addition, the SELADOC Committee of the Catholic University of Chile, Santiago, has published a collection of articles on the topic, *Iglesia y Seguridad Nacional, Panorama de la teología latinoamericana*, IV (Salamanca: Ediciones Sígueme, 1980).

16. Thomas E. Skidmore and Peter H. Smith examined the economic, social, and political development of the period in *Modern Latin America* (New York: Oxford University Press, 1984), particularly in chapter two, "The Transformation of Modern Latin America, 1880s-1980s," 46-69.

17. On the one hand, Segundo Galilea (*El mensaje de Puebla* [Santiago, Chile: Ediciones Paulinas, 1979], 12) described the unity of this first and less well known CELAM conference as defensive and pastorally traditional. On the other hand, Dussel (*A History of the Church*, 113-16) underlined its significance. Functionally, it treated important topics, among them lay involvement in Catholic Action, propaganda, relations with Protestants and other non-Catholics, social problems, missions, and immigrants. Symbolically, it represented the recovery of an ecclesial unity lost with the disintegration of colonial Christianity.

18. Enrique Dussel, "Current Events in Latin America," *The Challenge of Basic Christian Communities*, ed. Sergio Torres and John Eagleson (Maryknoll, N.Y.: Orbis Books, 1981), 77-78. Basic ecclesial communities will be discussed at greater length in Ch. IV.

19. John J. Considine, ed., *The Church in the New Latin America* (Notre Dame, Indiana: Fides Publishers, 1964), 219.

20. Mecham, 57.

21. Dussel, *A History of the Church*, p. 88. See the entire discussion, 87 ff.

22. During his two terms President Batlle set in motion extensive political and socio-economic reforms which remained and expanded after his presidency. The resulting democratic system, with its practice of capitalism, system of social services, and excellent educational programs resulted, particularly in Montevideo, in the partial breakdown of the boundary between upper and lower classes. At the same time, the government operated according to a largely paternalistic rationale which continued to reserve political power for a select few (Pike, *Spanish America*, 86-87; see also 18-20 concerning the rise of positivism).

23. Refer to Considine, 219.

24. See Pike, *Spanish America*, 21-24; Considine, 219.

25. Pike, *Spanish America*, 90. The Tupamaros represent a factor in the elites-masses, minorities-majorities dynamic operating in the national and ecclesial environment of Uruguay. Arturo C. Porzecanski has chronicled the activities of the group from its origins in early 1962 to its virtual dissolution in 1972-73 through military repression in *Uruguay's Tupamaros: The Urban Guerrilla* (New York, Washington, London: Praeger Publishers, 1973). Despite its earlier suppression, the Movimiento de Liberación Nacional-Tupamaro is active today in Montevideo. Its stated objective is now "Para la tierra, contra la pobreza" ("For the land, against poverty"), and the economic and political independence of the country.

26. *Encyclopedia Britannica, Micropaedia*, Vol. 12 (Chicago: University of Chicago Press, 1985), 211.

27. *Encyclopedia Britannica, 1987 Book of the Year* (Chicago: University of Chicago Press, 1987), 556.

28. *Tablet* 242 (May 14, 1988).

29. *Berdiaeff* (Paris: Montaigne, 1963).

30. *La cristiandad*, (Montevideo: Mimeográfica "Luz," 1964). The bibliographical information in this paragraph was taken from Alfred T. Hennelly, *Theologies in Conflict: The Challenge of Juan Luis Segundo* (Maryknoll, N.Y.: Orbis Books, 1979), 50-51, 66.

31. Such interdisciplinary efforts in Uruguay are not unique to Segundo. The Centro Latinoamericano de Economía Humana (CLAEH) in Montevideo, for example, also publishes in the social sciences and social development. Relative to this study see the three volume work by Carlos Zubillaga and Mario Cayota, *Cristianos y cambio social en el Uruguay de la modernización (1895-1919)* (n.d.), and *Promoción social y compromiso cristiano*, 1982 by Pablo Bonavia et al.

32. Father Andrés Asandri, S.J., described the history of the center in an interview in Montevideo, November 30, 1986. A founder with J. L. Segundo, he named such participating scholars as Roberto Viola in catechetics, Manuel Oliveira in sociology, Orlando Costa in politics, Paolo Friere in education, and himself in theology. The Peter Faber Center promoted the theology of liberation, and refrained from treating either popular religion or scientific Marxist analysis. Seeking to develop theology in its humanistic context, it was one among several centers established by the Jesuits in countries where they served, including also Venezuela, Colombia, Peru, Argentina, Chile, and El Salvador.

33. The first year of publication, 1965-66, the journal was called *Diálogo*. The second year the title changed to *Perspectivas de Diálogo*.

34. In the introduction to these volumes, Segundo described the format for the seminars, each three or four days of concentrated four-hour blocks, ordinarily over a holiday weekend. They included lecture, individual and group reflection, response to questions from the groups, and prayer.

35. Asandri, same interview.

36. For example, in May 1978, he presented a course in San Juan Bautista parish entitled, "That Man Jesus" ("Ese Hombre Jesus"), and in September 1984 to the same parish "Faith and Ideology" ("Fe e Ideología"). His series *Jesus of Nazareth Yesterday and Today*, trans. John Drury (Maryknoll, N.Y.: Orbis Books, 1984-88) originally appeared in 1982. The first volume was entitled *Faith and Ideologies*.

37. Segundo described the reflection groups in a conversation in Montevideo, November 20, 1986.

    Ms. Perla Vidal also described (November 21-30, 1986) the several types of currently active reflection groups. She is the only remaining member of Segundo's original four-person group. Among the many citizens who lived in exile during the dictatorship was one from his first group who returned to Uruguay in 1986. Ms. Vidal works with another group as well, made up of parishioners some of whom are directly inserted in a work of Christian or human promotion and all of whom are in a process of formation.

    Rev. Ismael Rivas, pastor of San Juan Bautista (Pocitos) parish in Montevideo where Segundo teaches each September, assists the twenty-two parish groups which meet weekly to integrate their faith and their daily lives. He stated (November 26, 1986) that the most important contribution of Segundo's theology is its emphasis on insertion into the work of the world.

38. Dussel, *A History of the Church*, 137.

39. Roger Aubert, *The Christian Centuries*, Vol. V, *The Church in a Secularized Society*, 627-28. Donal Dorr drew upon this information in *Option for the Poor: A Hundred Years of Vatican Social Teaching* (Maryknoll, N.Y.: Orbis Books, 1983), 295.

40. In their "Message to Humanity" the bishops highlighted the two issues of social justice and peace, trans. in *The Gospel of Peace and Justice: Catholic Social Teaching Since Pope John*, edited by Joseph Gremillion (Maryknoll, NY: Orbis Books, 1976), 353; see Dorr, 295.

41. See Donal Dorr, 118-19. Juan Luis Segundo discussed this social-geographical characteristic of the Council in *RC*, 13-14.

42. "Se puede decir que sólo *un* documento, sancionado al final, en 1965, provocó ese clima de entusiasmo, esperanza y renovación a que aludíamos: la *Gaudium et spes*,

o sea, la *Constitución sobre la Iglesia en el mundo actual*" (*Reflexiones críticas*, 12).

43. ". . . digamos que probablemente, y en líneas muy generales, ese estudio mostraría que los obispos latino-americanos captaron del Vatican II más un 'espíritu' o una 'mentalidad' — si se quiere, una 'actitud' — que una orientación estrictamente teológica" (*Reflexiones críticas*, 14).

   A profitable study of "the church and the poor" theme in the Vatican II documents could be made. The *Index Verborum cum Documentis Concilii Vaticani Secundi* (ed. Xavier Ochoa, Rome: Commentarium pro Religiosis, 1967) listed sixty-four references to **pauper** or derivatives with the majority of these clustering, not surprisingly, in *Lumen gentium* and *Gaudium et spes*. The contributing authors in Herbert Vorgrimler's *Commentary on the Documents of Vatican II* (5 vols., New York: Herder and Herder, 1967-69) examined the history of this theme as it developed through the documents. Gérard Philips noted, for example, that Cardinals Lercaro and Gerlier and Bishop Himmer advocated in October 1963 "the church of the poor" as a council theme (discussion of L.G., Ch. I, second draft; Vol. I, 112).

   Charles Moeller reported in the *Commentary*, Vol. V, that the impulse toward a schema on the church in the world came from Dom Helder Camara of Rio de Janeiro. A small group called "Church of the Poor," inspired by Abbé P. Gaulthier and in which Dom Helder Camara participated from the beginning, studied the problem from October 26, 1962, on. Moeller traced the work which resulted in *G.S.*, including the acceptance on December 4, 1962, of Cardinal Suenens' proposal that the schemata on the church be prepared around two poles, **ad intra** and **ad extra** (10-12).

44. "Es, por ejemplo, significativo que se citen poco o nada en Medellín aquellos pasajes más detonantes e innovadores de la *Gaudium et spes*. . .En cambio, un espíritu genérico de 'servicio al hombre,' y ello dentro de la historia humana, flota en todos o casi todos los documentos de Medellín" (*RC*, 14).

   Refer also to "Hacia una exégesis dinámica," *Víspera* 1 (No. 3, October 1967), 77-84, where Segundo discussed the challenge posed to the church by *Gaudium et spes*.

45. "En ellos [los Documentos de Medellín] podemos ya encontrar 'algo' que tendremos que definir ulteriormente; en todo caso, una versión geográficamente situada, del Vaticano II" (*RC*, 14).

46. The documents entitled "Justice," "Peace," and "Poverty of the Church" are numbers 1, 2, and 14 respectively of Vol. II, *Conclusions*.

   "Poverty of the Church" recalled the unjust situation prevailing in the Latin American countries and the charge made against a perceived "rich church" (art. 2). It reflected on the various levels of poverty, and the response made to each by a "poor church": The church opposes as evil the poverty that consists of a lack of necessities. The church advocates and fosters the poverty which equals an openness to God. And the church binds itself to the poverty entailed in a voluntary loving commitment to people in need (arts. 4-5). The appropriate pastoral response is to give "pre-eminence and solidarity" to the poorest and most miserable (arts. 9-11); to witness to this Gospel call, even at great cost (arts. 12-17); and to serve in the spirit of the poor Christ (art. 18).

47. A respected history of the development of liberation theology is *Liberación y teología: Genesis y crecimiento de una reflexión 1966-1977* by Roberto Oliveros Maqueo (Lima: Centro de Estudios y Publicaciones, 1977).

48. In March 1976, the Curia and Adveniat, the German bishops' aid organization for Latin America, cosponsored a meeting in Rome called "Church and Liberation Circle of Studies" to oppose the Medellín orientation. In November 1977, the same month as the CELAM consultative document, a group of German theologians who disagreed with Adveniat and the Curia prepared a Memorandum in support of the Latin American liberation efforts, a statement soon to be followed by similar affirmations by theologians of several nations. See Penny Lernoux, "The Long Path to Puebla," in *Puebla and Beyond: Documentation and Commentary*, ed. John Eagleson and Philip Scharper (Maryknoll, N.Y.: Orbis Books, 1979), 21-23.

49. Third General Conference of the Latin American Episcopate, *Evangelization in Latin America's Present and Future*, in *Puebla and Beyond: Documentation and Commentary*, ed. John Eagleson and Philip Scharper (Maryknoll, NY: Orbis Books, 1979), no 1135. See also Joseph Comblin, "La Conferencia episcopal de Puebla," *Mensaje* (Santiago; marzo-abril 1979), 119.

50. The tone of the consultative and working papers was highly conservative. CELAM General Secretary Lopéz Trujillo controlled the delegate selection, and the conference proceedings were segmented such that any theologians with a liberation perspective were excluded (see Moises Sandoval, "Report from the Conference," *Puebla and Beyond*, 29-39).

On the other hand, Pope John Paul II's presence and addresses at the conference, the work accomplished by the theologians "outside the walls," and the irrefutable reality in which the church was living made a powerful impact on the outcome of the conference (refer to Jon Sobrino, "The Significance of Puebla for the Catholic Church in Latin America," *Puebla and Beyond*, 292-96. The Spanish original appeared on pp. 44-55 in *Christus* 44 (1979), a theme issue by theologians "outside the walls" at Puebla.

51. Moises Sandoval described the votes on the pastoral overview of Latin American reality (Part One) and on the option for the poor. While the option for the poor received the necessary two thirds, only 56 bishops voted an unqualified "yes." See "Report from the Conference," 40.

52. Comblin, "La Conferencia episcopal," 119-20.

53. *Evangelization in Latin America's Present and Future*, 122-285.

54. The recognition that a pretheological commitment underlies any experience of reality is a principle of hermeneutical theory, of which Hans-Georg Gadamer is a major proponent; see *Truth and Method*, trans. and ed. G. Barden and J. Cumming (New York: Crossroad, 1975), especially 235-74. Gadamer depended on Martin Heidegger; see *Being and Time*, trans. John Macquarrie and Edward Robinson (London: SCM Press, 1962).

    Although with a different emphasis, Paul Ricoeur continued the hermeneutical approach. In "Preface to Bultmann," *Essays on Biblical Interpretation* (Phila.: Fortress Press, 1980), he defined the hermeneutical circle thus: "To understand, it is necessary to believe; to believe, it is necessary to understand" (58).

    Segundo employed the definition of theology as "critical reflection on praxis" on which Gustavo Gutiérrez based *A Theology of Liberation: History, Politics and Salvation*, trans. and ed. Caridad Inda and John Eagleson (Maryknoll, N.Y.: Orbis Books, 1973). Gutiérrez stated (11) that "theology is reflection, a critical attitude. Theology **follows**; it is the second step."

55. *LT*, 9.

56. Ibid.

57. " 'Entonces, en este continente practicamente cristiano durante cuatro siglos, los cristianos han dejado surgir esas <**favelas**> y pueden convivir tranquilamente días, meses y años con esa miseria. ¿Qué significado tiene entonces para ustedes la palabra cristiano?'," "Concepción cristiana del hombre" in *¿Qué es un cristiano?* (Montevideo: Mosca Hnos., S.A. Editores, 1971), 92. According to Alfred Hennelly (*Theologies in Conflict*, 52), "Concepción cristiana" was first presented as a lecture in 1962, and published (Montevideo: Mimeográfica "Luz") in 1964.

58. "Cuando la dominación pasa de lo anónimo a la represión abierta, el centro del imperio es atacado por preguntas. Y llega entonces para nosotros la hora de hablar. Porque toda arma empleada repercute en quien la emplea" (*De la sociedad a la teología*, Cuadernos Latinoamericanos [Buenos Aires, México: Ediciones Carlos Lohlé, 1970], 10).

59. *LT*, 9.

60. Humanization was the express purpose of Segundo's *The Historical Jesus of the Synoptics*, trans. John Drury (Maryknoll, N.Y.: Orbis Books, 1985; henceforth *HJS*). On p. 13 he said: "On the basis of the two human dimensions (**faith** and **ideology**) . . ., we will now try to determine methodically what contribution, if any, Jesus of Nazareth and the tradition stemming from him makes to the process of humanization."

61. *HJS*, 130.

62. *LT*, 89; emphasis Segundo's.

63. *Faith and Ideologies*, trans. John Drury (Maryknoll, N.Y.: Orbis Books, 1984), 189; henceforth *FI*.

    Nicholas Berdyaev, on whom Segundo wrote his philosophical dissertation, has continued to influence the latter's work, particularly through the emphasis on personal liberty. See *Berdaieff: Une réflexion chrétienne sur la personne* (Paris: Éditions Montaigne, 1963), especially 61-63.

64. *Grace and the Human Condition*, trans. John Drury (Maryknoll, N.Y.: Orbis Books, 1973), 127, 122-27; henceforth referred to as *GHC*.

    Segundo discussed his considerable debt to Leopoldo Malavez, particularly regarding the theology of history, in *Theology and the Church: A Response to Cardinal Ratzinger and a Warning to the Whole Church*, trans. John Diercksmeier (Minneapolis: Winston Press, 1985), 75-80. (Segundo noted in a conversation with me that the English translation is at times inaccurate, even to the point of theological error).

65. See above, note 54.

66. *The Humanist Christology of Paul*, trans. John Drury (Maryknoll, N.Y.: Orbis Books, 1986); henceforth referred to as *HCP*, 223. See also "Capitalism — Socialism: A Theological Crux," in *Concilium*, Vol. 96, *The Mystical and Political Dimension of the Christian Faith*, ed. Claude Geffré and Gustavo Gutiérrez (New York: Herder and Herder, 1974), esp. 115-16.

67. *HCP*, 172. See also footnotes 252-53, pp. 223-24.

68. "Soit dans le contenu du message, soit dans la tâche philosophique, la personne s'avère, dès maintenant, comme la clé de voûte de la philosophie prophétique de Berdiaeff" (66).

69. The Spanish title of the series is *El hombre de hoy ante Jesús de Nazaret*; Eng. translation published by Maryknoll, N.Y.: Orbis Books, 1984-88.

70. 13; emphasis Segundo's.

71. ". . . nous croyons que Berdaieff a particulièrement enrichi le domaine de la phénoménologie existentielle en éclairant tout un secteur de l'expérience humaine, et certes le plus positif: celui de l'amour, de la création, de l'extase, bref, de ces moments de plénitude où l'homme saisit l'accord foncier entre le liberté et l'être" (*Berdiaeff*, 410).

72. "Por un lado, el christianismo ve en la libertad de cada persona humana un valor irreductible. Dios es amor, y amar es siempre comenzar por querer libre al ser amado" (114).

Liberty epitomized for Segundo the mystery of God. In his article, "Disquisición sobre el misterio absoluto" ("Discourse about Absolute Mystery," *Revista latino-americana de teología* [El Salvador, Sept.-Dic. 1985]: 227), he acknowledged Berdyaev's continuing influence and said: "The mystery of God is, in its essence, the mystery of all liberty: only the self-revelation of this liberty as history, this beginning of love which consists in surrendering to 'being known', opens the true road to what is personal. Every person, even the human, contains this 'mystery', this 'I am who I am'."

("El misterio de Dios es, en su esencia, el misterio de toda libertad: sólo la autorrevelación de esa libertad como historia, ese comienzo del amor que consiste en darse 'a conocer,' abre el verdadero camino hacia lo que es personal. Toda persona, aun la humana, contiene ese 'misterio,' ese 'yo soy el que soy'.")

73. "... se le ha dado la verdad revelada: que Dios es amor y que todo amor efectivo se convierte en valor absoluto, en el único verdadero valor absoluto de la existencia humana" ("La concepción cristiana," 105).

74. *The Community Called Church*, trans. John Drury (Maryknoll, N.Y.: Orbis Books, 1973); henceforth referred to as *CCC*, 106.

75. "Le climat authentique de la philosophie a toujours été le combat héroïque de la conscience créatrice contre toute **nécessité** et toute condition de vie **obligatoire**" (Citation from *Le Sens de la création. Un essai de justification de l'homme*, trans. J. Cain [Bruges-Paris: Desclée, 1955], 52; in *Berdiaeff*, 41).

76. See "Etapas precristianas de la fe," 84-85.

77. *HCP*, 180; emphasis Segundo's.

78. In *LT* Segundo made the following observation about Marxist influence: "...There are problems with applying the label 'Marxist' to a line of thought or a source of influence. First of all, those who identify themselves with Marx and his thinking have a thousand different ways of conceiving and interpreting 'Marxist' thought. Aside from that fact, the point is that the great thinkers of history do not replace each other; rather, they complement and enrich each other. Philosophic thought would never be the same after Aristotle as it was before him. In that sense all Westerners who philosophize now are Aristotelians. After Marx, our way of conceiving and posing the problems of society will never be the same again. Whether everything Marx said is accepted or not, and in whatever way one may conceive his 'essential' thinking, there can be no doubt that present-day social thought will be 'Marxist' to some extent: that is, profoundly indebted to Marx. In that sense Latin American theology is certainly Marxist...." (35)

In her work, *From Theology to Social Theory: Juan Luis Segundo and the Theology of Liberation* (New York: Peter Lang, 1990), Marsha Aileen Hewitt closely examines the influence of Marx on Segundo's work. Chapters III and IV are key to her

conclusion that Segundo fails to construct a substantive Christian theology incorporating Marx's materialist conception of history (see pp. 100-1). In III she treats
Marxist influence upon Segundo's notion of ideology, while in IV she analyzes in
more detail the latter's appropriation of Marxist thought overall.

Two valuable secondary works on Marxism are *Marxism: An American Christian
Perspective* by Arthur F. McGovern (Maryknoll, N.Y.: Orbis Books, 1980) and
Marxist Analysis and Christian Faith by René Coste (Maryknoll, N.Y.: Orbis
Books, 1985), trans. Roger A. Couture and John C. Cort. Anthony J. Tambasco
gave a detailed presentation and critique of Segundo's use of Marxism in *The Bible
for Ethics: Juan Luis Segundo and First-World Ethics* (Washington, D.C.: University Press of America, 1981).

79. *LT*, 104.

80. *LT*, 116; emphasis Segundo's.

81. *FI*, 14; see 5ff. for a fuller explanation of the terms.

82. *FI*, 70-83.

83. *FI*, 16; emphasis Segundo's. Later in the book, he summarized two main usages of
"ideology" since the time of Marx: "The more **neutral** sense refers to everything
that lies outside the precision of the sciences, to the suprascientific or the super-
structural realm. In that sense it is only logical to talk about a 'Marxist ideology,'
even though one may recognize a 'scientific' area in it. . . . The second sense of the
term is clearly **negative**. It refers to all the cognitive mechanisms which disguise,
excuse, and even sacralize the existing mode of production, thus benefiting those
who profit from that mode of production" (97; see also 94-7.)

84. *FI*, 27. Tambasco delineated Segundo's uses of "ideology," in both negative and
positive senses in *The Bible for Ethics*, 91-106.

85. *FI*, 177.

86. *FI*, 178.

87. *FI*, 184.

88. *FI*, 100-103, 177-99. Segundo quoted Milan Machovec's definition of historical
materialism, the basis of its scientific criticism, as generally held in modern
Marxism on pp. 138-39.

Note Segundo's comment, p. 180: "The term 'mode of production' is much less
materialist than is often assumed by both its advocates and its opponents. As Marx
repeatedly stresses, the mode of production — or, the concrete economic structure — does not just take in the organization of the means of production: i.e., its
more quantitative and hence 'materialist' aspect. It also takes in the 'human

relations' generated by the type of production in question and by the appropriation of the means of production. And in these relations between human beings, effected in and through work, are included many elements which we could rightly call 'spiritual' and which are not nebulous idealizations." See also *LT*, 14-16.

89. *FI*, 194; emphasis Segundo's.

90. *FI*, 334.

91. For the atheism-theism question, see *FI*, 210, 241-42.

92. *GHC*, 82 ff.

93. *GHC*, 85. Here Segundo referred without a specific citation to *The Divine Milieu* (New York: Harper & Row; London: William Collins Sons & Co., Ltd., 1960), ed. Bernard Wall from *Le Milieu Divin* (Paris: Éditions du Seuil, 1957).

94. Mt. 5:47; parallel in Lk. 6:32.

95. *EG*, 113. Segundo frequently uses the terms "entropy" and "negentropy" from the science of thermodynamics. *The American Heritage Dictionary* defines "entropy" as "1. A measure of the capacity of a system to undergo spontaneous change. 2. A measure of the randomness, disorder, or chaos in a system." "Negentropy" represents the converse of this principle, and is therefore a measure of the ability to overcome such randomness and spontaneous change in order to form new, complex syntheses. See *FI*, 190-94, 199.

Concerning the church as contributor to evolution, see Segundo's article "La Iglesia en la evolución de un continente" in *De la sociedad a la teología*, 155-73.

96. After *EG*, the most explicitly evolutionary of Segundo's works was *An Evolutionary Approach to Jesus of Nazareth*, trans. John Drury (Maryknoll, N.Y.: Orbis Books, 1988; *EA*). The influence of Teilhard de Chardin was evident throughout the book, but was most pronounced in chapters I, II, and IV. The works of Teilhard most cited are *L'activation de l'énergie* (Paris: Éd. du Seuil, 1963) and *Le phénomène humaine* (Paris: Éd. du Seuil, 1955). He used a number of secondary sources on Teilhard as well.

97. While *Steps to an Ecology of Mind* (San Francisco: Chandler Publishing Col, 1972) was an important source, Segundo also drew in virtually every chapter of *EA* from Bateson's *Mind and Nature* (New York: Bantam Books, 1980).

98. *EA*, 79.

99. *EA*, 106-7. Bateson's evolutionary view included an "economy of energy" in which opposing movements limit the emergence of new forms. It also advocated language that preserves both the abstract, scientific, "digital" forms and the concrete, symbolic,

"iconic forms" in order to express adequately the values — the faith — of human beings. See Segundo's appropriation of these ideas in *FI*, 134-36, 155-59.

100. *LT*, 39.

101. *FI*, 224.

102. See *HJS*, 120-21, 125-31; also "La opción por los pobres como clave hermenéutica para entender el Evangelio," *Sal Terrae* (Junio 1986), 478-80.

103. *FI*, 224.

104. *HJS*, 132.

105. *LT*, 8.

106. *LT*, 231-32.

107. *LT*, 29.

108. *LT*, 66.

109. *LT*, 75. Marsha Aileen Hewitt argues (*From Theology to Social Theory*, 13) that Segundo so emphasizes the political aspect that theology collapses into politics or, more specifically, into a critical social theory based on the Christian ethical principle of loving one's neighbor. While much can be said for the points she makes, she states her thesis too strongly. While Segundo makes politics and ideological critique essential elements of his system, he does so **in the name of** a truer understanding of who God is and who the human being is. As he demonstrates with his hermeneutic circle, his critique serves a reconceptualization of theology as a whole and a renewed biblical interpretation (cf. *LT*, 9).

110. *FI*, 178.

111. *FI*, 179. Note (178) Segundo's description of the traditional antagonism between Christianity and Marxism, often perceived, respectively, as the faith and the ideology *par excellence.*

112. See *FI*, 179-84.

113. *FI*, 338.

114. Refer to *FI*, 338.

115. *FI*, 194.

116. *FI*, 241.

117. *LT*, 236.

118. *LT*, 39.

119. *LT*, p. 9.

120. *LT*, 31.

121. ". . .ese Dios es como un político que viene a instaurar un reino nuevo — ésa es la imagen que empleó Jesús para hablar del Padre — y no se preocupa en primer lugar de juzgar a los hombres, de determinar quiénes son buenos y quiénes malos, sino que va inmediatamente a aquellos que sufren más, a aquellos que están más marginados, más impedidos de ser verdaderamente humanos" ("La opción por los pobres," 477).

122. *LT*, 39.

123. In view of his creative treatment of scripture, what is Segundo's attitude toward historical critical method? He incorporated scripture most extensively into his early works "Etapas precristianas de la fe" and *La Cristiandad, ¿Una Utopía? II. Los Principios* (Montevideo: Mimeográfica "Luz," 1964), and into his recent *El hombre de hoy ante Jesús de Nazaret*, particularly volumes two and three. He appeared to do the greater part of the exegesis himself, drawing upon other exegetes and biblical theologians when he judged it appropriate.

The following exegetes were prominent in Segundo's references: Gerhard von Rad, C. H. Dodd, Joachim Jeremias, and C. E. B. Cranfield. For his exegesis of the Beatitudes, particularly important in *The Historical Jesus of the Synoptics*, Segundo depended upon J. Dupont and André Myre (*HJS*, 205, note 1; in reference to Jacques Dupont, *Les Béatitudes: Le problème littéraire,* 3 vols. [Bruges; Abbaye de Saint-André, 1954], especially Vol. III; and to André Myre, " 'Heureux les pauvres': histoire passée et future d'une parole," *Cri de Dieu: Espoir des pauvres*, ed. P.-A. Giguère, J. Martucci, and A. Myre [Montreal: Éditions Paulines, 1977], 67-134. (The latter article is erroneously listed in both the original and the English translation of *HJS* as "Développement d'un instantané christologique: Le prophète eschatologique," *Cri de Dieu*, 75-104. The content and the page references given by Segundo in the notes of *HJS*, however, do correspond to the page numbers in " 'Heureux les pauvres'.")

Overall, perhaps his note in *The Historical Jesus* best indicates his attitude toward historical critical method. After he presented the historical questions surrounding the synoptic gospels in "Introduction: A 'History' of Jesus?" he stated: "My effort here is not one of biblical exegesis. Hence in the following chapters I will use the criteria set forth in this Introduction without alluding specifically to them. I shall base my comments on the historical and exegetical data that seem more certain to me without burdening my readers with disquisitions and proofs that are alien to the aim of this book. My only purpose in this Introduction was to give readers a general overview of the scientific basis for everything that follows in this volume" (note 22, p. 198).

124. In *¿Qué es un cristiano?* (Montevideo: Mosca Hnos. S.A. Editores, 1971), table of contents, 18-19. The article had been presented first as a lecture and then in mimeograph form in 1964. See also *LT*, 112-15.

Alfred Hennelly, S.J., provided the first exposure in English to Segundo's early work, including "Etapas," in *Theologies in Conflict: The Challenge of Juan Luis Segundo* (Maryknoll, N.Y.: Orbis Books, 1979). He treated the stages of revelation/education on pp. 52-9.

Segundo carried forward this stage development of revelation into his article "Revelación, fe, signos de los tiempos" (*Revista Latinoaméricana de Teología* 5 [1988], 125-44).

125. "Pero lo que en realidad hace Jesús, durante esos tres años de convivencia con sus discípulos, es llevarlos a rehacer rápidamente las etapas religiosas por las cuales había pasado Israel durante diez siglos, a fin de volverlos capaces de comprender la Buena Noticia. También comunicó ésta, es cierto, pero la dejó como una semilla, semilla que la comunidad eclesial desarrollaría en sus inmensos alcances y expanadiría con su predicación" ("Etapas precristianas," 11).

126. ". . .la Escritura nos muestra **una historia sagrada revelada por Dios a diversos escritores**" ("Etapas precristianas," 12); emphasis Segundo's.

127. ". . .Digamos que cuando se ve más profundamente el contenido de la Escritura, ésta nos aparece como **la educación hecha por dios de la fe de su pueblo escogido, en las diferentes etapas de esa misma educación**" ("Etapas precristianas," 15); emphasis Segundo's.

128. "Etapas precristianas," 35.

129. *LT*, 118. "Etapas precristianas" predated Bateson's "Social Planning and the Concept of Deutero-Learning," in *Steps to an Ecology of Mind* (1972), 159-76. However, when Segundo spoke of biblical history as an educational process in *LT* in 1975, he referred explicitly to Bateson's theory of "deutero-learning."

Bateson explained his term: "Let us coin two words, 'proto-learning' and 'deutero-learning'. . . . Let us say that there are two sorts of gradient discernible in all continued learning. The gradient at any point on a simple learning curve (e.g., a curve of rote learning) we will say chiefly represents rate of proto-learning. If, however, we inflict a series of similar learning experiments on the same subject, we shall find that in each successive experiment the subject has a somewhat steeper proto-learning gradient, that he learns somewhat more rapidly. This progressive change in rate of proto-learning we will call 'deutero-learning'" (167). Cf. a "test-wise" student.

130. *HCP*, 171; emphasis Segundo's.

131. *HCP*, 171.

132. *HCP*, 172.

133. *HCP*, 172.

134. *LT*, 125.

135. *LT*, 78.

136. *LT*, p. 79.

137. *FI*, 41-2; emphasis Segundo's.

138. *FI*, 47.

139. *LT*, 81.

140. "La opción por los pobres," 478-80.

141. *LT*, 32. On this point Segundo cited Cone's *A Black Theology of Liberation* (Philadelphia: Lippincott, 1970), 156.

142. *LT*, 87.

143. "Pues bien, yo tengo una respuesta, la mía, a este problema hermenéutico: la opción por los pobres. No voy a abordar la opción por los pobres como un resultado de la Teología de la Liberación ni como uno de sus temas favoritos, sino como clave hermenéutica, es decir, como aquello previo para interpretar el Evangelio e impedir su letra mate. En ese sentido, propongo esta respuesta como algo universal que vale no sólo para América Latina, sino para todo el mundo" ("La opción por los pobres," 474-5).

144. "La opción," 481.

145. "La opción," 481-2.

146. "La opción," 476-77.

147. "La opción," 474-5.

148. *HJS*, 7.

149. *HJS*, 7. See also *The Sacraments Today* (*ST*), trans. John Drury (Maryknoll, N.Y.: Orbis Books, 1974), 32-34.

150. *LT*, 39.

2

IDENTITY AND ROLE OF THE POOR

The context out of which an author works and the method of the project itself significantly influence both the shape and the content of subsequent writings. Having examined in the first chapter the historical context of Juan Luis Segundo's theology and his theological method, this chapter will study the poor as they appear in his work, shaped by the developments of Latin American theology and embodying his highly nuanced hermeneutic circle. It will do this in two parts. First, it will explore the identity of the poor as Segundo referred to them in both general and specific ways. Second, it will investigate the role, both active and passive, of the poor in relation to history, Scripture, and Christian praxis.

IDENTITY OF THE POOR

GENERALLY UNDERSTOOD

From his earliest published work, Juan Luis Segundo wrote with an awareness of the impoverished situation of Latin America. Although he did not make frequent reference to "the poor" as such in his earlier writings, he alluded to them nevertheless when he discussed other themes such as membership in the church, grace, the sacraments, and theological method. Where he indicated who the poor are in this more general or implicit way, four characteristics stand out: the poor are persons lacking the necessities of life; deprived of liberty by oppressive structures; lacking in a critical consciousness of their situation; or in need of love and of the coming of the kingdom of God. These categories were not mutually exclusive and were frequently applied in combination to the persons or groups about whom Segundo spoke.

Persons Lacking Necessities

In *A Community Called Church*, referring to a Christian's more profound responsibility to be a sign of love, the author indicated some of the goods a person may lack: "be it a loaf of bread, a glass of water, a program for estabishing justice or communicating a revelation."[1] A few pages later he inquired into the appropriate response of the church to demands for efforts to assist the poor.[2] In other works he affirmed the historical context of sacramental ritual, which must confront "issues of suffering, violence, injustices, famine and death."[3]

Persons Deprived of Liberty by Oppressive Structures

Elsewhere, Segundo also referred to deficiencies which result from actual deprivation and subjection. He spoke, for instance, of "the most tangible and urgent enslavements: poverty, hunger, ignorance, exploitation, etc."[4] He referred to the lot of "the poorest, the most helpless, and the most oppressed."[5]

Segundo stresses the structural aspect of deprivation. When persons are forced to live and work according to an established morality which favors a small part of the population, they are alienated by the given structures.[6] Victims of unjust societies, such as Latin Americans in the period of crisis and desperation from 1950-75, are subject to both institutionalized and repressive forms of violence.[7] They are "those who have been deprived of [their full humanity], mainly by mechanisms of marginalization and exploitation that were grounded in religious ideologies."[8]

Besides structural violence and religious justification, global relationships become a part of the definition of deprivation. When as nations people are unable to sustain themselves, they constitute a "poor circuit."[9] From an evolutionary viewpoint in which all relationships participate in an economy of energy, Segundo called the situation of these nations "a poor circuit, and a catastrophic factor of inflexibility for the whole human species."[10]

Persons Without a Critical Consciousness of Their Situation

The lack of awareness, and specifically critical awareness, is a crucial deficiency in the people termed "the poor" in Segundo's thought. The subjective side of the alienation referred to above is that the majority of the Latin American population not only "cannot express their own thoughts as liberated subjects of history. They cannot even think their own thoughts."[11] Having assimilated a mentality which subjugates, they cannot serve as sources of a "liberating understanding" for themselves.[12] Their impaired comprehension extends to their view of God: oppressive, fatalistic, and idolatrous.[13]

Persons in Need of Love and of the Coming of God's Kingdom

In an ascending order of importance, the need for love and a readiness for God's reign appropriately culminates this resume of general or implicit references to the poor. In fact, the listing above of basic necessities ("be it a loaf of bread. . .") is set within a discussion of love as the ultimate principle of salvation and of the Church's mission as sign-bearer to this charity.[14] People's needs go deeper than the means for survival; they involve above all a yearning for love. It is to this level of need that the gospel proclamation speaks: "The kingdom of God comes first and foremost for those who, by virtue of their situation, have most need of it: the poor, the afflicted, the hungry of this world. . . ."[15]

SPECIFICALLY UNDERSTOOD

The Poor of the Old Testament

Segundo has made almost no references to the poor of the Old Testament period. The few he has made occurred in secondary or passing ways, chiefly in *The Historical Jesus of the Synoptics*. Concerning Jesus' proclamation of the kingdom he observes:

> It is no part of our purpose here to forget that the term 'kingdom' is qualified by the phrase 'of God' or that the poor in question here may well be, at least in principle, the very people who are also called the poor 'of Yahweh' in various passages of the Old Testament.[16]

While Segundo emphasizes the Old Testament tradition of God's special concern for the disadvantaged, he does not assume that the poor necessarily look solely to God for recourse. This was evident in his criticism of Jacques Dupont's conclusions about the "poor of Yahweh." While Dupont made trust in God a condition for the poor to expect God's intervention, Segundo considered the state of the poor as distinct from their moral attitudes:

> In their clearest and most ancient sense, [the Beatitudes] tell us that there is an intrinsic and positive relationship between the kingdom and the **situation** of **every** poor person, between the happiness brought by the kingdom and being poor (**period!**).[17]

Segundo also commented on the reference to Isaiah 61:1-2 in Luke's account of Jesus' initial Galilean preaching: " 'The spirit of the Lord is upon me; therefore he has anointed me. He has sent me to announce **good news to the poor**, to proclaim liberation to the captives and recovery of sight to the blind. . . .' " (Luke 4:18-19).[18] Again Segundo remarked on the Old Testament silence about a prerequisite moral or spiritual state in those for whom God acts. It is clear, therefore, that in the few instances where Segundo has made explicit reference to the poor of the Old Testament, they are those for whom God plans to act because of their unacceptable state of existence.

The Poor of Jesus' Day

In relation to the historical Jesus, Segundo's references to the poor have recently become much more frequent. They will be considered here according to two basic characteristics: (a) the poor were marked by a situation of poverty, and (b) the poor consequently were excluded as sinners. In the later section in this chapter on the role of the poor, they will be seen as well in relation to Jesus' proclamation of God's coming kingdom as those for whom the kingdom's arrival is "good news" and those to whom God chooses to reveal the divine Self.

First, the poor in the time of Jesus were those in a situation of poverty. In referring to the beatitudes, while Segundo recognizes the different redactions of the beatitudes made by Matthew and Luke, he prefers Luke's interpretation of the first statement of blessedness and its corollaries. In contrast to Matthew's "the poor in spirit" which indicated praise for a virtuous attitude,[19] Luke's simpler "blessed are you poor" indicated those who were poor because of their social and economic situation. Concretely for Luke, this meant "the poor and persecuted Christian community of his day."[20] After examining the pre-ecclesial and post-ecclesial context of the beatitude passages, Segundo concludes, however, that "the Beatitudes, in their earliest form, were probably addressed to the poor, those who were so in socio-economic terms."[21] They were the ones for whom Jesus initiated his historical project, "all those who have been the objects of scorn, injustice, and marginalization, whether they are good or bad."[22]

In his particular sensitivity to various forms of poverty, Luke among the evangelists provided some unique insights from within the Hellenistic context of preaching the gospel. His descriptions of poor people tended to be in relation to the wealthy, and his treatment of wealth revolved around its use. Since the appropriate use of wealth for Luke focused on the meal table, signifying both food and social relationships, it is easy to understand the central place he gave to the parable of Lazarus,[23] who "is participating in the eschatological banquet simply and solely because he is one of the poor."[24]

Second, the poor were excluded as sinners. Closely allied to the notion of poverty as a social condition was the exclusion suffered by the poor in Jesus' day. Because many of the economically poor Jewish people did not know nor observe the Law in its details, they belonged to a social class of the "impure," subordinate to the religious leaders and kept in an inferior social status for religious reasons. "Legal purity and impurity served the ideological function attributed to prestige, money, or power in other societies. The poor were called sinners, and they ended up regarding themselves as such."[25] As sinners the poor were ostracized.[26]

To sum up, who were the poor of Jesus' day as J. L. Segundo has presented them? They were the persons marked by their situation of socio-economic poverty, whose designation as "sinners" by the Jewish authorities relegated them to the margins of society. For these very motives, they will be seen as the addressees of Jesus' good news that God's reign is at hand to reveal the secret of God's personal, effective love for them which will change their inhuman condition.

The Poor Today

The contemporary reality of the poor is fundamental in Segundo's thought, ordinarily in the general senses discussed above. Certain specific meanings of "the poor" are significant, however, particularly in the recent *Reflexiones críticas*. For example in the first chapter, "Values 'versus' Solutions," Segundo advocates Christians sharing with certain groups (such as socialists) an active concern for "the liberation of peoples oppressed and impoverished by national and international structures" even though they do not always agree with the means these groups use.[27] In another instance, he speaks at length about the issue of the poor and the Indian devotees of the Virgin of Guadalupe. Here he criticizes a piety which has left people with virtually the same structural problems and poverty that they suffered four centuries ago.[28]

The allusions in *Reflexiones críticas* to the poor resemble those in Segundo's Pauline work. In a note to the Appendix, where he considers "Paul's Key and Latin America Today," he refers to the situation out of which one must do theology in Latin America. "Consider the ever increasing misery of the poor, their obvious lack of orientation, and the growing evidence and signs of further oppression and repression."[29]

An important sense of the "poor" for Segundo appeared in several of his later works: the poor as synonymous with the "people" and often with the passive and uncritical "mass." In *The Humanist Christology of Paul* he argued that it is futile to seek the desired liberation directly from "a simultaneously qualitative and quantitative power: 'the People', or more specifically, 'the Poor'."[30] He based this negation on his principle that the (qualitative) Christianity which stresses commitment and critical awareness is of a different order than the (quantitative) Catholicism which emphasizes minimally committed numerical membership. He saw these two orders as essentially incompatible. Thus he could not attribute to the "poor," who have uncritically internalized oppressive mentalities, the "historical (liberating) force," that the title of Gustavo Gutiérrez' recent book described.[31] Neither did he concur in the idea of a "discipleship of the poor" for similar reasons.[32]

How, then, does Segundo conceptualize the poor in today's world? The poor live a less than human existence because of hunger, violence, and multiple forms of injustice. Furthermore, they lack a critical awareness which can penetrate the ideological distortions which hold them captive. Thus, in a way similar to the poor of Jesus' day, the poor are the objects of the Christian message of love which fosters their becoming fully conscious human subjects.[33]

THE ROLE OF THE POOR

Now that the previous section has clarified who the poor are, implicitly and explicitly, in Juan Luis Segundo's treatment of social reality and scripture, the following part will discuss the role of the poor. As Segundo presented it, this role is sometimes in the background, sometimes in the forefront; if not multiple, it is yet complex. It will be developed here in relation to three areas: history, Scripture, and Christian praxis. The discussion assumes two other fields of inquiry, one preliminary and one consequent. The first is the hermeneutic circle, which figures continually in and about the role of the poor. The second is the relationship to the church, which will unfold at length in the next three chapters.

RELATED TO HISTORY

As a social and economic reality with religious implications being poor is by definition historical. The way that Segundo articulates the function of the poor within Christianity and theology exemplifies three important principles in his theology of history: love as the primary or absolute value of both human and Christian life; freedom as the arena in which human existence operates; and the sociopolitical character of history. The poor at different times express these basic truths positively or negatively, actively or passively, as model or as contrast.

Love as the Primary Value

Love in Segundo's theology first of all reveals who God is. Knowledge of God and love of neighbor are directly proportionate: "Where there is no love of neighbor, there is no knowledge of, or relationship with God."[34] When people turn away from the gratuitous faith which recognizes other persons as deserving of love, they are by this fact, and not by their failure to adhere to Christianity, idolatrous.[35] In turn, the freedom of God's love urges believers to work gratuitously for the integration of the marginalized and to collaborate with God in constructing a truly human existence for all women and men.[36]

Secondly, love was Jesus' absolute value. In his volume on the *Spiritual Exercises* of St. Ignatius, Segundo recalled "the conclusion that Jesus, in his 'ideologically' limited life and message, revealed that the absolute for him was love. . . , taking sides with the poor and marginalized against the established society and its protected favorites."[37]   When viewed in relation to the cross, this love is seen to show results even now: "One must accept the **transcendent datum** that the cross of Jesus is not a closed but an open door, through which life, justice, and love are already filtering and beginning to transform historical reality."[38]

The author arrived at the same point from the perspective of values, touching also on authentic knowledge of God vs. idolatry:

> . . .We may well see that the Christian message is living witness to the satisfaction one may find in joining the poorest, the most helpless, and the most oppressed. In that case the logic of **Christian** values may lead us to reject what we see to be a community of privileged beings. We may even go so far as to reject a God who seems to confer such privileges quite independently of the good will of the people involved.[39]

The third aspect of love as an absolute is that it constitutes the dynamism within universal evolution. In his fifth volume on Jesus Christ, Segundo called love "the qualitative vector of survival that is present in universal evolution from beginning to end."[40] The movement toward fulfillment and integration is far from a smoothly continuous one, however; creative forces always contend with degradation, negentropy with entropy. Yet Segundo relied on the power of gratuitous love: "We believe that grace dialectically integrates human sins in the creative human destiny."[41]

Before moving on to the topic of human freedom, a short summary is in order. How do the poor, according to Segundo, manifest the absolute importance of love within human and salvation history? First, because God chooses to reveal the divine identity through love of neighbor which participates in God's own gratuity, the poor disclose through others' response to them the knowledge of the true God. Second, the poor exemplify the absolute value of love at work in the life, message, and mission of Jesus who cast his lot with the poor and marginalized of his day. Third, as individuals but even more as groups and nations, the poor bring to light integrative dynamisms in tension with disintegrative forces within global evolution.

The Arena of Human Freedom

Freedom which enables movement toward a creative human destiny is of fundamental importance for Segundo both in general and in relation to the poor. Three dimensions of freedom, according to Segundo, will be explored here: (a) freedom is the ability to carry out what one chooses; (b) freedom confronts the conflict between sin and salvation; and (c) freedom requires conscious attention to the enslaving forces at work in history.

First, freedom involves the ability to realize one's goals. Thus Segundo defined freedom in *The Humanist Christology of Paul*, based on Romans 7.[42] As human beings, the poor bear title to liberty. In his early book, *Grace and the Human Condition*, Segundo emphasized the basic freedom which marks all human beings despite the myriad obstacles to its realization.[43] Later, in his Pauline work, he described the moment at the conclusion of the history of love when "the best and most precious part of us will be revealed: our freedom."[44]

Yet, quite obviously, this foundational aspect of human existence and accomplishment is far from realized. Segundo refers, for example, to the essential imbalance and disruption of the social ecology which exists because six percent of the world population consumes forty percent of the goods. Here the rich subject the poor to their patterns of consumption.[45] He notes also the continuing oppression suffered by Indians and the poor despite several centuries of Catholicism and devotions such as that to the Virgin of Guadalupe.[46] A majority of human beings, in other words, are not free to obtain the necessities for a dignified existence.

Second, on the field of human liberty, sin and salvation contend for the upper hand. The author's definition of "salvation" in *Grace and the Human Condition* emphasized the inner obstacles from which a person, poor or rich, is freed by grace: "inner slavery and fear, the corruption of the surrounding universe (destined for vanity otherwise), and the subjection of our body. Consequently, salvation from these four evils leads into the reality **par excellence: our liberty**."[47] The inner power of sin is real and lifelong. Nevertheless, the author calls attention to Paul's faith in the victory which Christ accomplishes over the enemies of human freedom. "It must be translated as a **resurrection**: the victory in all human beings of life, of the grace received in faith, and of an effective freedom that proves to be creative in love for others."[48]

Third, freedom entails awareness of the enslaving forces which threaten its attainment. The victory of grace still needs to be internalized and consolidated. Segundo has shown that Jesus worked to create this very awareness in those to whom he preached. While he proclaimed the arrival of God's kingdom **for** the poor out of God's gratuity, he drew the people toward freely accepting that action as genuine subjects.[49] Through his polemical parables he strove to destroy the distorted patterns of thinking by which the poor made their (popular) religious practice oppressive for themselves.[50] Jesus also addressed the social dimension of sin and grace: by a combination of self-propelling and self-justifying forces, the majority is dominated and the minority dominates.[51]

Segundo has pointed out how essential it is to uncover the ways that social patterns of behavior work to justify both the systems and the attitudes they express. It is necessary to discover what real or perceived benefits result for both oppressed and oppressor from given social structures. For in the poor people themselves distorted understanding and lack of consciousness obstruct an effective belief in 'Jesus who frees'.

For this reason, Segundo has pursued a theological orientation in which the poor, to the extent that they internalize the mental distortions and lack awareness of them, cannot be subjects of their own liberation or of theology. Rather, theology is at their service, exposing through the mediation of social science the structured injustices and underlying rationale — the ideologies — which oppress them.[52] Here the theologian must be open to the

> conversion which is required of the intellectual confronted with the interests and way of thinking of the people themselves. To some extent this conversion demands a renunciation of critical and creative characteristics which the intellectual can draw out of himself or herself, in order to be freely engaged as an instrument of the people.[53]

As the poor grow in conscious subjectivity, they overcome the alienation associated with their existence as "masses."[54] Undertaking their intended free role within history, they begin to realize their goals more effectively. They enter into a graced liberty which overcomes the powerlessness of sin. And, conscious of the forces which hold them captive, they more critically and effectively confront these powers.

The Sociopolitical Character of History

Near the end of *The Humanist Christology of Paul*, Segundo made a powerful statement about the sociopolitical quality of the relationship between the poor and history. Although he did not use the words "poverty" or "poor," the linkage of love and the concrete situation of oppression clearly included them:

> . . .Paul has helped us to see the central problem of our human condition today: the creation and maintenance of structures and power-centers that are bound to block all effective forms of loving our neighbors and our fellow human beings in either the public or private sphere. The crucial issue is not the existence of individual sins of frailty, even those involving conscious exploitation, which will ultimately be forgiven and forgotten. The crucial problem is the idol that has been erected above and against everything human, the global power that has been set up to endure, to enslave human beings, to strip them of their freedom to create, to make them useless and kill them. . . .[55]

Segundo has shown this idolatrous power at work in several spheres. One is the mission of the Church to evangelize. Over the centuries, alliances of convenience with economic powers have diluted the message of a God who promises the kingdom to the poor. History seems to say that "in order to be 'the church of the poor,' it must first be 'the church of the rich.' "[56] The dehumanizing force also operates in sacramental theology when it is practiced out of a vertical and ahistorical perspective which sets religious formulas and rites above issues of suffering, hunger, and violence.[57] Further, it functions in popular devotions when they endure passively alongside structural oppression.

Internationally, "advanced" nations, many of them professedly Christian, employ in the name of law "dehumanizing ideologies" in such areas as insurance, trade, and human rights policies.[58] On the personal level, individuals and small groups experience simultaneously a sense of 'structural sin' and a lack of effective instruments for combatting it.[59]

While Segundo does not discuss the poor in terms of a "class struggle" in the main body of his work, he responded to the charge in the Vatican *Instruction on Certain Aspects of the "Theology of Liberation"* that for some theologians "every affirmation of faith or of theology is subordinated to a political criterion which in turn depends on the class struggle, the driving force of history."[60] He noted in his reply that, while this definition of history is both inadequate and inaccurate, the recognition of class differences due to wrongful appropriation of common resources is more Christian than it is Marxist.[61]

Where does Segundo offer realistic hope for change in the situation of the poor? He points to the positive, evangelical value of human history and issues a challenge to assume the sociopolitical exigencies of human liberation. He argues from the viewpoints of social structure, of evangelization, and of Christian tradition.

History is sociopolitical in nature basically because it deals with society. Segundo wrote in his early volumes on the sacraments and grace from the conviction that individual liberation from sin does not automatically produce other liberations without changing sinful social and political structures. Particular freedom must be "concretized in ideological transformation and political action."[62] Since unjust societies as well as just ones constitute ecologies or social systems, they must be changed as structured entities.[63] The conclusion follows, then, that transforming inhuman conditions into situations compatible with a God of compassion requires concrete forms on the sociopolitical level.

The gospel's primary address to the poor implies a key point. Where true evangelization exists, Christians make different decisions:

> The good news becomes the basic wellspring, not only of their attitudes but also of their value judgments on the historical scene in which they are living. The surface appearance of events does not impress them as much as the affinity of a given political or social movement to the deeper values associated with the good news.[64]

Thus Christians link newspaper headlines about a rising or falling stock market to issues of international trade and of hunger in Brazil or Ethiopia.

Christian tradition also underscores the sociopolitical dimension of history. Since the role of the poor in relation to Scripture will be developed in the next section, suffice it here to make two observations.

First, based on his political reading of the synoptic gospels and his reflection on Paul's letter to the Romans, Segundo maintains that

> in Latin America . . . we have to be suspicious of any christological key that does not issue in political consequences as concrete and conflictive as those that Jesus himself dared to draw from his conception of God. We must suspect that such keys constitute culpable evasion and escapism.[65]

Second, Segundo draws out the political significance of Justin the apologist's writing on God's presence and activity in philosophers and legislators. Justin considered the political activity of the lawmaker, Christian or not, an exercise of saving grace. Segundo translates this to mean that "Justin is telling us that all those who are fighting for a more equitable distribution of wealth, for the betterment of man, and for the construction of a more fraternal social order, are responding to the summons of grace. . . ."[66]

Segundo has decried throughout his work "the creation and maintenance of structures and power-centers that. . .block all effective forms of loving our neighbors."[67] Such institutions, which he termed idolatrous, exist both within and outside the church. At the same time, he draws from the nature of society, the implications of evangelization, and the insights of Christian tradition the principles for new structures and power-centers which enable a love for the neighbor embodying authentic knowledge of God.

Before proceeding to the next section, a brief backwards glance is worthwhile. The poor in Segundo's work exemplify the historical character of human and Christian life. Sometimes as actors and agents, other times as recipients and victims, poor people make visible three important characteristics of historical reality: (1) love is the absolute value in history; (2) history comprises the sphere of human freedom; and (3) history is social and political by nature. In setting forth the interplay of the poor and history, Segundo speaks about the poor, yes, but about the rest of Christianity and the human race as well. In a way similar to the birth of a child in a family, a description of the event is not simply about the baby — nor a theological study of the poor solely about marginalized people. It is also an investigation into the history, with all its implications, of those in whose midst the baby or the poor live.

RELATED TO SCRIPTURE

The Revelation of God in the Old Testament

Segundo has not dealt extensively with the role of the poor from an Old Testament perspective. He has, however, outlined an approach to the early Scriptures which is significant for the overall question: the stages of God's revelation in the Old Testament. He used von Rad's typological theology as the framework for his own educational variation upon the theme.[68] God's progressive self-revelation was simultaneously a process of educating the chosen people. Furthermore, the process has continued into the New Testament era as God leads people through these prerequisite stages toward genuine Christian belief.[69] This section will, therefore, briefly summarize the four stages of the process found in the article, "Etapas precristianas," as they relate to the role of the poor. It will then review related Old Testament material from several additional works of Segundo.

The first stage corresponds to the period from approximately 1000-800 B.C., when the Yahwist and Eloist traditions developed. During this period the people came to understand God as the Absolute in the land of Israel, a God of mystery and awe. Beyond its immediate significance for that era, this stage brings a recognition of the absolute value of love. " 'God is Love' means: 'the Absolute is love' and consequently, 'love is the Absolute'."[70] An important drawback of this stage despite the key value is the exteriority of its reliance on ritual efficacy divorced from ordinary historical causes.[71]

The second stage focuses on the God of the covenant with Israel during the years from 800-550 B.C. Here God appeared as a moral providence who required upright conduct. This phase of understanding provokes a "crusader" zeal, both in the era of the chosen people and in later epochs. It lends itself, as well, to

> a justification . . . applied to the riches of the upper classes in the Christian countries. The morality, at least external, which characterizes them, contrary to the open passion which the lower classes allow to be seen, comes together in this historical explanation to formulate this judgment: 'God has blessed us', which is equivalent to the other: 'God has rewarded us'.[72]

The third stage takes on greater universalism. This period in Hebrew history from 550-175, B.C., showed God as transcendent and creator. It gave rise to the tension of attempting "to synthesize the historical task and divine transcendence," and generated the messianic notion of Israel.[73] The messianic concept has continued to influence thinking throughout history, perhaps especially the classical economic theories of liberalism.

> The acceptance of a growing inequality between poor and rich. . . seemed to [the founders of liberalism] acceptable as the will of God. For God, in a mysterious way, destines some people to riches and others to misery, and similarly brings upon some salvation and upon others infirmity or death.[74]

In addition, the passivity engendered in this stage weakens its movement beyond particularism.[75]

The fourth and final prechristian stage, originating between 175 B.C. and the time of Christ, is that of God as legislator of the universe. The writers of that era showed God to be creator of the good only, and so did not solve the problem of an upright life marked by suffering. Thus the basic insight found here is that God effects justice beyond the borders of human existence in eternal life. Personal liberty comes to the fore, as does the relationship between outward event and inner liberty.[76] As close as these understandings come to the Christian vision, Segundo noted that they still anticipate the gospel message. In particular, the notion of human existence as a test, the non-creative character of liberty, and a "certain resigned inhibition" in the religious person fall short of the development still to come.[77]

The *Theology for Artisans of a New Humanity* series presented related Old Testament material in the "Biblical Tapestries" found at the end of each volume. All of this material appeared against the background of Segundo's comprehensive view of salvation history, summarized above. In *The Community Called Church*, for example, he arranged Old Testament texts according to the theme, God's preparation of Israel for transformation into the church. Using Isaiah 1:9-17 he showed Yahweh's law for the covenant people to be a law of inner justice. He referred to the remnant of Israel as "a poor and lowly people" and reflected upon "the eternal hope of the poor."[78] He pointed to the wicked who confound this hope by playing out a gamble based on their own moral norms and justifying their oppression of others.[79]

The Sacraments Today addressed the question, Where is the sacred? Segundo pointed out Isaiah's admonition, in the midst of ancient Israel's search for God's true presence, to worshippers seeking to draw near to God: " 'Is this not what I require of you as a fast: . . . Is it not sharing your food with the hungry, taking the homeless poor into your house, clothing the naked when you meet them and never evading a duty to your kinsfolk?' "[80]

How, then, does the interpretation of salvation history in the Old Testament relate to the role of the poor as shown in Segundo's work? While in a few specific instances, such as the observation in "Etapas precristianas" concerning the liberal theory of economics, the author spoke of the situation of poor people in the world, his main contribution in regard to the Old Testament lay elsewhere. It portrayed the face of God manifested gradually to a people being readied to act in the manner of this God: with love, in a spirit of freedom, engaging creatively in the whole social and political complex of history on behalf of those whose lives God intends to transform, the poor.

The Revelation of God in the New Testament

The process of God's educating and the people's learning continued in the New Testament era. In the "Biblical Tapestries" given at the end of each

volume in the *Theology for Artisans of a New Humanity* series Segundo
offered a wide variety of New Testament references on the role of the poor.
The relevant texts centered almost exclusively on love. In exploring the
sign-function of the church, for example, Segundo maintained that "in trying
to form a sure conscience we must operate in terms of that which is the
fulfillment of the law: i.e., love of neighbor."[81] In the volume on grace, he
identified the opposition between fear and filial love as the "fleshly" threat
posed to a Christian outlook. The menace to filial love (1 Jn 4:16-21)
endangers in turn the love of brother and sister. Inversely, the same charity
forms the continuity between the present earth and the new one, for God
identifies with the neighbor to whom a glass of water is offered out of love.[82]
Similarly, the sacred place where the God of the new Israel dwells is the
human being in need of love.[83] Taken together, these Scriptural reflections
point to the poor as the paradigm for the presence of true Christianity and the
new creation.

In addition to affording an overview of God's continuing formation
process in the "Tapestries," Segundo draws upon two major New Testament
sources to illuminate the role of the poor: the historical Jesus in the synoptic
gospels and the christology of Paul found mainly in the letter to the Romans.
These two sources, then, form the basis for this section.

The Synoptic Gospels

Jesus proclaimed the coming of the kingdom of God as good news for
the poor. This fact, which Segundo developed most extensively in the
second book of the series, *Jesus of Nazareth Yesterday and Today*, represented for him the heart of the synoptic message. In *The Historical Jesus of
the Synoptics*, Segundo accomplished two important tasks: he identified the
components of Jesus' proclamation and he pointed out the political character
of the message. The following section will develop these two aspects of the
contribution which the historical Jesus made concerning the role of the poor.

Components of the Proclamation   Rather than existing as one discrete
action, Jesus' proclamation encompassed his whole life and ministry. Yet
three elements of this proclamation, which set Jesus' mission in clearest
relief, will be explored here: three crucial occasions which appear almost as
moments of one event, Jesus' parables, and Jesus' lifestyle itself.

Segundo identified within the synoptic gospels three events which in
their convergence "might be called a circle of meaning that brings us closer

to the heart of the question."[84] The first of these events was the summary of Jesus' first preaching found in Mark 1:15 and its parallels: " 'The time is fulfilled and the kingdom of God is near; change your outlook and believe in the good news'."[85]

The second moment was Jesus' reply to John the Baptist's question from prison about his identity, as it appeared in Matt. 11:2-6 and Luke 7:22-23. " 'Are you he who is to come, or shall we look for another?' Jesus responds to this question by pointing to signs of the proximate arrival or presence of the kingdom: 'Go and tell John what you hear and see. The blind receive their sight and the lame walk. . .'."[86] Here "he who is to come" signified for the author the reign which would accompany the one who arrives.

The third occasion, Jesus' solemn opening discourse (on the mountain in Matt. 5:3f., on the plain in Luke 6:20f.), bore particular importance in this convergence of events. Segundo gave careful attention to the discourse as the setting for the beatitudes. As noted above, he favored the Lucan version; Luke, he believed, "redacts the Beatitudes in line with the source as addressed exclusively to **the poor**, the hungry, and the mournful."[87] He added "The key word here is **poor** people, and the other two words spell that out."[88] The kingdom comes to **change** the situation of the poor. Thus it is in the conjunction of three closely related terms "('kingdom,' 'the poor,' and 'good news') that the prophetic content of Jesus' proclamation moves. This, in other words, is his message and the key to his outlook, ministry, and death."[89] Thus, while the kingdom, the poor, and the good news coincided with particular clarity in Jesus' initial sermon and the beatitudes, the three terms consolidated the summary of Jesus' early preaching, his reply to John, and the discourse into one key to Jesus' relationship with the poor.

In addition to the three focal occasions which contained the kernel of Jesus's central proclamation, the parables bore the same essential message. Segundo developed at length in *The Historical Jesus* the parable of Lazarus and the rich man, in which he found that

> here we have an almost literal reproduction of the first Beatitude, this time in vivid images, and even of the other two Beatitudes, which make it still clearer that the kingdom of God is coming to invert situations: so that those who now weep can laugh and those who are hungry now can have their fill.[90]

This parable made another point as well. Segundo understood that for Luke the social occasion of the meal table focused the meaning of wealth and its proper use. In the 'new creation' of the kingdom, the poor, like Lazarus and the street people of the wedding banquet parable, step from the margins into the center of dignity, human interchange, and joy in the abundance from which they have been excluded.[91]

The close link between parables and central proclamation extended still farther. Segundo devoted an important section in *Reflexiones críticas* to the parables, which "were spoken, for the most part, against the authorities of Israel and their way of understanding and handling the law, and in favor of the poor and sinners."[92] Yet if Jesus was to preach convincingly that God came to change the situation of the poor to a human, liberating one, he had to surmount an enormous ideological obstacle. He undertook this through the parables, which Segundo divided into four series according to aspects of the task.

The first series, which demonstrated the surprising and inevitable arrival of the kingdom, included the stories of the callous rich man (Lk. 12: 16-21), the watchful virgins (Mt. 25: 1-12), and the rich man and Lazarus (Lk. 16: 19-31). The second, announcing the kingdom's arrival for the poor, even if they are sinners, included the narratives of joy (primarily God's) over finding the lost: the sheep, the coin, the son (Lk. 15:4-32; Mt. 18:12-14).[93]

The two final series looked to the roots of the problem. The third, parables such as the Pharisee and the publican (Lk. 18:9-14) and the wicked vinedressers (Mk. 12:1-11 and parallels), reveal who the true sinners were in Israel. The fourth counseled responsibility to be exercised on behalf of the neighbor, such as the narratives of the talents (Mt. 25:1-12 and Lucan parallel) and the good Samaritan (Lk. 10:25-37). This last set forth the only true basis, love for the neighbor, for knowing who God is and understanding God's law.[94]

Jesus' lifestyle and activity also proclaimed the kingdom's arrival for the poor. The author described Jesus' and the disciples' style of life not as poor but as middle class, or perhaps more exacly, lower middle class. "In any case," he maintained "Jesus was not, nor could he become, one of the common people."[95] Yet the beatitudes Jesus addressed to the poor, and in fact his whole didactic and thaumaturgic activity, evidenced his non-indifference toward poverty.[96] While he refrained from treating the miracles extensively, Segundo noted: Jesus "had extraordinary powers to alleviate evils and heal illnesses, and he used those powers especially for the poor and needy; moreover, he did so to announce to them in a creditable way the nearness or presence of the kingdom of God."[97] He countered accusations of evil influence by showing that the place where the diabolical manifests itself is "infrahuman situations where liberty and purpose are lacking."[98]

The fundamental reason for Jesus' special consideration for the poor was God's own being. Jesus directed the promise of the kingdom unconditionally to the poor of his day because "their inhuman situation . . . [was] an affront to God: because they have been left on the sidelines in the religiously established society of Israel."[99] The poor constitute the occasion for God's profound and concrete self-revelation: "in this historical plan of making a certain type or group of people happy, God's heart will be revealed."[100]

The Message as Political   To speak about Jesus' stance toward the poor is to acknowledge the conflict which marked both what he taught and what he did. When he announced who would enter the kingdom of God and spelled out the criterion for a right understanding of the law, he cut to the heart of Jewish belief and practice. In this he "not only seeks but manages to sharpen the main conflicts latent in Israelite society."[101] Jesus accepted the uncomfortable and controversial lot of the prophet. He struggled to make "all the **systems** that affect human coexistence, from the psychological and interpersonal to the social and international" subject to the criterion of effective love.[102] He opposed the religious leadership by his support of the poor and sinners, thereby bringing down upon himself the full weight of the authorities' self-defense.[103] Jesus strove above all to bring people to consciousness of God's plan, and to lift the ideological burden which kept people less than human.[104]

Segundo showed, in the light of the synoptic evidence, that "**the kingdom itself** cannot be preached indiscriminately as good news, as gospel."[105] The proclamation was political or conflictual also in that it divided Jesus' hearers. Three groups emerge: those whom the kingdom threatens; the disciples who follow Christ's way on behalf of the poor; and the direct addressees, the poor.[106]

The first group is the rich; what does the news of the kingdom's arrival say to them? Just as the parables of Jesus affirmed and elaborated the joyful promise to the poor found in the beatitudes so, read from the reverse, they echoed the "woes" of Jesus' solemn opening discourse.[107] Jesus set up an opposition, declared a judgment. Segundo remarked that Luke, in his version of the beatitudes

is especially anxious to indicate and stress the corresponding negative side: the kingdom of God is a piece of bad news for the concrete groups that stand opposite the poor in the social spectrum. Its arrival sounds the death knell of the privileges that have so far been enjoyed by the rich, the satisfied, and all those who have been able to laugh in the world as it has actually been structured (see Luke: 24-25).[108]

The opposition touches every facet of life. The author continued: "Paradoxically enough, the aspect of political conflict becomes increasingly crucial and decisive as the line of preference shifts from social groups to others that would have to be classified in much more directly religious terms."[109]

For the bad news to become good news, a conversion is necessary through facing the conflict which results from Jesus' proclamation. Conversion requires that the rich persons side with the poor ones and work to dissolve the barriers which stand in the way of their living fully as human beings. These barriers, Segundo reasoned, are ideological and religious; their removal dictates a radically new viewpoint on who God is, what Jesus taught, and what God's will or plan truly demands.[110]

The second group is composed of the disciples who follow the mandates of Christ on behalf of the poor. Their role will be discussed at length in the next chapter.

The third group consists of the poor listeners themselves. Most importantly, they receive the good news that the kingdom will belong to them and will change their situation. God welcomes them not because of their moral worthiness, but because of God's own joy in effecting their true humanization. At the same time that Segundo viewed the poor chiefly as the objects and the recipients of God's action in the kingdom, he also saw them called to prophetic consciousness. Citing the passage 'Take my yoke upon you . . .' (Mt. 11:28-30) as an invitation to discipleship, he observed:

> Thus Jesus would be inviting sinners and the poor, for whom the kingdom is coming without conditions or distinctions, to become his disciples. And if they do, he promises them a light burden by comparison with the heavy burden laid on their weary shoulders by the Pharisees and the doctors of the law.[111]

Jesus desired that the poor become aware of God's liberating action in themselves and, particularly, in the oppressive structures of which they are a part.[112]

Pauline Thought

The second Scriptural focus in Segundo's work is Paul's christology, drawn mainly from the letter to the Romans. Paul did not write from a political perspective. Yet while he held a very different point of view on the gospel message than Luke did, Segundo found that Paul also offered profound insights into the reality of the kingdom and the poor.

Segundo recognized that Paul's "key" or interpretative tool differed significantly from that of the synoptics:

> The term 'kingdom' has disappeared, and so has the central position of 'the poor'. The term 'sinners' no longer serves as an ideological label for a specific social group; that is why the unexpectedly positive or favorable sense of the term in Jesus' message disappears in Paul's letter. . . .
>
> What is this new key [of Paul's]? It is clear enough, I think, if we take a close look at Paul's personification of the conflicting forces, which is a 'theatrical' device in the good sense of the word. In the context of those forces Paul makes clear the unique place of Jesus, the Christ, and his importance for the human being. . . . Such terms as sin, grace, justification, law, inner human being, etc., compel us to assay an **anthropological** or existential key in Paul.[113]

Reading Romans 1-8 according to this anthropological key, Segundo in *The Humanist Christology of Paul* examined each chapter by turn, drew conclusions about Christ and the human being, and lastly considered the way that Paul's key relates to Latin America today.

In Romans 1, Segundo named idolatry, punishment, and dehumanized relationships as the three essential aspects of sin in Paul's description.[114] When he highlighted the portrayal in Romans 3 of the person of faith, he identified attitudes consistent with a notion of the law that is more true both to the human being and to God: (1) a surrender of attitudes which harden the heart; (2) human needs as the criterion for understanding the law; and (3) the integrity which risks obeying the dictates of one's heart.[115]

From Romans 5, the author compared Paul's interpretation of Jesus' message and mission with that of the synoptics. He recalled the evangelists' emphasis that the coming kingdom overturns the inhuman situation of the poor "by destroying the power of the 'strong one' who was dehumanizing them: Satan." He recognized that "in a different key Paul also sees God's project as a battle, coextensive with humanity itself, against the infrahuman condition of human beings."[116]

At this point, the anthropological principle which has held special importance for both Paul and Segundo became prominent: human freedom, that quality which marks the mature human being and evidences the victory of Christ. For Paul, freedom and resurrection required each other. The arrival of God's reign "must be translated as a **resurrection**: the victory in all human beings of life, of the grace received in faith, and of an effective freedom that proves to be creative in love for others."[117]

This theme of effective, constructive love continued to play through Paul's exposition and Segundo's presentation of it. In discussing Chapter 8 of Romans and the divided or mixed character of human action, Segundo added insights from 1 Corinthians and Romans 14 to articulate a Pauline view of morality based on participation in God's act of building the world and human life.[118] He conceived of freedom as the human counterpart to the divine attribute of creation. The apostle, Segundo commented, "does not regard it as a pendulum oscillating between good and evil. Paul sees freedom as the ability to carry out the projects that the 'I' chooses to perform."[119]   Liberty was for Segundo simultaneously the principle of effective love, the power of creative collaboration, and the Pauline image for the kingdom.[120]

While the central chapters of *The Humanist Christology of Paul* set forth the principles — sin, faith, freedom, victory, construction of the world — which ground an understanding of the role of the poor, Segundo's appendix contained more explicit comments based on them. He and the group members with whom he has reflected on the letter to the Romans have articulated a twofold experience: "(1) the power of what has come to be called 'structural sin' and its stranglehold on our societies; (2) the absence or lack of the usual political instruments that were used in the recent past to combat that structural sin."[121]

In Paul's letter Segundo searched for a key to understanding Christ in a way that cuts through centuries-old self-deception and impotence and releases the message of Christian freedom in effective structures. He acknowledged that this key is necessarily as conflictive as Jesus' own stance was. Even though the poor number in the millions in Latin American, he declined to settle for a solution that depends on numbers at the expense of consciousness and commitment.[122]   In the end, the value he and his companion searchers found in Paul's christology was insight into the enslaving dynamic which held them and blocked effective love for the neighbor. This new understanding, born out of the deep longing for freedom for themselves and their society, enabled them to make their wager of faith at a deeper level. In their "religious **faith** in Jesus and the **transcendent data** brought by him" they could confront what exists in the name of the "more" to which Jesus witnessed.[123]

To summarize, Segundo's assessment of Paul's contribution in Romans to the question of the role of the poor applied to rich as well as to poor. The dehumanized relationships which constitute poverty amounted, for both subject and object of the oppression, to idolatry. Gentiles, Jews, and

Christians all knew from within themselves the inability to carry out their ideals and good intentions. Yet belief in Christ lent a new perspective to the universal experience of powerlessness. The act of love in which Jesus embodied to the point of death God's liberative, humanizing plan opened a new horizon in which the struggle was worth the cost.

RELATED TO CHRISTIAN PRAXIS

Authentic Christianity is historical; it is conscious; it is free. It witnesses to the arrival of God's kingdom as good news for the poor and to the triumph over sin by faith in Christ. It manifests itself in effective love. Did not these traits delineated by Juan Luis Segundo speak adequately of Christian praxis? They did, in fact, set forth basic tenets of the way Segundo understood responsibility for the world carried out according to Christ's project in relation to the poor.

The present section will deal briefly with certain areas of social reality which concern the role of the poor and in which Segundo employed his ideological criticism. Most of these topics he treated in articles (which frequently grew out of lectures); on some, however, he commented in longer works. The three areas to be touched on here are: development and socioeconomic systems, human rights, and education and the mass media.

Development and Socioeconomic Systems

America published an article by Segundo in 1968 with the somewhat misleading title, "Social Justice and Revolution." In it the theologian examined Catholic social doctrine in terms of implementation. He surveyed principles from the gospels and the patristic writers for an equitable social order, but found that "the Christian aversion to treating poor men and rich differently never came to be more than an 'inspiration' — there were no politico-economic means to put it into practice."[124] Ordinarily insightful Latin American bishops could castigate those immediately responsible for the misery of innumerable poor people and still not disapprove its underlying cause, which he saw as "the industrialized countries and the international capitalistic market."[125] He concluded by questioning whether the socialist emphasis on means to accomplish the ideal, as well on as the principle that all people, not just a tiny minority, have the right to the means of production necessary for life, was not compatible with Catholic social doctrine.[126]

In an article the following year on riches and poverty as obstacles to development, Segundo maintained that a definite system or structure exists which increases the global imbalance between rich and poor countries. "Riches and poverty are clearly not the results of different causes, but two aspects of one and the same reality, indissolubly linked."[127] The poor countries are the "remainder," so to speak, of an unjust global division of resources.

A few years later, *Concilium* published an article of Segundo's which continued the discussion of socioeconomic questions, "Capitalism-Socialism: A Theological Crux." He pointed out that even the ability to decide whether theology can contribute to a choice of capitalism or socialism depends upon the value one gives to the historical dimension of Christian faith.

Given a positive valuing of this dimension, then an "authentic historical functionality of the gospel"[128] requires criteria. Ultimately, Segundo postulated that these criteria are the 'signs of the times' to which Jesus referred his listeners: "concrete transformations effected by him in the historical present, and entrusted by him to his disciples for then and for the future."[129] In other words, where a liberating moment occurs, there is the action of God, there is the kingdom. "Historical sensibility to hunger and illiteracy, for example, calls for a society where the provision of basic food and culture to an underdeveloped people will be regarded as a liberation."[130]

Human Rights

In an article on human rights, evangelization, and ideology, Segundo agreed that human rights are based on the same ideal for human beings as Jesus' good news and the beatitudes were. To move directly from the gospel ideal to human rights programs, however, ignores the important step of education and conversion. Very importantly, the sphere of "human rights" also excludes major needs experienced by the hungry two thirds of the human race. Therefore, prophetic action is urgently needed to expose the structures which underlie both hunger and torture, and not to stop short at an ideological defense of human rights.[131]

Segundo criticized narrow and self-interested conceptions of human rights again in the final volume of his christologies. He considered the human rights issue too linear and inflexible when viewed in terms of the exchange of energy within an evolving universe. It takes for granted the move from ideal to realization without examining the vested interests represented by the means to the end:

> Indeed where or how are we to locate those responsible for this situation without entering into the area of ideologies? A whole nation can go hungry or fail to provide education for its citizens, without any authority at home or abroad having made a decision or actually violated a single right. No one can denounce the mechanism operative here because it does not issue from the theme of "human rights" as such.[132]

He emphasized as well that the rich countries can insist on protection for human rights in nations where the former continue to carry on, in the name of 'legality' and 'preservation of democracy', systematic violations at a deeper level. For these reasons, he was most reluctant to see Jesus entitled the "great defender of human rights."[133]

Education and Mass Media

In a paper delivered at an inter-American seminar on the relationship between liberating education and the communications media, Segundo compared the "new person" fashioned by the media with the "new person" created by revelation. He focused particularly on the potential of the media to produce an educated populace, and the danger that it may instead further a mass, uncritical, manipulative society. Within this discussion he set in bold relief the negative effects of the media upon the underdeveloped countries: stimulating artificial needs, urging greater consumption in countries where basic sustenance is barely attainable, and reinforcing "an implicit but terribly effective political decision to make the underconsumption of some pay for the development of others, by means of a structure imposed on the international market."[134]

The internalization of the oppressive system was for Segundo the most destructive aspect of these effects. Therefore, the greatest potential of the media lay also at this precise point: liberation through critical awareness.

> All of which means that, both on the individual and social level, a political decision is called for, here [in Latin America] far more than in the developed countries, to limit the communications media at a certain point or to provide some institution to criticize their message.[135]

SUMMARY

This chapter has explored two interrelated questions: Who are the poor of whom Juan Luis Segundo has taken account in his theology? How are they, as Segundo has conceived them, involved in the flow of history, the meaning of scripture, and the responsibility of committed Christian living?

The reality of poverty and oppression, particularly in the Latin American countries, impelled Segundo into his theological endeavor. Even when the term "the poor" was implicit, their situation was never far from his writing. The poor were people in need, often of the most basic means for survival. Yet their misery and the lack of freedom to remedy it most often stemmed from structures more than from individual actions. Frequently unaware of how they were held captive by patterns of action which claim justification in reason and in religion, poor people continued to struggle within the familiar ways of acting and thinking. In need of love most of all, they possessed the strongest claim on the God who promises happiness in exchange for their woe.

The identity of the poor came into clearer focus in the scriptures, particularly in the gospel proclamation. Set within the historical process of God's teaching the chosen people about the gratuity of divine love, Jesus' message addressed first of all those persons around him suffering from their concrete situation of need and the sorrow of being excluded as sinners from the Jewish society that "counted." Those with whom Jesus sided have their counterparts in contemporary society as well, those whose inhuman conditions are founded upon distorted personal, corporate, and global relationships and twisted understandings of God and humanity.

And how were the poor involved for Segundo in history, the meaning of God's word, and the concrete practice of the Christian faith? They revealed important aspects of history: the preeminence of love, the crucial dimension of human freedom, and the necessarily political character of that history. This is a history about which God is concerned and in which God chooses to be involved. It is the forum of God's reign, as Jesus announced, which overturns accepted values and vindicates those excluded from the centers of power. It is the building on which, by God's act of freeing love, people collaborate with God in the construction. Social and economic systems which make accessible the means for a dignified human existence, education and communication, international affairs: all are touched by the power of God's action at work in free, conscious, committed human beings. In his description of this state where it is absent in the current lot of the poor, as where it is present in God's promise to them, Segundo carried out his theology.

And he did it by means of the hermeneutic circle. Recall the dynamics of his method: reality provokes questions which uncover and challenge self-interested, ineffective structures. The resulting loss of naiveté creates new understandings of the whole theoretical framework of society, and in particular of theology and scripture. The new conceptions open the way for a more genuine knowledge of God which generates a truer practice of love of neighbor. The way that the church is called to this free, critical, effective love is the subject of the following chapter.

NOTES

1. The *Community Called Church*, trans. John Drury (Maryknoll, N.Y.: Orbis Books, 1973), 83; henceforth referred to as *CCC*.

2. *CCC*, 96-7; see a similar reflection on the challenge to the church posed by economic development, 118-20.

3. *The Liberation of Theology*, trans. John Drury (Maryknoll, N.Y.: Orbis Books, 1976), 43; henceforth *LT*.

4. *The Sacraments Today*, trans. John Drury (Maryknoll, N.Y.: Orbis Books, 1974), 107; henceforth *ST*.

5. *Faith and Ideologies*, trans. John Drury (Maryknoll, N.Y.: Orbis Books, 1984), 77; henceforth *FI*.

6. See the author's clarification on "The Social Dimension of Grace and Sin" in *Grace and the Human Condition*, trans. John Drury (Maryknoll, N.Y.: Orbis Books, 1973), 37-39. Henceforth referred to as *GHC*. The discussion on p. 39 focused on the movement from an "established morality" to a "creative morality."

7. *FI*, ch. XI, especially 282.

8. *An Evolutionary Approach to Jesus of Nazareth*, trans. John Drury (Maryknoll, N.Y.: Orbis Books, 1988), 62. Henceforth referred to as *EA*.

9. *EA*, 83.

10. *EA*, 83.

11. *LT*, 188.

12. *The Historical Jesus of the Synoptics*, trans. John Drury (Maryknoll, N.Y.: Orbis Books, 1985), 138; henceforth referred to as *HJS*.

13. Note this theme in *Teología abierta*, Vol. III, *Reflexiones criticas* (Madrid: Ediciones Cristiandad, 1984), ch. X, particularly 295-6; this work will be noted as *RC*.

14. Especially pertinent here are pp. 82-3 of *CCC*.

15. *HJS*, 62.

16. *HJS*, 88. Segundo looked to Gerhard von Rad as an important source of his own biblical theology. Of interest here is von Rad's comment in *Old Testament Theology*, Vol. I, trans. D. M. G. Stalker (New York: Harper & Brothers, 1962),

400-1. He spoke of persons praying the psalms of lamentation who designated themselves as "poor" and "wretched": "The conviction that those whose legal standing was weak and who were less privileged in the struggle of life were the objects of Yahweh's particular interest reaches far back into the history of the people of Yahweh. This conception of the poor practically contains a legal claim upon Yahweh; and it was precisely this which later made it a self-designation of the pious before Yahweh. In fact, a great number of references understand these poor quite frankly and directly as those who can justifiably expect the divine protection."

Segundo made reference to the "poor of Yahweh" in *The Hidden Motives of Pastoral Action*, trans. John Drury (Maryknoll, N.Y.: Orbis Books, 1978), 92; henceforth referred to as *HM*. He was commenting on their strength of conviction and their hope in Yahweh: "In the prophetical writings of the Bible, therefore, the 'poor of Yahweh' are not the vast majority of the Israelites but God's 'remnant'. They make up a heroic minority of strong-willed people."

17. *HJS*, 108-9. In this discussion, Segundo cited J. Dupont, *Les Béatitudes: Le problème littéraire*, 3 vols. (Bruges: Abbaye de Saint-André, 1954), 435.

18. *HJS*, 110. The translation and emphasis are Segundo's.

19. Segundo viewed Matthew's translation of the "poor" into the "poor in spirit" as an incorporation of Jesus' basic teaching into the catechesis of the church, legitimate but farther from Jesus' probable original message than Luke's edition (see *HJS*, 63). Segundo carried over this exegetical option into the rest of his theological interpretation and, with few exceptions, dissociated his theology from the concept of the "poor in spirit." He treated poverty as a dehumanizing condition from which God desires to deliver people.

An exception to this principle appeared in the second part of Segundo's theological dissertation, *La Cristiandad, ¿Una utopía?*, II, *Los principios* (Montevideo: Mimeográfica "Luz," 1964), 5. "From a point of view which could be called existential, it is going to be from within that 'remnant', those poor in spirit, those humble ones, those who thirst for justice, that the appearance of the Word will be given in the moment of definitive drawing near." ("Desde un punto de vista que podría llamarse existencial, va a ser, en efecto, dentro de ese 'resto', de esos pobres en espíritu, de esos humildes, de esos sedientos de justicia, donde se dará la aparición del Verbo en el momento de su acercamiento definitivo.")

A second exception occurred in *Masas y minorías en la dialéctica divina de la liberación*, Cuadernos de contestación polémica (Buenos Aires: Editorial La Aurora, 1973), 102. The author was speaking of political commitment on behalf of the oppressed: "The commitment is changed into that open and poor heart which is the only kind, according to Christ himself, that can grasp his message as good news, as gospel." ("El compromiso se convierte en ese corazón abierto y pobre que es el único que, según Cristo mismo, puede captar su mensaje como buena noticia, como evangelio.")

20. *HJS*, 62; discussion of the objective situation of poverty on pp. 62-4 was echoed frequently throughout this work, e.g., 105-6 and 110. Segundo acknowledged that Luke evidently addressed the poor and persecuted early Christian community rather than the poor at large. He maintained, however, that the original Q form of the beatitudes was directed to the socioeconomic poor, even though religious reasons supported their marginalization (62, 114).

    Pertinent to the whole discussion of the poor in Segundo is John P. Meier's paper, "The Bible as a Source for Theology" (*Proceedings CTSA* 43 [1988] 1-14). On this point, Meier questions the degree of socioeconomic deprivation which Segundo posits in his references to "the poor." Meier points to Qumranic evidence that calls for a more complex analysis of poverty in Jesus' time than Segundo carries out (11-12).

21. *HJS*, 64. Segundo qualified this definition by following it with the parenthetical note "even though the religious factor played a role in their marginalization." This qualification, which will come to the fore later in this paper, nevertheless does not negate his basic definition in terms of socio-economic status.

22. *The Christ of the Ignatian Exercises*, trans. John Drury (Maryknoll, N.Y.: Orbis Books, 1987), 92; henceforth *IE*.

23. Segundo developed these ideas at some length in *HJS*, 110-14.

24. *HJS*, 114.

25. *HJS*, 94. Further elaboration of this point occured on 92, 116-118, 122-23, and n.19 on 207. The later volume in the series, *EA*, also discussed it on 62-3.

26. *HJS*, 116; see 117 as well. Segundo follows Joachim Jeremias and others in identifying the poor with sinners in Jesus' day. See *New Testament Theology: The Proclamation of Jesus*, trans. John Bowden (New York: Charles Scribner's Sons, 1971, 108-21. On pp. 112-13, Jeremias said, ". . . Jesus' following consisted predominantly of the disreputable, the '*amme ha-ares*, the uneducated, the ignorant, whose **religious** ignorance and **moral** behaviour stood in the way of their access to salvation, according to the convictions of the time. . . .

    "Jesus looks with infinite mercy on these beggars before God when in Matt. 11.28 he calls them 'those who labour and are heavy laden'. Their burden is doubly hard: they have to bear public contempt from men and, in addition, the hopelessness of ever gaining God's salvation."

    E. P. Sanders, however, strongly disagreed with this position. In *Jesus and Judaism* (Phila.: Fortress Press, 1985), 179-80, he argued: "The problem with Jeremias's position is that the term 'the wicked' (in Greek, 'sinners') — which is used with complete consistency in the Gospels and in Jewish literature from Ben Sira to the close of the Mishnah, a period of 400 years — does not include the '*amme ha-arets*.

. . . I maintain that there is absolutely no passage in the entirety of [Rabbinic] literature . . . which in any way supports the assertion that the scrupulous and learned regarded the ordinary people as 'the wicked', those who flagrantly and persistently disobeyed the law."

In an extended discussion in Ch. 6, "The Sinners," Sanders also denied the probability of conflict between Jesus and the Pharisees over his association with the ritually impure, nor of confrontation with the ruling authorities of Judaism. Note his summary, 209-11.

Drawing on Sanders' research John Meier criticizes Segundo's identification of the poor and sinners in *HJS* and *RC*. "Jesus . . . was concerned with the poor. But in Jewish eyes, the damaging charge against him was not that he associated with the poor, but that he associated with the wicked" (12).

27. *RC*, 31.

28. Segundo's reflection, in *RC*, 203-12, was provoked by an article by Arnaldo Zenteno, ". . . un comentario del pueblo al relato al guadalupano," *Servir* (Jalapa, México, 1981), 297-319.

29. *The Humanist Christology of Paul*, trans. John Drury (Maryknoll, N.Y.: Orbis Books, 1986), 224, note 254. Henceforth referred to as *HCP*.

30. *HCP*, 179. Compare the similarity of "the poor" as used throughout the foregoing section and "mass" in this summary statement which occurred in *HJS*, 147: "From this person — whom his enemies called a glutton, a drunkard, and a friend and cohort of publicans and sinners — the masses learned that God was preparing something marvelous for them. . . ."

It was in this vein that Segundo spoke of "popular" and "mass" in his critique of popular religion, more recently in *RC*, 140-48, but also much earlier in ch. 7 of *LT*.

31. Segundo wrote adamantly on this point, e.g., in *HCP*, 224, note 254; *RC*, 127 and, especially, 210-11. His idea was similar in *HJS*, 138.

His reference to Gutiérrez came from the title *The Power of the Poor in History*, trans. Robert R. Barr (Maryknoll, N.Y.: Orbis Books, 1983). Segundo's use of the title was closer, however, to the original Spanish, *La fuerza histórica de los pobres* (Lima: Centro de Estudios y Publicaciones, 1979).

32. The author discussed this notion explicitly in *HCP*, 224-5, note 257; *RC*, 138; and "Notas e comentários: Nota sobre ironias e tristezas, (Resposta a Hugo Assmann)," *Perspectiva teológica* (São Leopoldo, Brasil) 15 (no. 37, 1983), 387.

33. See, for instance, *RC*, 161, 199.

34. *CCC*, 66; 65-67.

35. Segundo interpreted Rom. 1:21,23 with this definition of idolatry in *GHC*, 110. The whole of *GHC* discussed grace in the sense of the "gratuity" of God's gift (see 9).

36. See *EA*, 63-4, on gratuity and the integration of all humanity in love; *HCP*, 130-1, on cooperating in God's "work."

37. *IE*, 27.

38. *HJS*, 9. Segundo strongly opposed a romanticized or fatalistic interpretation of the cross. He made this comment about the passage from Leonardo Boff's work with which he begins *HJS*, from *Passion of Christ, Passion of the World* (Maryknoll, N.Y.: Orbis Books, 1987) 130-33. (The citation in *HJS*, however, was a translation made from a Spanish edition by Cristiandad, Madrid, of Boff's original.)

39. *FI*, 77.

40. *EA*, 61.

41. "Creemos que la gracia integra dialécticamente los pecados humanos en el destino creador del hombre" (*RC*, 275).

    See also *EA* and its discussion of "Jesus and the recapitulation of the universe," esp. 106.

    This interplay of good and evil in the movement toward Omega recalls an important point made by Segundo in the conclusions to his study of Nicholas Berdyaev. The former listed as polar opposites a number of elements treated by the philosopher: "the primacy of liberty over being/ the primacy of being over liberty"; "dualism/ monism"; etc. Then he posed the question whether Berdyaev declared himself for the first list of elements over the second. Segundo presented the other's answer that, while a **prophet** could emphasize the first over the second, a **philosopher** had to strive for the integration of the two at the risk of being enslaved by one or the other. *Berdiaeff: Une réflexion chrétienne sur la personne* (Paris: Editions Montaigne, 1963), 403, 408-9.

42. See *HCP*, ch. VII and esp. 117. Cf. Rom. 7: 15, 19: (trans. from Segundo's Spanish) " 'I do not recognize what I accomplish because I do not perform what I want to do, I perform what I hate. . . . I do not perform the good I want to do; I perform the evil I don't want to do.' "

43. Segundo discussed this basic reality as part of a reflection on concupiscence and of Paul's contribution to the topic, in *GHC*, especially 21-25.

44. *HCP*, 125.

45. See *EA*, 13-14, 83-4.

46. The fuller treatment occurred in *RC*, 205 ff.

47. *GHC*, 156-7.

48. *HCP*, 98. Further discussion of the experience of sin as described by Paul in Romans will take place below in relation to "Scripture: Pauline thought."

49. Refer to *HJS*, ch. IX, particularly 144, for more on prophetism and conscientization.

50. *HJS*, 132, outlined Jesus' basic strategy.

51. Recall the discussion of "determinisms" in *GHC*, 37-9.

52. This issue, and the types of theology which proceed from it, concerned Segundo greatly. In *RC*, 132 ff., he strongly criticized Leonardo Boff and Jon Sobrino for attributing to the poor the position of subjects of their history and of theology without acknowledging also the need for a critical view of their perceptions and judgments.

    He devoted the whole of *RC* ch. V to "Two Theologies of Liberation." He aligned himself with the (chronologically) first, which "considers the people as the theological source to which the whole task of understanding the faith tends as **object.**" The second, which has developed later, "considers this same people as the collective **subject** from where the correct understanding and interpretation of the faith begins." ("Si una considera al pueblo como lugar teológico al que tiende como a su **objeto**, toda la tarea de comprender la fe, la otra considera a ese mismo pueblo como el **sujeto** colectivo de donde parte la correcta interpretación y comprensión de la fe.") *RC*, 129.

    Several articles, as well, presented the author's thinking on the subject-object question and the two types of liberation theology. "Ideas y orientaciones: Las teologías de la liberación," *Pastoral misionero* (Madrid) 18 (1982), 352-74, reproduced a talk given at the Instituto Superior de Pastoral in February 1982. "Two Theologies of Liberation," *Month* 17 (October 1984), 321-27, also represented a lecture given at Regis College, Toronto. "Les deux théologies de la libération en Amérique latine," *Études* (Paris) 361 (Septembre 1984), 149-61, presented the translation of the Toronto talk. "Les deux tendances actuelles de la théologie de la libération," *La documentation catholique* 81 (7 Octobre 1984), 912-17, was a report and interview which appeared the same season.

53. "Two Theologies of Liberation," *Month*, 325.

54. See *LT*, 188.

55. *HCP*, 175.

56. *HM*, 44.

57. See the section "The Ideological Infiltration of Dogma" in *LT*, esp. 42-3.

58. See the fuller discussion of the church's practice regarding human rights in *RC*, especially 212.

59. Segundo referred to the experience of his own reflection group in its prolonged work on Romans; *HCP*, 173.

60. Congregation for the Doctrine of the Faith, *Origins* 14 (September 13, 1984), IX, article 6.

61. *Theology and the Church: A Response to Cardinal Ratzinger and a Warning to the Whole Church*, trans. John W. Diercksmeier (Minneapolis: Winston Press, 1985), 108, 164; henceforth *TC*.

62. *GHC*, 39. See the related treatment in *ST*, particularly 107.

63. This comment occurred in relation to the necessary institutionalization of values in *FI*, 285. Earlier in the same work, Segundo emphasized that for a value to be absolute, it must engage with historical reality; see 129.

64. *HM*, 130-31.

65. *HCP*, 170.

66. Justin Martyr, *First Apology* 46:2-5; *Second Apology* 10:1-5. Cited in *GHC*, 104.

67. *HCP*, 175.

68. See Gerhard von Rad, Part Three, Ch. A, "The Actualisation of the Old Testament in the New," in *Old Testament Theology*, Vol. II, trans. D. M. G. Stalker (New York: Harper & Row, 1965), 319-35. Themes from von Rad, particularly from prophetic history, which recur in Segundo's theology include: the (prophetic) message addressed to a situation in a certain historical moment (e.g., see 129); the prophets' linkage of world politics and God's action (182); the search for God's plan and will in history (183); and a sense of historical continuity mingled with "fresh starts" (Ch. A, passim).

    The prophetic manner of applying dogma or religious teaching to political events, as described by von Rad, was of importance to Segundo in his article, "Capitalism — Socialism: A Theological Crux," in *The Mystical and Political Dimensions of the Christian Faith*, ed. Claude Geffré and Gustavo Gutiérrez, *Concilium*, Vol. 96 (New York: Herder & Herder, 1974), 105-23, in particular 116.

69. The main source on the four stages was Segundo's article, "Etapas precristianas de la fe," in *Qué es un cristiano* (Montevideo: Mosca Hnos., S.A., 1971); the article had been presented first as a lecture and then in mimeograph form in 1962.

In *Reflexiones críticas* the author reviewed the Old Testament as the learning process which prepares humanity for the Christian message in Ch. VI, "Lo cristiano dentro del proceso bíblico," especially 170-95.

Alfred T. Hennelly, S.J., provided the first exposure in English to Segundo's early work in *Theologies in Conflict: The Challenge of Juan Luis Segundo* (Maryknoll, N.Y.: Orbis Books, 1979. He treated the stages of revelation/ education on 52-9. In addition, the published dissertation of Gerald J. Persha, *Juan Luis Segundo: A Study Concerning the Relationship Between the Particularity of the Church and the Universality of Her Mission (1963-1977)* (Maryknoll, N.Y.: Orbis Books, Probe Series, 1980), 56-72, also presented the stages of faith in the Old Testament.

70. "'Dios es Amor' significa: 'el Absoluto es amor' y, por consiguiente, 'el amor es el Absoluto' " ("Etapas," 35).

71. On this point, see particularly 34-5, 37.

72. "Etapas," 50.

73. ". . . no aparece fácil sintetizar tarea histórica y trascendencia divina" ("Etapas," 68-9).

74. "[Max Weber ha señalado que las teorías económicas del liberalismo clásico nacieron en el terreno protestante merced, precisamente, a la impregnación bíblica y véterotestamentaria de sus fundadores.] La aceptación de una desigualdad creciente entre pobres y ricos . . . les parecía aceptable como voluntad de Dios que, de una manera misteriosa, destina a unos hombres a la riqueza y a otros a la miseria, lo mismo que trae sobre unos la salud y sobre otros la enfermedad o la muerte" ("Etapas," 69).

75. See "Etapas", 68-70.

76. "Etapas", 77-80, outlined the features of this stage.

77. Segundo's evaluation of this stage appeared on p. 81 of "Etapas". He summarized the O. T. process as education for liberty in the article "Education, Communication, and Liberation: A Christian Vision" in *IDOC International*, No. Am. Ed. (Nov. 13, 1971), 86-9. It was a translation of a short work which appeared in mimeograph form, *Visión cristiana: Educación, comunicación social y liberación* (Mexico City: Centro Crítico Universitario, 1971); the O. T. summary was found on pp. 15-18.

78. *CCC*, 157, 158.

79. See *CCC*, 158-9.

80. *ST*, 143-4; Segundo cited Is. 58:1-8.

81. *CCC*, 166; he referred here to Rom. 13:8-10.

82. In *GHC* Segundo presented these ideas related to Mt 25:34-46 and 1 Jn 3:14 on pp. 200-1 and 203 respectively.

83. See the related material on "The New Beginnings of the Sacred" in *ST*, especially 150.

84. *HJS*, 86.

85. *HJS*, 86; Segundo's text translated of Mark 1:15 and par.

86. *HJS*, 86.

87. *HJS*, 91. As well as on Dupont, Segundo depended also on the exegete André Myre, " 'Heureux les pauvres': histoire passée et future d'une parole," in *Cri de Dieu* (Montreal: Paulinas, 1977), 80-1. (Refer here to Segundo's comment on his use of biblical scholarship in *HJS*, 198, note 22.) Myre maintained that God's predilection for the poor depends on God's aversion to their condition of poverty and not on the worthiness of the poor.

88. *HJS*, 114.

89. *HJS*, 87.

90. *HJS*, 114. In *RC*, 75, the author pointed out that finding the key to the parables equals getting to the heart of Jesus' message concerning the kingdom.

91. See Segundo's discussion of the meal table, the situation of the poor, and the eschatological banquet in *HJS*, 112-14.

92. "Las parábolas fueron dichas, en su mayoría, contra las autoridades de Israel y su forma de entender y manejar la ley, y a favor de los pobres y pecadores" (*RC*, 76).

    John Meier is extremely critical of Segundo's interpretation of the Jewish authorities' attitude, based on an inaccurate conception of Judaism in the first century A.D. In "The Bible as a Source for Theology" he maintains that Segundo reads Matthew's polemical post-A.D. 70 view of the Pharisees and Sadducees back into Jesus' own time. Meier adds, "I think [Segundo] lets his reconstruction of first-century history be dictated by his desire to draw parallels between the political oppression of Jesus' day and political oppression in Latin America today" (10).

93. *HJS*, 120-25, and *RC*, 79-85, contained the detailed reflection on these parables.

94. *HJS*, 125-31, and *RC*, 79-80, 87-99, continued the examination of the parables in Jesus' proclamation.

95. "En todo caso, Jesús no fue ni podía ser ni 'hacerse' **pueblo**" (*RC*, 122). Pp. 120-24 discussed Jesus' and the disciples' style of life.

Cf. *RC*, 118-21, where he stated that "evangelical poverty" is nonexistent because it contradicts God's desire for humanization. See also *Our Idea of God* (*OIG*) (Maryknoll, N.Y.: Orbis Books, 1973), 160.

IE, 101, commented on the second week of the Exercises and the need to understand the Incarnation in terms of the arrival of God's reign with its consequences: "Jesus' life was more uncomfortable than poor. . ., and more conflict-ridden than ignominious. Moreover, both features are framed within a purpose or project, as are the pain and suffering of his passion."

96. The author contrasted the traditional definition of "indifference" in the Spiritual Exercises with this new concept of "non-indifference" based on the active preference for persons and things in accord with Jesus' project; *IE*, 94-97.

97. *HJS*, 140.

98. *HJS*, 142.

99. *HJS*, 123.

100. ". . . En ese plan histórico de hacer felices a cierto tipo o grupo de hombres, Dios revelará su corazón" (*RC*, 70). Cf. 99, and *HJS*, 109-10.

101. *HJS*, 76. In the initial volume in the series, *FI*, Segundo explained this conflict in terms of the basic values-means question. Jesus carried on his polemic against religion in the name of **doing good** as prior to obeying religious commandments. See 46-50.

   Here again, John Meier questions the political character of Segundo's conclusions to the extent that these derive from a mistaken linkage between the poor and sinners in Jesus' time.

102. *HJS*, 81; cf. *RC*, 56.

103. Notice particularly *HJS*, 211, note 5. In *RC*, 56, the author emphasized that Jesus was a friend of sinners and the poor not simply as a comrade but as an advocate who took their part at a cost.

104. Segundo reaffirmed this prophetic-critical function in *HJS*, 148-9.

105. *HJS*, 90; emphasis the author's.

106. *HJS*, 119.

107. Recall Segundo's discussion of the parables in four series in both *RC*, 75-99 and *HJS*, 120-31.

108. *HJS*, 91.

109. *HJS*, 91.

110. See *HJS*, 109-10, and *RC*, 70-72, concerning God's self-revelation in making the poor happy; also *HJS*, 131-2, in regard to a true knowledge of God's commands.

111. *HJS*, 134. Cf. the Meier critique as noted above.

112. Consult *HJS*, 108-40, for a fuller discussion.

113. *HCP*, 9-10.

114. See particularly *HCP*, 17, 23.

115. Refer to *HCP*, 54-8, especially 57.

116. *HCP*, 96.

117. *HCP*, 98.

118. In a related point the author offered his interpretation of the traditional "faith and works" debate: "By **work** in the singular Paul means the free prolongation of the human being in reality through the one and only project that is truly free: i.e., that which unites the human being with God in real, effective love of brother and sister humans" (*HCP*, 131). Segundo treated the "work" — "works" question also in the corresponding note 184, p. 213.

119. *HCP*, 136.

120. *HCP*, 136.

121. *HCP*, 173.

122. See *HCP*, 170 ff.

123. Thus Segundo interpreted Paul's message to slaves, the essence of which summarized Paul's relevance to the contemporary experience of enslaving structures; *HCP*, 180.

124. "Social Justice and Revolution," *America* (April 27, 1968), 575.

125. "Social Justice and Revolution," 575.

126. Refer to "Social Justice and Revolution," 576-8.

127. "... aparece claro que riqueza y pobreza no son resultados de causas diferentes, sino los dos aspectos de una misma realidad indisolublemente ligados." "Riqueza y Pobreza como Obstáculos al Desarrollo," *Perspectivas de diálogo* (Abril 1969), 57.

128. "Capitalism-Socialism: A Theological Crux," *The Mystical and Political Dimension of the Christian Faith*, ed. Claude Geffré and Gustavo Gutiérrez, *Concilium*, Vol. 96 (New York: Herder and Herder, 1974), 110.

129. "Capitalism-Socialism," 118-19.

130. "Capitalism-Socialism," 121. In the course of the article, Segundo presented the choice between capitalism and socialism in a carefully qualified way. "The choice we have to make is not between society as it exists in the USA or society as it exists in the Soviet Union"; it is from the vantage point of underdeveloped countries (100). The author also defined the terms of the choice: "We give the name of socialism to a political regime in which the ownership of the means of production is removed from individuals and handed over to higher institutions whose concern is the common good. By capitalism we understand the political regime in which the ownership of the goods of production is open to economic competition" (115).

131. "Derechos humanos, evangelización e ideología," *Christus* 43 (Noviembre 1978), 29-35.

132. *EA*, 82.

133. *EA*, 84.

134. "Education, Communication and Liberation: A Christian Vision," *IDOC International*, North American Edition (November 13, 1971), 76. The original paper appeared as *Visión cristiana: educación, comunicación social y liberación* (Mexico: Centro Critico Universitario, 1971).

135. "Education," 77.

3

THE CHURCH AND THE POOR: FIDELITY TO THE GOSPEL

Juan Luis Segundo published in 1984 a critical reflection on his first series, *A Theology for Artisans of a New Humanity*, which had appeared in Spanish between 1968 and 1972.[1] In the later commentary, *Reflexiones críticas*, after examining the origins of the church in the historical Jesus and setting forth the two current trends of liberation theology, Segundo stated: "The church, if it wants to be faithful to the gospel, can only be a prophetic community at the service of the poor, marginalized, and dehumanized people of the earth."[2] His statement synthesizes, at this point in his theological writings, the significance that the poor hold for the church. Therefore, this chapter will expand the first component of his definition, faithfulness to the gospel. Subsequent chapters will develop the remaining two: the prophetic community, and the service of the poor, marginalized, and dehumanized.

Three foci emerged as Segundo developed the notion of faithfulness to the gospel: the gospel foundation for the church's mission on behalf of the poor, the nature of the faith response, and the question whether the response to the Christian vocation can be that of a majority.

The description given above concerning the church and the poor developed over time in the writings of Segundo. For this reason it is helpful to trace the earlier forms of his inquiries that gave rise to the central question of this dissertation. He observed the secularization and dechristianization occurring in his country and on his continent, and was impelled to ask: What, in fact, is Christianity? What is salvation? What does the gospel have to say in the face of the life struggles in Latin American today? The answers which he forged to these queries in dialogue with both unbelievers and believers in turn provoked further questions. It is important to follow this trail briefly, particularly noting the landmark concepts of authentic love as universal criterion, the gospel link to human development, and the minority's service to the majority.

THE GOSPEL FOUNDATION

CALL FOR A NEW FOCUS ON EVANGELIZATION

Two of Segundo's earliest publications probed the experience of secularization and dechristianization in Latin America, particularly Uruguay and Argentina, at mid-century. Both works explored the meaning of Christianity at a deeper level than the immediate experience of these related phenomena. *Función de la Iglesia en la realidad rioplatense* (1962) examined the church "at the service of authentic love," a church willing to accept the complexity of utilizing realistic means to reach its ends.[3]

La Cristiandad ¿una utopía? (1964), Segundo's published dissertation, reexamined dechristianization through complementary approaches.[4] Part One discussed Christianity as a reality of personal conviction rather than of forces in history, even religious history, which produce effects as a matter of course. Part Two searched the dialectics of flesh/spirit in Paul and of world/ liberty in John. Segundo's findings led him to oppose "making ecclesial institutions an 'historical movement' which flow naturally into Christian civil institutions as the way to achieve the promised universality."[5] Instead, he pointed to the image of the body of Christ, which human beings constitute precisely as "simultaneously loving and egotistical, free and slave, just and sinners, minority and majority."[6]

In both *Función* and *Utopía* Segundo rethought the purpose and function of the church. Then in *The Hidden Motives of Pastoral Action: Latin American Reflections* he articulated even more clearly the call which he heard at the depths of the Latin American reality: the invitation to a new focus on evangelization. Evangelization represented for him the truest and most effective alternative to the mass orientation of Christendom. He outlined three key dimensions of it: "1) Communicating only the essentials of the Christian message. . . . 2) Communicating it as good news. . . . 3) Adding nothing further except at a pace that will allow the essential element to remain precisely that."[7] The proclamation must be an experience of "good news" here and now, with its accompanying joy and freedom, to be genuinely the gospel. Furthermore, when persons are truly evangelized, they base their sociopolitical decisions on gospel values.[8]

RELATIONSHIP OF EVANGELIZATION TO HUMAN DEVELOPMENT

Segundo's view of the gospel message revealed an essential connection between evangelization and human development. He saw that pastoral dilemmas arise from the tension, even the alleged opposition, between work for "the salvation of souls" and work for social development. In *Grace and the Human Condition* he sought to resolve these dilemmas, based on belief in the universal presence and action of grace.[9]

Segundo pointed out first that "evangelization is deeply and intimately bound up with human development as such."[10] Secondly, while the above is true, pastoral activity is not synonymous with human development. The Christian points to the ultimate values which the gospel represents, and "drawing on revelation, will try to relate human development to the absolute dimensions given to it by God's Incarnation in our history."[11]

Segundo, third, underlined the incarnation by stressing that pastoral activity needs to attend to the 'signs of the times' in concrete history as the place where the Spirit is at work. "In other words, it must reveal the ultimate meaning of this history, the dimensions of personal involvement to which every person today is called."[12] Fourth and last, pastoral activity leads the evangelized to express their faith anew in symbols, formulations, and signs which suit the age and culture of the believers. This impulse to share the faith is a service to the world, the way by which God's revealed word draws the world and human history to their culmination in Christ.[13]

UNDERSTANDING THE GOSPEL MESSAGE

Involvement in the process of human development is fundamental to understanding the revealed word of God. In a 1972 work, *Masas y minorías*, Segundo asserted that "**starting from the reality**, that is from the commitment with the exploited in the relations of production" is the sole way of meeting the Christian message free of ideology.[14] Here he based the ability to comprehend God's word upon commitment to those oppressed in economic relationships. The definitive link between this commitment and evangelical understanding[15] also recapitulated his hermeneutic circle:

> Let the readers understand that the political commitment, in making us 'put the truth to work', is going to illuminate not only our profane praxis, but our very understanding of the Gospel message; we are here faced with a proposal as radical as, or more so than, that of Bultmann.[16]

Segundo held that the task of "putting the truth to work," of translating values into realistic expressions for life, is a process of "learning to learn" which demands a community. In the Christian faith tradition this community is the church. It is the body of Jesus' disciples continually challenged to grapple with the ideologies, that is, the systems of means, which best concretize the gospel message for a given place and time.[17] In the process they themselves come to an authentic understanding of the scriptures.

It is time to summarize, then, the gospel foundation of the faithfulness to which the church is called. While the disintegration of Catholic religious practice in Latin America in recent decades seemed to threaten the very existence of Christianity, Segundo interpreted it as a needed opportunity for renewal in the real meaning of Christianity. He pointed up the renewed call to evangelization, the invitation to accept the message of the gospel in freedom and the responsibility it entails for sharing the good news through service. Concomitant with helping people live a more human existence is a truer understanding of God's word.

THE RESPONSE OF FAITH

Evangelization evokes a commitment in faith. As cooperation with the gospel which has special significance for the poor, this response will be considered here in three of its facets: adopting Jesus' values, siding with the oppressed, and making the values effective.

ADOPTING JESUS' VALUES

To understand what this faith response meant for Segundo, it is helpful to recall his definition of faith. In *Faith and Ideologies* he referred to it as taking "a chance on life, choosing as his or her supreme goal something whose value is not known in a personal, experiential way."[18] When a person's scale of values is determined by Jesus' proclamation of God's coming reign with its consequences for the poor and by the evidence of other persons' lives consistent with Jesus' values, then that individual's human faith is also a religious and, specifically, a Christian faith.[19] The first aspect of the faith response to the gospel is thus apparent in the person: alignment with the values and meaning of Jesus' life.

In *Faith and Ideology* most directly but in other works as well, Segundo portrayed Jesus strongly resisting the practice of religion conceived as a set of sacred instruments.[20] In other words, Jesus distanced himself from a set of beliefs or prescriptions that had value in and of themselves. He rejected as well a notion of faith as cultural tradition, imparted through the life of a given group or environment.

In contrast, Jesus proposed to his followers a structure of meaning and value based on God's desire to see people fully human. He established a community on the basis of this genuine religious faith, whose contrast with cultural faith is shown in Segundo's description:

> Remember that we are talking here about an authentically religious faith, such as the one described in the case of Jesus. That sort of religious faith seems to be more in opposition to, than in continuity with, religious traditions which have become culture. . . . This approach leads people to first accept certain human values and then recognize the sacred as such, i.e., as something supernaturally effective; only then, and usually indirectly, does it propose to adopt the values implicit in that sacred set of instruments.[21]

While the nature of this community will be further explored shortly, it is evident that Segundo considered the sharing of Jesus' values to be the foundation for the disciples' response of faith to the gospel message.

SIDING WITH THE OPPRESSED

To highlight the adoption of Jesus' values as key to the Christian faith response is to recall Jesus' own proclamation to the poor and the consistency of his life and ministry with this proclamation. In *Faith and Ideology* Segundo related alliance with the poor to the truth of the gospel from the perspective of values:

But consider what may happen if we look at the Christian message from the standpoint of the realm of values. If we do that, we may well see that the Christian message is living witness to the satisfaction one may find in joining the poorest, the most helpless, and the most oppressed.[22]

Segundo explored Jesus' own option to accompany the poor in his life and ministry. He also considered it as a factor of discipleship which enables the follower of Jesus to understand the gospel rightly. Having done these two things, he underlined the gratification which derives from espousing this Christian value. He pointed throughout to the conclusion that commitment on behalf of the oppressed, concretely expressed, is prerequisite to a faithful response to the gospel.

MAKING THE VALUES EFFECTIVE

As Segundo has defined it, the human dimension of faith has its counterpart in the realm of ideology, that is, of efficacy or the means to the goal. How, in fact, do Jesus' disciples put his values to work in concrete situations? In *Grace and the Human Condition*, Segundo drew upon *Gaudium et spes* 11 to describe this process as translation: the Christian must "translate it [revelation] in such a way that it will allow us to point up the pathways to fully human solutions in the very warp and woof of activity in history."[23] Similarly, the author stated in *Reflexiones críticas* that "the function of the faith is to translate divine revelation into more human historical solutions for that very people, poor and exploited."[24]

In *Faith and Ideology*, where he emphasized the importance of ideologies for a vital faith, Segundo called the process of concretizing faith in history the "creation of ideologies." Such creation brings together the value and the historical reality, without which the value cannot be considered absolute. It draws upon revelation to show believers themselves how to construct ideologies.[25]

In summary, Segundo's principle is clear that a living faith response, shaped by the values of Jesus and allied with the oppressed, requires taking the means or creating the ideologies to express Jesus' values in historical terms. In light of the discussion to this point, the progression which he described in *Masas y minorías* is notable in its linkage of discipleship, social change on behalf of the poor, and understanding of the gospel message:

... That which grounds my faith in him and not in some other person ... appears against an horizon of political commitment and of revolutionary political commitment in favor of the oppressed.

The commitment thus becomes. . . the commitment lived out in the changing of structures in favor of the mass; it is converted, as I said, from a "state of grace" to go toward Christ into an hermeneutical "state of grace" to inquire of the authentic Christ. . . . The commitment is changed into that open and poor heart which is the only one which, according to Christ himself, can grasp his message as good news, as gospel.[26]

A FAITHFUL MULTITUDE?

As the third aspect of the church's faithfulness to the gospel, this section asks who can make such a faith response to the gospel message and the challenge to carry it throughout the world. Can a majority of people make this gospel commitment on behalf of the poor? Or is this a task for a minority of persons? In order to show Segundo's thinking on the question, the section will touch on the Medellín documents as he commented on divergent orientations found there. Then in the light of these orientations, of the limitations of mass responses, and of a fear among pastoral leaders for the salvation of the masses, the present section will discuss the gospel exigencies in relation to majorities.

TWO ORIENTATIONS WITHIN THE MEDELLÍN DOCUMENTS

Segundo found inconsistencies in the Medellín documents, particularly "Pastoral Care of the Masses." The authors of section II of the document, Theological Principles, were unwilling to deny arbitrarily "the character of true belief and of real ecclesial participation, no matter how weak, to every action which manifests spurious motives or temporal motivations, even selfish ones."[27] Segundo read in this reluctance a desire to maintain the church's identity as universal and nonsectarian at any cost. In his view, such a position, based to a significant extent on the religious sociology of Renato Poblete,[28] sacrifices the value of a conscious and committed faith to an inadequate notion of the church's universality.

Segundo contrasted this notion of church membership and mission with the views expressed in the documents of the same conference dealing with commitment to justice and peace. He refused to accept the pejorative connotation of "sect" which he perceived in Poblete's use of the term. Instead he maintained that the involvement envisioned overall in the Medellín documents is incompatible with a nondiscriminating thrust toward the large scale membership or practice.[29] This implied that genuine Christian life which expresses the faith in concrete efforts for justice is not mass produced.

LIMITATIONS OF MASS RESPONSE

Yet because Christian identity in Latin America has traditionally emphasized minimum conditions for belonging to the church, Segundo noted that the mass of people lacked a sense of committed, socially involved faith. Traditional society handed on Christian understandings of life, faith, and church practice as a cultural whole. In effect, "that society constituted a closed environment; and as such it manufactured generations of Christians for centuries without the church having to worry about obtaining a personal conviction from the individual apart from environmental influence."[30]

Segundo went on to observe that, surprisingly, the cultural crisis which exploded the closed universe of traditional Catholicism did not cause the rapid disappearance of the latter. Instead, it encouraged the retention of beliefs and practices which afforded security in the midst of upheaval. As a result the crisis did not automatically move Catholicism to the level of personal conviction with clear choices to be Christian or not. Thus the challenge remained, now with an added nuance, of how to arrive at the committed, socially involved faith which the gospel mission to the poor implies.[31]

UNWARRANTED FEAR FOR THE MASSES

Another factor was at work for Segundo in the matter of faith or salvation for the masses. If the Catholic church is the sole agent of salvation, then it is very important to work toward the ideal of incorporating everyone into the church. If, on the other hand, the church is only one — albeit important — means of salvation, then inclusion of all people at whatever

level of participation compromises its basic character. That Segundo sub-
scribed to the second notion was clear throughout his work, perhaps most
explicitly in *The Community Called Church, The Hidden Motives of Pastoral Action*, and *Reflexiones críticas*.[32] Such a notion of universal salvation
promotes an open, confident approach to pastoral action, in contrast to a
more fearful, protective manner typical of the first.

Yet Segundo saw fear and protectiveness prevalent in Latin American
Catholicism. It seemed to him that the majority of Catholics needed
Catholic organizations, institutions, and structures to guard and bolster their
faith. They lacked the initiative and vitality that the power of the gospel
fashions out of their freedom and the freedom of those with whom they share
the good news. Segundo considered the fear "for the salvation of the
masses" unfounded precisely because its basic motives remained unex-
amined.[33] In fact, while a specifically Christian life implies commitment to
the radical alleviation of poverty, God's saving power still encompasses the
multitudes unable to make this same commitment or to make it in a
concerted way.

EXIGENCIES OF THE GOSPEL: MINORITY BY DEFINITION

A variety of elements led Segundo to reject a mass or majority approach
to evangelization. The weakness of efforts to win the masses was evident
from several quarters: disparities even within the renewal-oriented Medellín
documents, a historically superficial manner of forming Christians, and
efforts to foster Catholic belief and practice through structures based on fear
for the people's spiritual wellbeing.[34] He concluded that the mass means
used have been inadequate to the task of carrying the gospel into the world.
A committed minority is needed.

In Chapter Eight of *The Liberation of Theology*, "Mass Man — Minority Elite — Gospel Message," Segundo argued for the minority character of
Christianity from four vantage points: ecclesiastical, socio-political, scientific, and biblical. He found that the church over the centuries used methods
of conversion and education, despite its faith in the universal saving victory
of Christ, which placed on a multitude obligations better suited to a small
number. In the social, political realm he maintained that important social
changes as represented by revolutions require a critical consciousness which
surpasses the simplification and desire for immediate results characteristic of
the general population.

On the scientific level, he saw in the mass-minority question a field where the principles of inertia, the distribution of energy, and the degradation of energy all operate. "**Masses** and **minorities** are precisely what they are because they represent the two necessary poles of the economy of energy that rules the universe."[35] Biblically, Segundo called attention to the grace or *charis* given to a Christian. He then pointed to the extraordinary response asked of the Christian in the name of this divine gratuity. Yet the "few" implied by this call are not separated from the "many," as Segundo summarized in a conclusion:

> This minority effort among the masses is not meant to impose elitist demands on the latter, nor is it meant to construct a society based on minority exigencies. The aim is to create, for oneself and others, new forms of energy that will permit lines of conduct that are necessarily mechanized to serve as the basis for new and more creative possibilities of a minority character in each and every human being.[36]

Segundo has maintained throughout his project that prophetic Christian service is an engagement made by a minority for the benefit of the majority. The required awareness and service, including awareness of God's predilection for the poor and resulting willingness to serve them, originate not from the disciple's own self but from the gift of revelation: "Jesus does not locate his church in the people, but at their service out of a knowledge, become message, of the 'secrets of the reign' " of God.[37] Segundo held that the crowds of Jesus' day did not know how to understand his teaching and meet its radical demands. Accordingly, he concluded that "the demands which the function of the church imposes on its members seem to exclude from it, as in the time of Jesus, the most poor and abandoned."[38]

SUMMARY

Critical social conditions in the world today urgently call Christians to their ecclesial mission of evangelization. This mission participates in Jesus' own vocation to proclaim the coming of God's reign. God's act of establishing the kingdom transforms the lot of the poor and dehumanized, whose oppression often includes a "mass" or uncritical mentality. The church carries out its mission when Christians respond in faith by embodying Jesus' values, stand with the oppressed, and actualize these values in society. Segundo has concluded that such a stance by the church for gospel justice and freedom, concretely expressed and assumed with all its risks, demands heroic minorities who serve for the benefit of impoverished humanity.

The following chapter will now consider the second element of Segundo's definition, "The church, if it wants to be faithful to the gospel, can only be a prophetic community at the service of the poor, marginalized, and dehumanized people of the earth." Poverty demands a prophetic community.

NOTES

1. *Reflexiones críticas*, Vol. III, *Teología abierta* (Madrid: Ediciones Cristiandad, 1984); henceforth, *RC*. This is the yet untranslated final volume of a new edition of this series.

2. "... la Iglesia, si quiere ser fiel al evangelio, sólo puede ser una comunidad profética al servicio de los pobres, marginados y deshumanizados de la tierra" (*RC*, 159).

3. (Montevideo: Barreiro y Ramos, 1962). Chapter II, 28-40, is entitled "The Religion of Authentic Love," and Chapter III, 41-63, "The Church at the Service of Authentic Love."

   Segundo saw simplification and immediacy as two characteristics of mass behavior, and conversely, complexity and mediacy (or the acceptance of mediations) as marks of minority action. On p. 74 he described Christianity as "the message of authentic love with its total, even opposed, demands." Christianity is the more complex in its ability to hold opposites in tension: justice and charity, institution and spirit, community and universality, etc. It is more mediate, as well, in its resistance to quick results at the expense of important aspects of the reality.

   "[Cristianismo] es el mensaje del amor verdadero con sus exigencias totales, aun opuestas. El más complejo, el más tenso de los ideales, el que insiste en un extremo y en el otro con la misma firmeza: justicia y caridad, esperanza y tenacidad, institución y espíritu, comunidad y universalidad. ... Es el más mediato, porque se resiste tenazmente a dejar de lado cualquier aspecto valioso de la realidad para obtener una eficacia más rápida" (74).

4. *La Cristiandad ¿una utopía?* (Montevideo: Cursos de Complementación Cristiana, 1964).

5. "Nuestra hipótesis consiste en decir que no es haciendo de las instituciones eclesiales un 'movimiento histórico' que se continúa naturalmente en las instituciones civiles cristianas como se va a alcanzar la universalidad prometida" (*Utopía*, Part Two, 19-20).

6. "La obra del Verbo, es decir la comunicación de su vida o, lo que es lo mismo, la comunicación de la posibilidad de amar verdaderamente, se realiza en la medida de la proximidad — prójimo — , es decir, en la medida en que los hombres constituyen un solo cuerpo entre ellos, una sola carne. Y lo constituyen por dos razones aparentemente opuestas — pero incluídas ambas en la significación del término **carne**: porque aman y porque son egoístas. Porque son libres y porque son esclavos. Porque son justos y pecadores, minoría y masa a la vez" (*Función*, Part II, 75).

7. *The Hidden Motives of Pastoral Action: Latin American Reflections*, trans. John Drury (Maryknoll, N.Y.: Orbis Books, 1978)., 111, 113, 115-16; henceforth *HM*.

8. See *HM*, especially 113, 130-31.

9. *Grace and the Human Condition*, trans. John Drury (Maryknoll, N.Y.: Orbis Books, 1973); henceforth *GHC*.

10. *GHC*, 128.

11. *GHC*, 128.

12. *GHC*, 128-9.

13. See *GHC*, 129.

14. "¿No será entonces la única manera de encontrarme con el mensaje cristiano desideologizado el **comenzar por** la realidad, es decir por el compromiso con el explotado en las relaciones de producción?" (*Masas y Minorías en la dialéctica divina de la liberación*, Cuadernos de contestación polemica [Buenos Aires: Editorial La Aurora, 1973], 78; emphasis Segundo's).

15. Understanding intimately related to practical love was a constant theme for Segundo. Knowledge of the mystery of God's saving action at work in the world was integral to his view of the church and of Christian identity. ". . . . The Christian, who receives that message [of the salvific character of love] and believes in it, is distinguished from the person who practices love spontaneously, in that the Christian **knows**."

   "Acabamos de ver . . . que el cristiano, el que recibe ese mensaje y cree en él, se distingue del hombre que practica espontáneamente el amor, en que **sabe**" (*Función*, 48).

   The author expressed the same understanding in *The Community Called Church* (*CCC*) as well. He summarized Chap. I in these words: "The redemptive work of Christ, carried out within history, goes beyond the limits of time and dominates the whole unfolding development of the universe — both its past and its future.

   "But there is something that begins with Christ and that moves out solely toward the future: namely, the revelation of this plan that suffuses all time. The Christian is not the only one to enter into this plan. But he is the one who knows it. He knows the plan because he has received not only redemption but also revelation.

   "The Christian is **he who knows**" (11; emphasis Segundo's).

16. "Comprendan los lectores que si el compromiso político, al hacernos 'obrar la verdad', va a iluminar no sólo nuestra praxis profana, sino nuestra misma comprensión del mensaje evangélico, estamos aquí ante un planteo tanto o más radical que el de Bultmann." (*Masas y minorías*, 92).

17. Note Segundo's remarks in *The Liberation of Theology*, trans. John Drury (Maryknoll, N.Y.: Orbis Books, 1976), 125-6; henceforth *LT*.

18. *Faith and Ideologies*, trans. John Drury (Maryknoll, N.Y.: Orbis Books, 1984), 6; henceforth referred to as *FI*.

19. See *FI*, 70-76, for a summary of the two determinants of religious faith, transcendent data and a tradition of witnesses.

20. In *FI*, 336, Segundo contrasted that "authentically religious faith" which Jesus praised with cultural religion. See the remainder of the chapter, and particularly 326-29 and 334-38.

    The author also spoke quite explicitly about sacred instrumentality in *The Sacraments Today* (trans. John Drury; Maryknoll, N.Y.: Orbis Books, 1974; henceforth *ST*). See 29-32 and the related note 5, p. 41. In *HM*, 26-32, Segundo attributed rites exercised for direct heavenly access to a religious adherence out of the need for security. He did so also in his treatment of popular religion in *LT*, particularly 186-88.

    Likewise in *RC*, 125, he set Jesus' hermeneutical principle, a wager on behalf of one's dehumanized neighbor, against the law and religious institutions as standards unto themselves (". . . la única premisa que permite entender la palabra de Dios consiste en la apuesta humana del hombre por su hermano deshumanizado. **Sólo** desde esa actitud previa se comprende dónde habla Dios (las señales de los tiempos) y qué es lo que pretende con la ley y las instituciones religiosas en ella contenidas").

21. *FI*, 336.

22. *FI*, 77.

23. *GHC*, 13. The author spoke here of two languages needed by the Christian, that of revelation and that of Christian practice. He cautioned, however, against neglecting the first and moving too rapidly to the pragmatic consideration of a matter's social, economic, and political effects.

24. "Y unimos a este principio negativo el positivo, señalado también por el Concilio, de que la función de la fe es traducir la revelación divina en soluciones históricas más humanas para ese mismo pueblo, pobre y explotado" (*RC*, 213).

25. Note especially *FI*, 129-30, the concluding pages of a section entitled "Faith without Ideologies?", 120-30. See Ch. One above, 37-38.

26. ". . . la que funda mi fe en él y no ya en otra personal alguna. . . aparece en un horizonte de compromiso político y de compromiso político revolucionario en favor de los oprimidos.

    "El compromiso se vuelve así el compromiso vivido en el cambio de estructuras en favor de la masa, se convierte, decía, en un 'estado de gracia' hermenéutico, de 'estado de gracia' para ir hacia Cristo, para preguntarle al auténtico Cristo. . . . El compromiso se convierte en ese corazón abierto y pobre que es el único que, según Cristo mismo, puede captar su mensaje como buena noticia, como evangelio" (*Masas*, 102).

A note about the phrase "revolutionary commitment" may be in order. A thorough treatment of the theology of J. L. Segundo in relation to revolution is impossible here. Yet since "revolution" is so emotionally colored a term, a description given in the Medellín *Conclusions* (Second General Conference of Latin American Bishops, *The Church in the Present-Day Transformation of Latin America in the Light of the Council*, 3rd ed., Vol. II, Washington, D.C.: NCCB, Secretariat for Latin America, 1979) may help preclude unwarranted assumptions about Segundo's thought.

"Pastoral Concern for the Elites," *Conclusions*, art. 8, p. 100, classified influential persons according to function in the process of social change, and gave the following description: "The revolutionaries question the socio-economic structure. They desire a radical change in goals as well as in implementation. For them, the people are and must be the subject of this change in such manner that they take an active part in decision-making for the reordering of the entire social process. This attitude can most frequently be found among intellectuals, scientific   researchers and university people." Segundo's theological approach harmonizes with this definition of "revolutionary."

27. *Medellín Conclusions*, "Pastoral Care of the Masses," art. 6, p. 93; cited in *LT*, 192.

   In *HM*, 88-9, Segundo commented on important differences in terminology in the Medellín documents in regard to "masses." In the one under consideration here, e.g., in arts. 1-4, "masses" refers to "passive majorities." In contrast, the document "Pastoral Care of the Elites" uses "masses" for those who lack skills and influence in the areas of culture, society, politics, education, and other professions (arts. 1-2).

28. Segundo referred in LT, 193-6, to Bishop Luis E. Henriquez' presentation to the Medellín conference ("Pastoral Care of the Masses and the Elites," *The Church in the Present-Day Transformation of Latin America in the Light of the Council*, Vol. I, *Position Papers* (Washington, D.C.: NCCB, Secretariat for Latin America, 1979), 186 ff.

   A major source for Bishop Henriquez' paper was the article by Renato Poblete, "Religión de masa, religión de élite," *Mensaje* (Santiago; 1965).

29. Segundo made this point in *LT*, especially 193, but in a more general way on 183-96.

   While the author did not cite Medellín documents which exemplified the contrast with "Pastoral Care of the Masses," this reference from "Justice," art. 6 (*Conclusions*, p. 35) illustrates the different emphases: "Our pastoral mission is essentially a service of encouraging and educating the conscience of believers, to help them to perceive the responsibilities of their faith in their personal life and in their social life. . . ."

30. *HM*, 27.

31. See discussion in *HM*, particularly 30-1.

32. In *CCC*, see as examples the concluding paragraphs of Ch. One and Two, 11 and 32. In *HM*, while this assumption underlies the entire book, a clear summary occurred in the final chapter, 135-41.

    In *RC*, Segundo began with a review and evaluation of Vatican II's significance. He remarked that "that maturity [to which the church was called through reform] implies that it stop considering itself in possession of the monopoly on eternal salvation. . . ." "De ahí la insistencia del Vaticano II en llevar la reforma a la Iglesia misma al darse ésta cuenta, 'por su experiencia de siglos, cuánto debe aún madurar in su relación con el mundo' (*GS* 43). Esa maduración implica que deje de considerarse en posesión del monopolio de la salvación eterna (*GS* 22). . . . " (pp. 15-16).

33. See the argument presented in *HM*, 88-92.

34. The church as a minority is a major theme in Segundo's theology. He has treated this aspect most extensively in *Masas y minorías* and in *LT*, Ch. 8. The theme, however, appears consistently in his other works as well. See, for example, *Función*, 47-48, 74 ff.; *Utopía?*, I, 42, 66-7, 90-2; II, 20-1, 32, 61-3, 91; *CCC*, pp. 4, 6-11, 53, 80-6; *HM*, pp. 138-9; and *RC*, pp. 27, 38-9, 161, 213 ff.

    See also the published dissertation of Gerald L. Persha on one aspect of the church as minority: *Juan Luis Segundo: A Study Concerning the Relationship Between the Particularity of the Church and the Universality of Her Mission* (1963-1977) (Maryknoll, N.Y.: Orbis Probe Books, 1979).

35. *LT*, 224. Segundo continued, "[Masses and minorities] are the quantitative and qualitative poles present in any and every human group, **but equally present in the patterns of conduct of each and every human individual**" (emphasis Segundo's).

36. *LT*, 231.

37. Note the discussion in *RC*, 140: ". . .Aquel pueblo de pobres que, en el Israel de Jesús, si bien fue objeto de las bienaventuranzas y de la buena nueva, no supo comprender y aceptar la enseñanza y las exigencias radicales de la comunidad de Jesús. Y así quedó fuera de ésta, aunque todo en Jesús estuviera y quedara, en principio, a su servicio y apuntara a volverlo sujeto."

38. "Las exigencias que la función de la Iglesia impone a sus miembros parecen excluir de ella, como en el tiempo de Jesús, a los más pobres y desamparados" (*RC*, 161).

4

THE CHURCH AND THE POOR:
A PROPHETIC COMMUNITY

The first part of Segundo's synthetic definition of the church's relationship with the poor unfolded in the previous chapter, "to be faithful to the gospel." The chapter examined three aspects of this call to faithfulness: the gospel foundation, the response of faith, and the minority character of the faith response. The present chapter will continue to explore the definition by focusing on "a prophetic community." It will look first at the church as community of Jesus' disciples and then at the consequences which flow from the choice to love effectively, the vocation to prophecy and the conflict which attends this vocation.

THE COMMUNITY OF JESUS' DISCIPLES

Segundo regards the community of faith as a direct result of Jesus' life and ministry. Jesus' followers extend his action on behalf of God's reign, and in so doing make the Christian community a sign of authentic love in the world.

DISCIPLES WHO MULTIPLY JESUS' ACTION

Segundo has not discussed at any length the questions whether Jesus expected an imminent coming of God's reign nor whether he intended to found a church.[1] But he affirmed that Jesus did gather followers and that he "want[ed] to unite his disciples to his activity as servant on behalf of the designees of the reign."[2] As shown in the synoptics, the work of curing the sick, raising the dead, cleansing lepers, and expelling demons is a community effort.[3] Segundo noted in *The Historical Jesus*: "Jesus is seeking **to place historical causality in the service of the kingdom.** And not only does he invest his all as *perfectus homo* in that service; he invests his disciples' all as well."[4] And the disciples' all, like Jesus' own — committed for the sake of the poor — was simultaneously conflictual and liberative.

A significant change in orientation occurred in the years following Jesus' resurrection. Jesus' teachings, particularly the beatitudes and the parables, which had originally been delivered in situations of controversy with the Jewish religious authorities over the latter's treatment of the poor and sinners, came to be directed to the Christian community itself. Luke adopted second person address in his account of the beatitudes ("Blessed are you poor. . . ."), for example, connoting that "as the continuer of Jesus' work, the church would be poor, hungry, afflicted, and persecuted."[5]

Segundo portrayed the early Christians interpreting the good news differently than Jesus had done. Instead of Jesus' emphasis that God's reign transforms the inhuman situation of the poor, the early Christian preaching stressed Jesus' relation with God and his power to save.[6] The political key disappeared, and Segundo observed that "the first Christian community, then, preaches nothing conflictual in political terms, nothing which can inspire a concrete fear originating from the community mission."[7] While this major change was true, the community nevertheless continued to care for those members who lacked the necessities of life. Yet one may summarize thus the transposition which occurred in Jesus' invitation to his disciples in the following way. The beatitudes and other aspects of early church preaching changed from Jesus' focus on the arrival of God's reign for the poor to an emphasis on the situation of the church itself as it preached salvation.

SIGN OF AUTHENTIC LOVE

Segundo also viewed the nature and purpose of the community gathered to extend Jesus' mission from the perspective of genuine and effective love visible in the world. While this principle undergirded Segundo's theological project from the beginning, two distinct stages have emerged in his thought on the church as community. Although no clear break set the two apart, the first was most evident in his works up to 1972 (through the fifth volume of *A Theology for Artisans of a New Humanity*) and the second became increasingly apparent from 1975 forward (with *The Liberation of Theology*), as he explored the role of evangelization in the process of social change.

The first phase was founded solidly on the integral relationship of faith and morality to love of neighbor. In *The Community Called Church* Segundo briefly traced the scriptural writers' constant association of idolatry with sins against the neighbor, and conversely the knowledge of God with love of others.[8] He carried the principle through *Grace and the Human Condition*, pointing out that Paul characterized the pagans as idolatrous. He so designated them not in respect to Christian orthodoxy but in respect to the faith, freely given by God, which recognizes other persons as deserving of love. Segundo found that Paul's conception of Christian moral life then followed logically: the moral life is not an external law but the mandate to love in creative ways according to the needs of the neighbor.[9]

But in Jesus' work for the reign of God, individual lives of faith and love — as individual — are insufficient; thus Segundo also stressed the essential social dimension. Recall the question posed to the latter by an African delegate to a Young Catholic Worker conference in Rio de Janeiro: What do the *favelas* of Rio say about four hundred years of Christianity?[10] Yet even earlier than the work in which he narrated this inquiry, he reflected:

> Who, then, can in truth love the other person without truly loving God's own Self? Not by the effect of an intention which transcends the human being, but by the indescribable community of love which prevails between people and God, the intimate community in which no one can wound without wounding God and the rest of the members, in which no one can love without loving God and the rest.[11]

Segundo went on to point out that the love at issue is fundamentally God's love which surges to visibility in its effectiveness: "The church appears visibly, founded by Jesus Christ, better to carry into action the work of salvation which the love of God brought about among the human race from the beginning of the world."[12] Segundo asserted the importance of both elements, the love and its visibility, and developed the idea further in *The Community Called Church*. After recounting Karl Rahner's image of the signs of love exchanged between two lovers, Segundo noted: "The Church, the visible community with its formulas of faith and its sacraments, is to the cosmic community of God's People what the aforementioned signs [which nourish love] are to the reality they signify and convey."[13]

To summarize, the charity proper to the community of Jesus' disciples is authentic love made visible. By inserting itself into the dynamic of love and saving grace already at work in the world, the church functions as a sign of this love.

The second stage increasingly stressed the Christian community as **prophetic** sign of love.[14] The element of knowing the secret of God's saving action was no longer primarily knowledge; it became a matter of critical awareness. Since the next section will examine in detail the prophetic dimension, it will only be noted here. The pertinent point here is the changed emphasis which took place within Segundo's notion of the church as sign community. It was also in his writings from 1975 on where he commented more frequently on basic ecclesial communities.

In 1971, Segundo discussed base communities in *The Sacraments Today*. He urged a renewal of the community nature of the church so that the sacraments could function as genuine signs:

> Restoring the sacraments once again to the finality which Christ gave them means restoring the Church to its character as a community. Put more concretely, it means restoring the Church's character as a congregation of many 'base communities' (i.e., grass-roots communities at the local level). For it must be a congregation of real, concrete communities.[15]

Yet even from 1975 onward, Segundo ordinarily discussed the base communities in relation to other topics he was addressing, often the question of popular religion, rather than as a theme in its own right. That was the case with his remarks in *The Liberation of Theology* which expressed at the same time the author's prophetic thrust:

> If the concrete experience of grass-roots communities proves anything at all, it proves that taking cognizance of the liberative function of the Church does not lead to liturgical preciosity and merely intraecclesial reformism. Instead such communities become the fiercest and most effective opponents of the compromises the Church is forced to make when it tries to expropriate the masses as such and thereby impedes the liberation of the latter.[16]

Segundo commented most explicitly on basic ecclesial communities in his 1984 work, *Reflexiones críticas*. His observations throughout the book manifested the tension between the ecclesial importance of the communities (an importance underlined at Medellín) and the mass or popularizing tendencies which he saw at work. He attributed the origin of the name "base" communities to a recognition not of the "popular" aspect of the church but of the replacement of the clergy by the laity at its center.[17] He affirmed Medellín's definition of the Christian base community as the "initial cell" of the institutional church and the "focus of evangelization."[18] As a nucleus, the base community represents a new power of the church to gather people who will express their faith within the social and poltical reality. Segundo viewed this renewed potential as a challenge to restructure the church according to the values of faith and practical commitment. In fact, he considered the basic ecclesial community normative for Christian life.[19]

Such a community, Segundo observed, has a hermeneutical significance as well. Jesus' followers are able to imitate their leader's way of interpreting scripture according to God's purpose to humanize and liberate. After the pattern of the first Christian faithful, the disciples of today exemplify the hermeneutical circle: the responsibility they have shouldered leads them to hear and understand in the manner of Jesus:

> [Scripture] was . . . a powerful instrument because of the way Jesus used it. He interpreted it to liberate the poor and marginalized of Israel from their inhuman situation, thus gathering up a deep-rooted and visible human need of the majority and filling his sails with it.[20]

Thus Segundo has sharpened the image of the church as sign of authentic love. Assembled for the sake of Jesus' cause, the inauguration of God's reign for the poor and oppressed, the disciples form a community of love which shows to the world the reality of God's saving plan for the human race. The basic ecclesial communities, their members aware and committed, focus the prophetic vocation of the church. While on the same journey with every other person in the slow and painful growth of this love, the community of Jesus' disciples is distinguished by an understanding, the gift of God's revelation, of God's transforming salvation.

PROPHECY AND CONFLICT

The implications of the discipleship which manifests genuine love, especially for those most in need of love, are serious ones. This section will trace the demands made on Jesus' followers in three stages: Jesus' own prophetic vocation, the changed emphasis in the first centuries of the church, and the prophetic challenge today — particularly in regard to the institutional church.

PROPHETS AS JESUS WAS

Both Jesus' deeds of power and his teaching which sought to dismantle the oppressive religious ideologies around him served to make the coming of God's reign believable to those for whom it was coming. Jesus' conflicts in the political arena testified to the seriousness of God's intention to transform the lives of the poor.[21]

Segundo emphasized most strongly the prophetic[22] character of Christianity in the same work where he commented most explicitly about basic ecclesial communities, in *Reflexiones críticas*. This conjunction of themes underlined Jesus' creation of a prophetic community at the service of the people at large and especially the poor.[23] In *Reflexiones* Segundo described the prophetic responsibility which Jesus asked of the disciples for the benefit of the poor:

> Look at the service here: Jesus and his disciples (not the people) constitute a community of prophets. And, insofar as they are prophets, they serve the people, identifying themselves with their cause against that of their adversaries and oppressors. Prophet and people are in an intimate and complementary relationship, but are not confused.[24]

He elaborated on the difference between the demands Jesus made upon the common people and those he exacted from his disciples according to texts in Matthew's gospel:

> What happens is that the context of the first exhortation [". . . my burden is light"] shows that Jesus is addressing himself to the "simple ones," while the second ["carry one's cross"] reveals in the clearest way that he is defining the conditions for full prophetic discipleship.[25]

At the end of the chapter Segundo summed up and reaffirmed Jesus' call to the disciples to be prophets as he was:

> He creates a prophetic community, exacting and unselfish, at the service of the people and of the poor. He does not locate them in their totality in its midst. Nor would that be humane, on the other hand, given the type of service which he requires and the risk that this implies.[26]

SHIFT OF EMPHASIS IN THE EARLY CHURCH

Proclaiming the arrival of God's reign was for Jesus politically conflictual in his challenge to religious ideologies. The tone changed, however, after Jesus' resurrection. Although he died as a condemned political figure, it would be a long time before the Christian community which originated with him incurred political opposition by its advocacy of the poor and sinners.[27]

The early church changed the way it handed on Jesus' teaching. Even Luke, in his presentation of Jesus' controversy on behalf of the poor, shifted his point of view to the the social situation in which the church was living. Luke continued to manifest a strong interest in the poor and afflicted. He nevertheless transferred the beatitudes from their polemical context with the religious authorities to an interpretation that would promote the upbuilding of the early church. A similar transposition occurred for the parables and other teachings of Jesus.[28] Segundo summed up the transformation in these words, demonstrating that the early church retreated from the political and religious conflictivity of Jesus' ministry:

> The first Christian community preaches nothing conflictual in politi-
> cal terms, nothing which can inspire a concrete fear springing from the
> community mission. It says nothing about the poor and the rich.[29]

PROPHETIC CHRISTIANITY TODAY: PROPHECY VIS-À-VIS INSTITUTION

For centuries the prophetic face of Christianity remained largely veiled. But the Second Vatican Council, particularly *Gaudium et spes*, called for a new encounter between the church and the world. The bishops at Medellín identified the present time as crucial for the people of their continent. It is an invitation to reappropriate dimensions of the gospel message that have been overlooked or supplanted in preceding eras. In this context Segundo has argued that living the gospel today entails restoring Jesus' own politically conflictual key to interpreting events.

Segundo's understandings of personal liberty and the distinction between faith and ideology are essential to the argument. In light of the diminished capacity of Latin American culture to pass on Christian values, he insisted that the church "must stop relying on the surrounding milieu and start transmitting the gospel message to **each individual person.**"[30] The faith must become increasingly a matter of free, personal commitment.

For Segundo the failure to distinguish between faith and ideology is responsible for two types of errors concerning Christianity.[31] The first is the opposition of many church authorities to all "ideologies," in the popular sense of the word. The second is the failure of Christians to seek out and adopt effective historical means to implement the values which they hold.[32]

The ability to make this crucial distinction enables a more realistic view of the church's mission of reconciliation. Segundo notes that this mission does not mean being uninvolved in the concrete struggles of the poor or failing to take stands on their behalf for the sake of harmony. Rather, "the (eschatological) reconciliation sought by his [Jesus'] message will entail the unmasking and accentuation of that conflict and its hidden mechanisms, in order to turn its victims into conscious, active subjects in the struggle."[33]

Segundo considers the ideological, political interpretation of Jesus' message the essential means to a more effective living of Christianity on his continent. The implications of this key are serious:

> In Latin America . . . we have to be suspicious of any christological key that does not issue in political consequences as concrete and conflictive as those that Jesus himself dared to draw from his conception of God. We must suspect that such keys constitute culpable evasion and escapism. The dimensions of Sin are too obvious to pass unnoticed, to excuse those who emphasize something else.[34]

In effect, Segundo delineates a far-reaching political role for the church based on the God whose reign is coming in its fullness and on Jesus who proclaimed this reign and inaugurated it. Segundo believes strongly that such a role, conflictual in its prophetism, best conforms to the mission of Jesus which the church continues.

What happens when one tries to relate the prophetic character to the institutional aspect of the church? After all, even if this prophetic service has been curtailed for centuries, the institutional church has obviously continued to function during this time. Segundo has treated three points at which the prophetic challenge touches the institution. To be discussed here in turn, they are the standards for church membership, the recognition of roles within the church, and the church's function in society.

Criteria for Belonging to the Church

One level on which Segundo addressed this question was that of criteria for church membership. He acknowledged that the church as institution is obliged to define its limits of membership. It can in principle specify these limits in such a way that the entire population belongs. Yet if it does so, he maintained that its teaching tends to center on a creed conveyed through mass-oriented catechetics, liturgy, and preaching. This teaching applies generically to all who describe themselves as "Christians."[35] Such assumed and undifferentiated criteria for membership do not support the type of personally committed, prophetic involvement in society that Segundo outlined for the sake of God's project of humanization in the kingdom.

Intra-Church Roles

In *The Liberation of Theology* Segundo began Chapter IV with these words:

> For if our remarks are indeed a logical conclusion from theology accepted at the Medellín Conference, then we must have a new kind of authority in the Church, a new ecclesial structure, a new kind of faith and pastoral effort, and a new role for the laity in the very process of defining what authentic Christian faith is.[36]

His observation recalls a major point he had made in *¿Qué es un cristiano?*, that in comparison with religions which reserve ritual power exclusively to the priesthood, Christianity represents "a lay and aclerical revolution."[37] He views Christianity as granting absolute value to the human, based on its understanding of God, with all the consequences this would imply for the mutual roles of laity and clergy.[38] While Segundo was not directly addressing the question of the prophetic service to which Christians are called, this theme of the value of ordinary life and (extra)ordinary love amounted to setting aside traditional clericalized views of ecclesial structures to allow room for prophetic demands.

In emphasizing the lay character of the church, however, Segundo did not equate "lay" with "popular." In *Reflexiones críticas* he stated strongly:

> We are concerned in particular with the form in which the ecclesial institution is related to the people, not with individual persons of the

population, but with the people as such. For unintentionally, it seems
to think that the people, and especially the most poor, will be so much
the more protected and helped in their human necessities in the
measure in which they form part of the church. It seems to think this
even though this belonging is vitiated by spurious temporal and even
egotistical motivations. What service, we ask, can arise from this type
of motivation?[39]

At the same time he recognizes the tension which exists because "the
structures of the church which we would desire to change and put in closer
relation with the gospel conception of real practical service to the Christian
community are inextricably linked in Latin America with the phenomenon
of popular religiosity."[40]   Although popular religion tends to maintain
traditional practices and structures, Segundo sees hope for renewal in "the
creative help of the laity. . . from lay persons who possess a transforming
vision of the church and of its function."[41]

Segundo, after 1975, did not treat in detail the roles of clergy and
hierarchy. Two points he had made earlier in *The Sacraments Today*,
however, relates to prophecy and institution. First, he identified the crisis in
priestly ministry, particularly since Vatican II, as part of the political
radicalization which was occurring within the Christian community as it
opened itself to social problems. The priest was faced with the choice to be
a maintainer of social stability or an agent of social change.[42] Secondly, as
the lived and spoken expressions of the gospel in contemporary Christian
life multiplied, Segundo delineated the role of hierarchy and magisterium as
one of harmonizing the variety of evangelical interpretations, while re-
specting the diversity, into a unity of one faith, one baptism, and one
church.[43]

To summarize, although Segundo has not elaborated in detail the ways
he envisioned the institutional church adjusting to a new prophetic focus, he
pointed out directly and indirectly that the theology accepted at Vatican
Council II and at Medellín implies new ecclesial roles and structures for
laity, ordained ministers, and hierarchy and magisterium.

The Social Role of the Church

Segundo is more specific about the implications of the prophetic role of
the church in regard to social action than in regard to internal roles and
structures. His basic assessment of the prophetic relationship between
church and authorities in social-economic-political life was stark:

> . . . prophetism comes into conflict with **established authority and power**. It threatens the latter and the latter responds with violence, provoking the death of the prophet. And there can be only one good reason why the reason of state systematically comes into conflict with prophetism: because the latter intervenes and interferes in the sphere of the former, even though the claim and power of prophetism have their ultimate origin and validation in the religious sphere.[44]

Segundo's remarks in *The Community Called Church* on social assistance programs arose out of his sacramental model of the church and predated his more pronounced emphasis on prophetism. Yet in a significant way they exemplified values which linked his earlier and later thinking. He noted, for example, official declarations on behalf of laborers and other oppressed people, such as the letter by twenty Brazilian bishops in 1966 supporting the claims of impoverished sugarcane workers in a Northeastern state.

When the church provides social assistance to promote human betterment, it does so in a particular way. Segundo asserted that such a task is appropriate for the institutional church only in a substitutive capacity. He insisted that the official church assume the task, when it does so, totally in a spirit of service rather than of power, and in an attitude of respect for plurality rather than of a desire to shield persons from a diversity of views.[45]

Segundo reacted strongly toward the area of church teaching commonly known as its social doctrine. In different contexts, he criticized it along three lines: (1) efficacy, (2) linearity, and (3) ideology. First, in *Faith and Ideology* he faulted the social encyclicals as good statements of principle but poor instances of lived faith. He explained that "something is missing in the social encyclicals themselves because they do not provide the mediations needed to implement their imperatives."[46]

Second, Segundo considered in *An Evolutionary Approach to Jesus of Nazareth* the social doctrine of the church from an evolutionary perspective. The point at which he discussed this doctrine occurred immediately after he considered the ways that God, Jesus, and creation itself integrate both degeneration and growth, entropy and negentropy, death and life. With this realization he turned his attention

> to the official Church position on [human rights], suggesting that it derives from a christology in which the efficacy of Christ is conceived in linear rather than circuit terms. I shall suggest that the Church, once again, is trying to move straight from ideal to reality, to avoid the limitations and meanderings of ideologies which are such a necessary part of the process.[47]

Both human and salvation history require concrete, if limited, means to express values. Thus even values of social justice must follow this slower route to realization.

Third, it was in *An Evolutionary Approach to Jesus of Nazareth*, although written prior to *Reflexiones*, that Segundo dealt with precisely the ideological biases, and the lack of awareness of them on the part of church officials, which flaw social teaching. When policies concerning rights are administered from within "advanced" nations, and even when those rights are advocated by the church in the name of justice, one often gets the impression that the policies conform more to the interests of the administering nations than to the cause of the victims.

SUMMARY

Segundo has been at pains to show that both the church's social assistance practices and its social doctrine need to be rethought in circular rather than linear terms. They also need to be aware of biases tied to the social, economic, and political ground on which the teaching authorities stand. Social teaching must take means to put its principles into practice, indicating concrete, specific ways to concretize the values it advocates.

NOTES

1. Segundo acknowledged the questions but touched on them only briefly. Concerning an imminent coming of the kingdom, see *The Historical Jesus of the Synoptics*, trans. John Drury (Maryknoll, N.Y.: Orbis Books, 1985; henceforth *HJS*), 148. His comment in regard to "successors" to Jesus appeared in *Reflexiones críticas*, Vol. III, *Teología abierta* (Madrid: Ediciones Cristiandad, 1984), 102-3; now *RC*.

2. "No hay que olvidar, en efecto, que Jesús quiere unir a sus discípulos a su actividad de servidor en beneficio de los destinatarios del reino," *RC*, 108.

3. See *RC*, 103.

4. *HJS*, 149; emphasis Segundo's. He explained his frequently used phrase "historical causality" explicitly on pp. 158-9. He said (158), "Contrary to all the familiar apocalyptic perspectives, the coming of the kingdom does not evoke a merely **passive** hope . . . . Human beings **collaborate** in its coming." He concluded from the texts Mt. 11:12/ Lk. 16:16 and Lk. 12:31/ Mt. 6:33 that "there is a causal connection, however small and secondary, between the establishment of the kingdom and human activity directed toward it."

   See also Segundo's discussion of human work, referred to in 1 Cor. 3:10-15, in *The Humanist Christology of Paul*, trans. John Drury (Maryknoll, N.Y.: Orbis Books, 1986, 130-31; henceforth *HCP*.

5. *HJS*, 106.

6. Note Segundo's observations in *RC*, 113-115; see also *HCP*, 3-5, regarding the shift evident in 1 and 2 Thessalonians.

7. "Pues bien, la primera comunidad cristiana no predica nada conflictivo en términos políticos. Nada que pueda inspirar un temor concreto proveniente de la misión comunitaria" (*RC*, 114).

8. See *The Community Called Church*, trans. John Drury (Maryknoll, N.Y.: Orbis Books, 1973), 63-7; henceforth *CCC*.

9. Note the discussion of Paul's thought in *Grace and the Human Condition*, trans. John Drury (Maryknoll, N.Y.: Orbis Books, 1973), esp. 110, 21-28; henceforth *GHC*.

10. Segundo described this encounter and his reflections on it in *¿Qué es un cristiano?* (Montevideo: Mosca Hnos. S.A. Editores, 1971), 92.

11. "¿Quién puede amar entonces de verdad a otro hombre sin amar de veras a Dios mismo? No por el efecto de una intención que trascienda al hombre, sino por la inefable comunidad del amor que reina entre los hombres y Dios, comunidad

entrañable en la que nadie puede herir sin herir a Dios y a los demás, en la que nadie puede amar sin amar a Dios y a los demás" (*Función de la Iglesia en la realidad rioplantense* [Montevideo: Barreiro y Ramos, 1962], 34).

12. "La Iglesia aparece visiblemente, fundada por Jesucristo, para realizar mejor la obra de salvación que el amor de Dios realizó desde el comienzo del mundo entre los hombres" (*Función*, 42)

13. *CCC*, 54. The citation from Karl Rahner appeared on 53, from *Theological Investigations*, Vol. II, *Man in the Church* (London: Darton, Longman and Todd; Baltimore: Helicon, 1963), 129-30.

14. It is notable in this regard that the Uruguayan military seized power in 1973 (see Ch. One, 5). One pre-1975 article, however, that typifies the second or prophetic phase of Segundo's writing more than the first was "Capitalism — Socialism: A Theological Crux," in *Concilium*, Vol. 96, ed. Claude Geffré and Gustavo Gutiérrez (New York: Herder and Herder, 1974), 105-23.

15. *The Sacraments Today*, trans. John Drury (Maryknoll, N.Y.: Orbis Books, 1974), 32; henceforth *ST*. Segundo described the reflection groups he leads in relation to basic ecclesial communities in a private conversation in Montevideo, November 20, 1986. "In Uruguay, over half the people are not baptized. The proletariat, the working class is non-Christian. For this reason it is impossible to speak of basic Christian communities here in the way they are spoken of in Brazil, for example.

"An important shift has occurred in the meaning of 'basic Christian communities' from its meaning at Medellín. At Medellín, 'basic' meant 'at the base or foundation of the church'. The church is made up of many types of groups, in contrast to large, anonymous institutional parishes and dioceses.

"But at Puebla, 'basic' took on the meaning of 'popular or grassroots'. In Brazil, if you speak of a community of middle-class persons, they will say that this is not a basic Christian community because it is not made up of poor people.

"In Montevideo, Christianity is a middle-class result. It is impossible to have a basic community in a single locale. Actually, a group of this kind is too heterogeneous. It is better to draw people together from many different places who have a similar commitment. That is why I go all over the city for the different reflection groups. In these groups, persons who are not Christian are interested also. They consider this kind of Christian reflection and action more important than formal membership in an institutional church. So the groups are not really basic Christian communities even in the sense of Medellín."

16. *The Liberation of Theology*, trans. John Drury (Maryknoll, N.Y.: 1976), 203; henceforth *LT*.

17. See *RC*, 143, note 21. On p. 148, Segundo noted the "gray area" between the origins of some basic communities in the convoking power of the church itself and the

impetus from political and economic interest groups which want to use the groups for their ends.

18. Latin American Episcopate (Medellín, Colombia), "Joint Pastoral Planning," *The Church in the Present-Day Transformation of Latin America in the Light of the Council*, 3rd. ed., Vol. II, *Conclusions* (Washington, D.C.: United States Catholic Conference, 1968), art. 10, 185; citation in *RC*, note 21, 143.

19. Segundo elaborated these ideas in *RC*, particularly 148 and 215-17. Note as well on p. 157 his caution to distinguish the CEB's (*comunidades eclesiales de base*) from mass-oriented practices, such as equating them with mini-parishes.

On pp. 215-17 he commented on the requirement such affirmation (as Medellín) places on the church at large to restructure itself, and thus be better able through such communities to "accompany the rhythm, distinct in each case, of the process of consciousness and humanization among the people" (. . . la imposibilidad, para la Iglesia-institución, de acompañar el ritmo, distinto en cada caso, del proceso popular de conciencia y humanización," 216).

20. *An Evolutionary Approach to Jesus of Nazareth*, trans. John Drury (Maryknoll, N.Y.: Orbis Books, 1988), 17; henceforth *EA*.

21. See *RC*, 99: ". . . tanto las 'fuerzas' que se revelan en las **obras** de Jesús, como el desmantelamiento de la ideología religiosa opresora que se opera con su **enseñanza**, convergen hacia un mismo objetivo: hacer creíble a sus propios destinatarios la venida del reino a la historia" ("Ambas son tareas 'políticas' en las que Dios **se revela** como el rey que viene a humanizar a los más pobres y oprimidos de Israel").

22. While Segundo has not defined "prophecy" as such, its main elements were apparent in his use of it. These may be summarized as four, exemplified in *HJS*: (1) participation by Jesus and his disciples in the tradition of the Old Testament prophets (78-9); (2) requiring critical consciousness (136-9); (3) involving political conflict (80-5); and entailing opposition and suffering (80).

23. Note the author's observation in *HJS*, 87, about Jesus' central proclamation: "It is within this [circle], which closely associates three terms ('kingdom', 'the poor', and 'good news'), that the prophetic content of Jesus' proclamation moves."

(The Spanish original had "círculo," the English translation "article"; "circle" renders the meaning more accurately.)

24. "He aquí el servicio: Jesús y sus discipulos (no el pueblo) constituyen una comunidad de profetas. Y, en cuanto profetas, sirven al pueblo identificándose con su causa contraria a la de sus adversarios y opresores. Profeta y pueblo están en relación íntima y complementaria, pero no se confunden" (*RC*, 109).

25. "Lo que ocurre es que el contexto de la primera exhortación ['. . . mi carga ligera'] muestra que Jesús se está dirigiendo a 'los sencillos', mientras que el de la segunda

['cargue su cruz'] manifiesta de la manera más clara que está definiendo las condiciones del discipulado profética pleno" (*RC*, 109-10). The first text cited was Mt. 11:28, 30; the second was Mt. 16:24.

La Biblia (Madrid: Ed. Paulinas; Navarra: Ed. Verbo Divino, 1972) showed the linguistic parallels which Segundo made in *RC* within Mt. 11 and between Mt. 11 and 16.

A problem appears, however, when one tries to follow the same linkage of terms in the Greek text. In Mt 11: 28, 30, the parallels in Segundo's usage matched those in the Greek. "Heavy-laden" was rendered as "*sobrecargados*" by Segundo and by "*pephortismenoi*" in Greek. "My burden is light" appeared as "mi *carga* [es] ligera" and "to *phortion* mou elaphron estin."

Segundo traced the verb "*cargar*" through to Mt. 16:24 ['cargue su cruz'], where the Greek text did not use the same verb as in Mt. 11. Rather, "let a person take up the cross" was "*aratō* ton stauron" in Mt. 16 which corresponded to "take my yoke" in Mt. 11, "*arate* ton zygon."

It is pertinent to note here, however, that two years earlier in *HJS*, 134, Segundo had used the Mt. 11 text, "my yoke is easy and my burden light," not to describe relief from the life burden which the poor carried, but to Jesus' invitation to the poor to follow him. They would find the weight of discipleship under him easier to carry than the duties imposed by the Jewish religious leaders.

26. ". . . Jesús crea una comunidad profética, exigente y desprendida, al servicio del pueblo y de los pobres. No coloca a éstos, en cuanto globalidad, dentro de ella. Ni ello sería, por otra parte, humano, dado el tipo de servicio que se exige y el riesgo que ello implica" (*RC*, 128).

27. See *HJS*, 182-88, esp. 183.

28. Consult *RC*, particularly 49-52. "Por ejemplo, las bienaventuranzas que Lucas coloca en segunda persona y que aparecen, así, dirigidas a los discípulos pobres y perseguidos (no a la multitud que seguía a Jesús). Lo mismo ocurre con enseñanzas de Jesús, que han sido desplazadas de su contexto polémico con las autoridades de Israel para darles una interpretación edificante en la Iglesia naciente, lo que ocurre, como se verá más adelante, en la mayoría de las parábolas. En algunas se percibe cómo los redactores de los evangelios han llegado a modificar, para este fin, la 'moraleja' con que la parábola concluye" (52, note 12).

29. "Pues bien, la primera comunidad cristiana no predica nada conflictivo en términos políticos. Nada que pueda inspirar un temor concreto proveniente de la misión comunitaria. No dice nada sobre los pobres o sobre los ricos" (*RC*, 114).

30. *LT*, 128.

31. Recall that Segundo defined "faith" fundamentally as the human dimension of "a meaning-structure, . . . a scale of values, a life-meaning." This human faith can then become a religious or specifically Christian faith. He defined "ideology" as "all human knowledge about **efficacy** (or **effectiveness**)," or perhaps more exactly, "a systematization of objective knowledge about efficacy." See *Faith and Ideologies*, trans. John Drury (Maryknoll, N.Y.: Orbis Books, 1984), 27; henceforth *FI*. See also Ch. One above, 36-9.

32. See the important discussion in *LT*, 126-33. Segundo synopsized on p. 126 his view of ideology in relation to the church: "It can be said that the Catholic Church in Latin America was the first Catholic community to set out resolutely on the new pathway opened up by Vatican II. The new pathway was based on the assumption that faith has as its function the task of guiding the human mind towards more fully human solutions in history; that the Church does not possess those solutions in advance but does possess elements that have been revealed by God; that these revealed elements do not preserve the Church from ideologies; that instead the Church must take advantage of those elements to go out in search of (ideological) solutions to the problems posed by the historical process; and that such solutions will always remain provisional."

33. *HJS*, 133. See also 126.

34. *HCP*, 170.

35. For this discussion, see *RC*, 213-14. "La institución eclesial puede (y debe) definir sus propios límites (institucionales) de acuerdo con su función. Puede entender que el pueblo entero le pertenece. Pero, en tal caso, lo que no puede es 'dosificar' su enseñanza en función de su aporte a la humanización. En efecto, la institución Iglesia se concentra en torno a un **credo** que pasa a todos sus miembros mediante la catequesis, los sacramentos y su preparación, la predicación dominical y el ciclo anual de la liturgia. Así, todo el paquete de datos trascendentes cristianos pasa, en forma indiscriminada y constante, a **todos** los que se consideran 'cristianos'."

36. *LT*, 97.

37. "Y en el sentido en que el sacerdocio suele en las diversas religiones reservarse la exclusividad del poder ritual considerado decisivo, el cristianismo significaba una revolución laica y aclerical. Más aún, pensando en la reacción que ello suscitaba en un mundo donde el sacerdocio pretendía de hecho esa exclusividad, hasta se podría emplear el término que usa Escarpit: 'laica y anticlerical" (*¿Qué es un cristiano?*, Montevideo: Mosca Hnos. S.A. Editores, 1971, 101).

This point served as the theme for section II of *¿Qué es*, 99-105. Notice that Segundo modified the description by Robert Escarpit (*École laique, école du peuple*, Paris: Calmann-Lévy, 1961, 43). Where Escarpit had described a renewed church as "lay and **anti**clerical," Segundo said "lay and aclerical"; emphasis added.

38. Cf. the conclusion to the section of ¿*Qué es* under discussion: "El cristianismo, tal como lo hallábamos en sus fuentes auténticas, era una revolución laica en lo religioso. . . . Ninguna magia sagrada, ningún conocimiento de un camino especial escondido a los demás, deberán sacarlo de ese combate, puesto que para ese combate y no para otra cosa se la ha dado la verdad revelada: que Dios es amor y que todo amor efectivo se convierte en valor absoluto, en el único verdadero valor absoluto de la existencia humana" (105).

39. "Nos preocupa en particular la forma en que la institución eclesial se relaciona con el pueblo. No con personas del pueblo, sino con el pueblo como tal. Por de pronto, parece pensar que el pueblo, y en especial los más pobres, estarán tanto más protegidos y ayudados en sus necesidades humanas en la medida en que formen parte de la Iglesia. Aunque esta pertenencia esté viciada por motivaciones temporales espúreas y aun egoístas. ¿Qué servicio, nos preguntamos, puede surgir de este tipo de motivaciones?" (*RC*, 213-14).

40. "Las estructuras de la Iglesia que desearíamos cambiar y poner más en relación con la concepción evangélica de un servicio real y práctico a la comunidad cristiana, están en América Latina inextricablemente ligadas al fenómeno de la religiosidad popular. . . ." (*RC*, 332).

41. "Por otro lado, en todas partes de América Latina las autoridades eclesiásticas necesitan para innumerables funciones imprescindibles—aun en lo que toca a la propagación de la fe—de la ayuda creadora del laico. . . . En todas partes ese apoyo viene, cada vez más, en forma claramente mayoritaria, de laicos que poseen una visión transformadora de la Iglesia y de su función" (*RC*, 332). Surprisingly, this description contained clerical/hierarchal overtones in its reference to helping the ecclesiastical authorities, but it did lay stress on the body of the faithful.

42. Note the discussion in *ST*, especially 106.

43. This idea appeared in *ST*, 34.

44. *HJS*, 80.

45. See *CCC*, 93-7.

46. *FI*, 127.

47. *EA*, 79.

5

THE CHURCH AND THE POOR:
A MINISTRY OF SERVICE

The previous chapter focused on two dimensions of the church as a prophetic community. It expanded on the church's identity as the community of Jesus' disciples who extend in the world Jesus' mission of effective love, especially to those on the periphery of society. It also looked closely at the conflict which attends those who cast their lot with Jesus, who was put to death in the manner of the Old Testament prophets. This chapter turns to the third and final part of Segundo's definition: the prophetic community is "at the service of the poor, marginalized, and dehumanized people of the earth." After examining the question of the subjectivity of poor people themselves, it will discuss servant discipleship.

THE STATE OF THE QUESTION: SUBJECT OR OBJECT?

Along with other Latin American theologians, Segundo has reflected at length on the meaning of the Christian faith and the church on a continent where a majority of the people endure a less than human existence. Despite this common concern, theologians have come to different conclusions about the relationship of poor people and the church. Segundo's most comprehensive discussion of this inquiry, preceded by several articles, occurred in *Reflexiones críticas.*[1]

Therefore, this section of the paper will treat two aspects of the question: "Can the church truly be a church of, in the sense of arising out of, the poor?"[2] It will review Segundo's replies to Leonardo Boff, Jon Sobrino, and

Gustavo Gutiérrez, three prominent Latin American theologians who emphasize that poor people are subjects of theology and, by implication, subjects in the church because they are bearers of the gospel message. It will then consider what difference the church makes to the ordinary populace in light of the way the popular church relates to other popular movements in Latin America.

RESPONSE TO ADVOCATES OF THE POOR AS SUBJECT

Segundo based his reaction to the stance of Leonardo Boff mainly on an article Boff published in the *Revista Eclesiastica Brasileira* after a stay in the jungle area of Acre, Brazil. In the introduction to the article, Boff raised the question, " 'Who evangelizes the theologian? It is **the very testimony of faith of the faithful people,** their capacity to insert God in all their struggles, their force of resistance against all the oppressions which they habitually suffer.' "[3] When Boff narrated his attempt to lead the people to a more positive understanding of salvation and of suffering, he commented, " 'A Jesus who is only sorrowing does not liberate; he generates misery and fatalism. It is important **to replace in the minds of the people** the **rightful** place of the cross. . . .' "[4] Segundo maintained that, with a faith so tinged by fatalism and by an "oppressive ideology," the people cannot truly evangelize.[5] It takes a person carefully prepared to recognize these distortions to convey an authentic understanding of salvation.

Segundo's response to Jon Sobrino on the subject-object question centered on three chapters of Sobrino's book, *The True Church and the Poor.*[6] Sobrino, comparing European political theologies with Latin American liberation theologies, described the latter as more self-conscious of their status as a field of knowledge and more self-critical than the former. Segundo remarked that even such self-criticism implies a certain distance, a certain kind of standing outside the people in the events being criticized.[7] To Sobrino's reflection on the church of the poor as the place of conversion, where "it is 'easier' to be aware of one's own status as a sinner in the midst of sinful poverty. . .,"[8] Segundo replied that "it is not a matter of the conversion **of** the poor, but of conversion **toward** the poor and their cause."[9]

Sobrino, unwilling to accept a church which stands outside the people and offers them help, maintained that a church of the poor as exemplified by Bartolomé de las Casas indicated the right relationship.[10] Segundo, however, countered that both Sobrino's example of the Spaniard De Las Casas and his advocacy of the social sciences to benefit theology indicated a stepping outside the mentality of the people themselves to assist them.[11]

Segundo also responded critically to a statement made by Gustavo Gutiérrez in **The Power of the Poor in History**.[12]

> The gospel, read from the viewpoint of the poor, from the viewpoint of the militancy of their struggles for liberation, convokes a popular church — that is, a church born of the people. . . . It is a church rooted in a people that snatches the gospel from the hands of the great ones of this world. It prevents it from being utilized henceforward as an element in the justification of a situation contrary to the will of the Liberator-God.[13]

Because the poor of Jesus' own day could not "snatch God's revelation, the Law and the Prophets, from the hands of the great ones of Israel,"[14] Segundo failed to see how Gutiérrez could realistically expect the Latin American poor of today to do so.

In summary, Segundo did not analyze the work of these three theologians comprehensively, nor even the articles to which he referred here. He nevertheless found the given instances indicative of the theological current which recognizes the poor to be subjects of theology, of evangelization and, by inference, of the church. He was convinced that all three failed to make crucial distinctions and therefore were unconvincing in their argument for the poor as subjects. He named the significance he saw for the church in this issue when he made the statement which forms the theme for Chapters Three to Five: "the church, if it wants to be faithful to the gospel, can only be a prophetic community at the service of the poor, marginalized and dehumanized of the earth."[15]

WHAT DIFFERENCE DOES THE CHURCH MAKE FOR THE PEOPLE AT LARGE?

At the beginning of *The Community Called Church* Segundo quoted the Greek philosopher Porphyry: "'If Christ is the one and only savior, as his followers claim, then why did he come so recently?' "[16] The thinker's question might be paraphrased as follows: If the church is a sign and instrument of love and a prophetic community of service to the poor, then why did it come so recently? This theme recurred frequently in Segundo's works. He found in the long history of the world without Christianity and the small number of Christians in the total world population a further argument against identifying the church as a church (historically) of the poor. In *Reflexiones críticas* he questioned pointedly:

> And if we suppose that those long earlier periods represent precisely those in which humanity was subject to the most urgent necessities of survival, as the lowest classes of society are today, should we not call that portion of humanity accompanied by Christianity something like a "middle class"? There must be something intrinsic in it which destines it to that spacial-temporal context: why, otherwise, did Christianity from the beginning not accompany the slow and laborious route of the "proletariat" of humanity?[17]

Segundo argued, as well, that the ponderous and undifferentiated character of popular religion militates against social changes that benefit the poor.[18] The church has tended to accept popular religion as a means to keep the multitudes within its embrace and allowed devotions such as that to the Virgin of Guadalupe to act "as a religious 'alleviation' which does not transform their misery."[19] Even the ambivalence of the Medellín documents on the question of popular religion[20] does not serve the true interests of the poor majority.

The discussion above seems to produce quite a pessimistic conclusion concerning the contribution of the church to the good of the people. It is true that, by virtue of both theological principle and historical observation, Segundo maintained that Christianity does not appear as the essential way to salvation for those at the poorest levels of society. And to the extent that the church defines itself and its pastoral task in terms of popular religion, its effectiveness is very limited and even somewhat negative. On the other hand, where genuine commitment in a faith oriented to service, exemplified by basic ecclesial communities, increasingly constitutes the life of the church, Segundo's conclusion became most positive:

> Here we would no longer be in the presence of an alienated people whose religion brings it to acceptance and passivity. The church in this continent would have recovered its potentiality for assembling, and for significant changes, a people which acted as a subject. If one is talking about proposed changes by popular political movements, the church accompanies the mobilization of the people. If one is dealing with its own base communities, the church seems to be, in good part, the instigator of the mobilization.[21]

SERVANT DISCIPLES

THE CHURCH AT THE SERVICE OF THE WORLD

Segundo's basic and consistent ecclesiological principle has been that the church was founded to benefit the whole of humanity. The Christian assumes more profoundly the responsibility for the love which is the ultimate principle for all existence. This conviction has undergirded equally his theology of the church as sign of authentic love and his understanding of prophetic community.

The mission of service as articulated in *The Community Called Church* recapitulated key points from his earlier *La función de la Iglesia en la realidad rioplatense*:

> On the day of final judgment, man will hear some such statement as this from his judge: "Come, blessed of my Father, because I was hungry and your love had sufficient scope and hope to feed me. . .
>
> Herein lies the necessity of the church. Here we see why it is so indispensable in the salvation plan for humanity. In the midst of the human race there must be people who know the mystery of love, who will meet and dialogue with those who are moving toward the gospel and confronting the questions raised by love. . . . And this dialogue is essential for what Teilhard called the "piloting of history."[22]

In *The Hidden Motives of Pastoral Action*, the author stated simply the first of three elements of an alternative ecclesiology: "The church was established in the world to benefit the rest of humankind."[23] In his work on the historical Jesus, he again linked history and the reign of God, this time from the other direction: "Jesus is seeking **to place historical causality in the service of the kingdom**. And not only does he invest his all as *perfectus homo* in that service; he invests his disciples' all as well."[24] The author pointed out that, while Paul's interpretive key changed to an anthropological-existential one for the gospel, the key was still open to an historical and political causality. The foundation of a church at the service of universal sister- and brotherhood is undergirded by God's gift to all people throughout history of being sisters and brothers because daughters and sons. While this reality appears with particular clarity in the church, it is not limited to the church.[25]

In the most recent of his works, Segundo still maintained the same focus for the church:

> Once the supposed monopoly of grace and salvation which Christians
> would retain was excluded, there remained no other specificity for the
> church and its mission in the world than that indicated by Vatican II:
> that which could arise from a service which would be reserved to it or
> in which it would have a decisive contribution to make. . . .
>
> To translate the faith into a concrete humanization for people, in
> circumstances always new and in dialogue with the rest. . . .[26]

Recall Segundo's consideration of the task of the church in Argentina
and Uruguay. Segundo has shown that he views the church not as an
absolute in itself, but as one means for approaching the absolute.[27] In
working for that development of the church which would establish it in
equilibrium with other elements in the concrete history of these two countries, he had expressed more specifically the principle which he has held
throughout. The Christian is a servant disciple in a church which helps the
world reach its full humanization.

EFFECTIVE SERVICE

The service to which Jesus' disciples are called is oriented not inward to
the community itself but outward to the world. It gives a clear sign of God's
love at work on earth. It engages people in collaborating in the project which
God carries out for the poor. Yet all of this must produce an effect; thus, the
question of means comes into play. Segundo's concern for efficacy marked
his earlier as well as his later works. In *Masas y minorías*, he reflected:

> But, in what does committing oneself in favor of the poor consist?
> Without a doubt, in **doing everything possible** to halt their oppres-
> sion. . . . We begin immediately with the problem of means.
> **Everything possible** does not mean the same thing to an ordinary
> Marxist as it does to an ordinary Christian.[28]

The same question concerned Segundo in *The Liberation of Theology* as
in *Masas*. Yet after examining concrete examples within the political life of
Latin America, he admitted:

> And so we come to the end of this chapter with a question still
> unanswered. We started out considering what a political option taken
> in the name of Christian theology might be, and we ended up with the
> conclusion that there is no such thing as Christian theology or a

Christian interpretation of the gospel message in the absence of a prior
political commitment. Only the latter makes the former possible at
all.[29]

For Segundo, the faith which serves to stimulate concrete historical
solutions with the aid of revelation "is a liberative process. It is converted
into freedom for history, which means freedom **for ideologies**" — his term
for systems of means to actualize a value.[30] Therefore the disciple, who has
taken the side of the poor, seeks the most effective means possible on their
behalf.

This search for effective means requires participation in changing structures. Recall the corollary to the method for a creative morality, described in
Grace and the Human Condition above: human liberation "is concretized in
ideological transformation and political action."[31] In addition to the extensive analysis of ideology which concretizes faith in *Faith and Ideology*,
Segundo noted that "even unjust societies constitute **ecologies** in the long
run. They constitute social systems with a complicated equilibrium, and
hence they must be changed **as such**."[32] The individual faith response is
insufficient by itself, just as relieving only the symptoms of social ills is
inadequate:

> . . . It seems evident that his [Jesus'] commandment of love and his
> countless examples and admonitions concerning it must be translated
> to an era in which real-life love has taken on political forms. . . . To
> suggest that almsgiving should continue to be the Christian response
> to the whole problem of wealth and its relationship to love is also to
> seriously distort the gospel message.[33]

Segundo was convinced that the history of Jesus demonstrated the
reciprocity which exists between the religious and the political:

> Here we have the great paradox, the unexpected finding: the more the
> Beatitudes allude to the simple, anguished situation of the poor, the
> afflicted, and the hungry, the more **political** they turn out to be; but, at
> the same time, the more they are dissociated from any intrinsic
> relationship with the moral, spiritual, or religious dispositions of
> human groups, the more **religious** they become. For it is thus that they
> enable us to probe much deeper into the 'heart' of God, into the
> mystery of God's will on earth. And only thus do we glimpse the
> realm of values for which God opts and then makes the object of
> God's reign.[34]

The author offered examples where implementation of values was an issue. He reflected on the Christian Democratic movement and the questions about a specifically Christian contribution to which it gave rise.[35] He took up the crisis in priestly ministry in *The Sacraments Today*, situating it within the church's new openness to social problems. In this context, he stated that:

> It would be a delusion to pretend that **liberation of the individual from sin**, expanded in scale, could bring about all the other needed liberations in an effective, rapid, or even realistic way; that there is no need to call into question the sinful sociopolitical structures which are responsible for the most tangible exploitation, etc. These can only be overcome by an attack on structures. That is to say, the attack must be directed at the source from which they come.[36]

Segundo also commented on slavery, from 1 Cor. 7:20-22, in relation to goals and means. While the language of Paul's letter seems harsh, the author argued that the loving service which Paul urged between slave and overseer necessarily included removing hindrances to this love. Therefore, "all that **virtually** implies the abolition of slavery as a societal structure."[37]

In short, the issue of means, of how to "do everything possible," in service to one's sisters and brothers permeates every aspect of the love to which Jesus' disciples are called. For the liberation of individuals is neither possible nor sufficient without the conversion of sociopolitical structures responsible for such manifold enslavements as poverty and hunger.

SACRAMENTALITY: SERVICE SIGNIFIED

Segundo's theology of the sacraments exemplified his basic conviction that the Christian community is to be an effective sign of love in the world. In *The Sacraments Today*, he stated it this way:

> In order to make its own specific and divine contribution to universal salvation, the visible Church *qua* community must be a sign: a sign of the universal salvific plan, of the recapitulation for which the whole universe is waiting, of a message that God sends through his Church in order to contribute toward solutions of man's historical problems that are truly human.[38]

All that Segundo said about sacramental rites depended on this principle. On the one hand, the sacraments indicate that God chooses to give grace as "grace 'of the Church': i.e., as grace which fashions a Church in the service of the rest of the human community."[39] From the other — human — side, the sacraments represent the community response to a deepened understanding of and commitment to human liberation proceeding through history.[40] It is imperative for Segundo that the sacramental rites not be viewed or enacted as "magic," as instruments which can bring about favorable responses from God.[41] That is to say, religious rites must allow the questions of "suffering, violence, injustices, famine and death" to be seen as the critical issues they are.[42]

Little has appeared in recent years from Segundo on the sacraments. In *Reflexiones críticas*, however, he affirmed that his thinking had remained essentially the same since *The Sacraments Today*,[43] and remarked mainly on the question of ministry. He observed that the internal renewal of the church has not kept pace with the new outward thrust of Vatican II. In fact, he judged that the liturgical reform has, on two points, left the church in a worse state than before.

First, the adoption of the vernacular, instead of engaging Christians more profoundly in their historical setting, has served to sacralize and clericalize liturgical practice even further:

> Today we find on the one side those who, without devoting much attention to the content, rush gladly upon the opportunity to perform cultic and sacred functions which were reserved until very recently to the clergy. Thus a clericalization on the part of the laity has been produced — particularly visible at the level of the *diaconate* — which was certainly not the intention of Vatican II.[44]

In the second place, the Latin of preconciliar liturgical practice had managed to hide a vacuum that existed. While the rites emphasized the tradition of many centuries and the celebration of divine mysteries, they lacked almost entirely the dimension of present history and the situation of the human beings who are worshipping this God:

> . . . The theology — the understanding of the faith — transmitted by the liturgy dated from earlier ages and did not reflect the function of the Christian in the face of the joys, the hopes, the moans, and the afflictions of their contemporary brothers and sisters. This has occurred in that the sacramental and liturgical crisis, the crisis of the "celebration" of God, of God's grace and reign, has not been in some way overcome by a liturgical revision which has been presented as already concluded. As a result, many of the most profound and creative Christians stay away from something so intimately constitutive of a Christian community: celebration.[45]

Segundo has chosen not to address the internal structures of the church
and its sacramental practice for two reasons: because of both anticipated
failure and already achieved success. The prospect of failure is tied to the
ponderous character of popular religion, which weighs upon any attempts to
change. The success is due to the growing vitality of laypersons throughout
Latin America who are already furthering the transformative vision of the
church which is being fashioned as a sign community of effective, prophetic
love in the world.[46]

SERVICE AS MORAL CRITERION

When service is as fundamental to a theology as it is to Segundo's, it
appears in all dimensions of that theology, the moral as well as the sacramental. Segundo addressed the questions of moral criteria, grace, and sin early in
his writings. In *Grace and the Human Condition*, he discussed the pressure
which social reality exerts on the person through patterns of thought,
attitude, judgment and action. These determinisms or compelling influences
both represent concepts of human relationships and stand for vested interests
in the system of relationships. A certain ideology (used here in the sense of
a justifying rationale) supports the system. When Segundo addressed the
effect that this social dimension produces on moral criteria, on the boun-
daries of grace and sin, he concluded that becoming aware of one's "unconscious determinisms" is an essential aspect of human liberation. He
continued:

> [This liberation] takes concrete form when [the person] shoulders the
> task of moving from an established morality that he did not choose to
> a creative morality involving the formulation of a new societal
> scheme, and then engages in action to transform the structures which
> are perpetuating his alienation. In short, it is concretized in ideologi-
> cal transformation and political action.[47]

While his main emphasis in *Evolution and Guilt* was original sin,
Segundo has treated historical moral choices at a few points. In terms of
evolution and energy, he identified the mass aspect of human existence as
sinful, because this tendency toward "simplistic, mechanical syntheses"
involves a person's "rejection of a creative but costly liberty."[48] In other
words, the person's capacity for service or effective love is curtailed. When
he turned to the question whether a universal, timeless Christian morality

actually exists, he based his answer on Jesus' teaching that only what comes from within can defile a person (Mark 17:19-20):

> Jesus' principle revolutionizes the whole of morality: things do not come into the sphere of human activity already bearing the moral label of 'good' or 'bad'. Ethical value adheres to the whole project within which they are inscribed as means and ends.[49]

This notion of the project is central in Segundo's work. In *The Humanist Christology of Paul*, he placed collaboration in God's project being accomplished in history at the crux of the struggle between God's reign of love and human sinfulness. Including 1 Corinthians in his reflection on Romans, he remarked: "In deciding what is 'suitable,' human beings must consider what 'builds up' their brothers and sisters. . . . Love consists in collaborating with God in the work of building or constructing a human existence for human beings."[50] Yet the ongoing struggle to realize God's reign entails more than individual resistance: "Even after Christ and Faith, the vast majority of our works follow the 'natural' course toward the easy way out. They are caught in the mechanisms that separate intention from performance."[51]

In *The Christ of the Spiritual Exercises*, Segundo ratified the theology of project, present inchoately in Ignatius, which he had developed in the previous volume, and rejected the theology of test. He based his project morality upon the ultimate criterion described in Matthew 25 that God will use to judge all human beings:

> Suddenly we see that the fact that God is love, a fact derived from christology, leaves behind any conception of human existence as a **test**. It plants us before a common human and divine **project** that is unfolding in the history of human beings and their dire needs.[52]

Because the project as standard of judgment is essentially social, so is any sin. In Jesus' own life, this criterion was "how to make happy the poor and sinners, who were one and the same group."[53] For Jesus' servant followers, while the application of the principle may not be clear and simple, the principle itself is direct and to the point.

In short, human life is social both in its context of human relationships and in its connection with God's reign. Christian morality is an interior response of personal liberty; it is the creative participation in God's project of the coming kingdom. When the reign is at hand, God will judge all peoples by the standard Jesus used in reference to it: how is the misery of the poor abolished?

SUMMARY

"The church, if it wants to be faithful to the gospel, can only be a prophetic community at the service of the poor, marginalized, and dehumanized people on the earth." This statement from *Reflexiones críticas* synthesizes three decades or more of Juan Luis Segundo's thought on the church and its relationship with the poor. It has also provided an opportune framework for examining in these three central chapters many direct and indirect aspects of his thinking on the topic.

"To be faithful to the gospel": The gospel has newly challenged the church of Latin America. Christians have experienced through the death of much traditional religious practice a fresh call to hear the gospel in freedom and to commit themselves to actualize it in their concrete settings, where multitudes suffer the lack of the most basic human necessities. Christians are invited to share the good news in service to others, especially the most deprived, and thus come to understand it with increasing profundity.

The response in faith is the transformation entailed in making Jesus' values one's own. As Jesus took his stand alongside the poor so that they might know the new order which God's reign establishes for them, so the disciples take their stand on behalf of the poor today for whom God still acts. Not everyone can hear or follow this radical call with the complexity and risk of continually seeking ways to enflesh in history the message of God's coming reign. Therefore the disciples constitute an heroic minority whose whole reason for being is the full humanity which the gospel offers to all people.

"A prophetic community": Gathered in community in Jesus' name, the disciples are commissioned to manifest God's saving plan at work in the world. While they walk the same road as their human brothers and sisters, Jesus' followers are distinguished by their knowledge of God's liberating action, which seeks out particularly the poor and oppressed. Christians' understanding impels them to collaborate in God's action by sharing in Jesus' prophetic role inside and outside the church. Retrieving the tradition which Jesus assumed from the Old Testament prophets, they are called to face the conflict that necessarily attends the confrontation of God's reign with powers on earth which oppress and dehumanize. Aware of the gospel import of their action, they enter into the political controversies surrounding the issues of poverty in society today.

"At the service of the poor, marginalized, and dehumanized people of the earth": Because poor people are deprived of what makes them most human, not only material sustenance but also the capacity to think and decide for themselves, they are to that extent unable to act truly as subjects of their own history, of evangelization, of theology, and of ecclesial life. Therefore Christians are called to loving solidarity with the poor. They are impelled to assist them in the light of the gospel to an awareness of their own dignity and of the forces which deprive them of it. They are challenged to collaborate in changing the structures which obstruct the attainment of this dignity.

Such service undertaken as a reponse to the gospel forms the basis of both sacramental and moral expressions of Christianity. Through concrete love particularly for the most dehumanized, the church becomes truly an effective sign, a genuine sacrament, of God's salvific love. Through engagement in God's own transforming project for the poor of the earth, Christians assume more consciously the universal criterion of love by which all women and men will be judged on the day when God's reign is fully established.

NOTES

1. *Teología abierta*, Vol. III (Madrid: Ediciones Cristiandad, 1984), 129-59; henceforth *RC*. Refer also to Ch. Two above, note 52, which gives an overview of Segundo's thinking on the "two theologies of liberation" as they deal with the subject-object question.

2. Segundo articulated the question in two ways in *RC*, 148: "Can the Church of Jesus of Nazareth contain within itself the masses, which means the immense majority of the poor and marginalized? Or, in other words, can the Church truly be the Church of, in the sense of arising out of, the poor?" ("¿Puede la Iglesia de Jesús de Nazaret contener dentro de sí las masas, es decir, la inmensa mayoría de pobres y marginados? O, dicho en otras palabras, ¿puede la Iglesia ser verdaderamente la Iglesia [que surge] de los pobres?").

3. Segundo's translation from Boff's original appeared in *RC*, 131: "¿Quién evangeliza al teólogo? Es el **propio testimonio de fe del pueblo fiel**, su capacidad de insertar a Dios en todas sus luchas, su fuerza de resistencia contra todas las opresiones que de costumbre padece." The citation is from "Teologia à Escuta do Povo," *Revista eclesiastica brasiliera* 41 (1981), 55.

4. "Un Jesús sólo doliente no libera; genera dolorismo y fatalismo. Importa **recolocar en la cabeza del pueblo** el lugar **debido** de la cruz" (*RC*, 131; he cited Boff in "Teologia à escuta do povo," 65).

5. *RC*, 131-2. Segundo was speaking particularly of the theologian; the principle as he presented it applies also to the Christian in the church, who must be able to distinguish genuine from adulterated expressions of faith.

6. *The True Church and the Poor*, trans. Matthew J. O'Connell (Maryknoll, N.Y.: Orbis Books, 1981. The three chapters were articles written in 1975, 1978, and 1979; Segundo considered this span of time significant because the second theology of liberation that he had described was taking shape during those years; see 132.

7. *RC*, 133-34; the citation is from *The True Church*, 36 (Eng. trans.).

8. *The True Church*, 145, cited in *RC*, 134.

9. "Es obvio que no se trata de la conversión de los pobres, sino de la conversión **hacia** los pobres y su causa" (*RC*, 135).

   Segundo did use the phrase "church of the poor" in the sense of "church in the interests of the poor" on pp. 9-10 of the article, "Evangelización y humanización (Progreso del Reino y progreso temporal)," *Perspectivas de Diálogo* 5, 41 (Marzo 1970), 9-17: ". . . something which comes directly from the gospel: the awareness that the Church is at the service of the poor or, more exactly in our contemporary situation, of the impoverished, the victims of a violence which leaves them not only without a voice but also without consciousness, without a human face. . . . Perhaps we think that the church does not travel fast enough on this road which brings it to be a **church of the poor**" (emphasis added).

("... algo que viene directamente del Evangelio: a la conciencia de que la Iglesia está al servicio de los pobres o para ser más exactos en nuestra situación actual, de los empobrecidos, de las víctimas de una violencia que los deja no sólo sin voz sino hasta sin conciencia, sin rostro humano. . . . Tal vez pensamos que la Iglesia no recorre con rapidez suficiente ese camino que la lleva a ser Iglesia de los pobres.")

10. *The True Church*, 92, 112. On p. 92, Sobrino cited I. Ellacuría, "La Iglesia de los pobres, sacramento histórico de liberación," *Estudios Centroamericanos* 31 (1977), 717.

11. *RC*, 135-39.

12. *The Power of the Poor in History: Selected Writings*, trans. Robert R. Barr (Maryknoll, N.Y.: Orbis Books, 1979).

13. *The Power of the Poor*, 208; cited in *HCP*, 226, note 262. Segundo included in this footnote a citation from P. Libanio, without a specific reference, taken from the press coverage of the conference on basic ecclesial communitiees in São Paulo, Brazil, February 1980. Segundo's comment was actually in response to both Libanio and Gutiérrez.

14. *The Humanist Christology of Paul*, trans. John Drury (Maryknoll, N.Y.: Orbis Books, 1986), 226; henceforth *HCP*. Segundo used the phraseology of G. Gutiérrez here, from *The Power of the Poor*, 208.

15. *RC*, 159; see note 2 above for original text.

Segundo declined to call all small Christian communities "basic ecclesial communities" in the sense in which he defined them. He spelled out his distinction, based on a political commitment generated by faith, on 142-43: "A una cierta invitación o convocatoria de la Iglesia, el pueblo o, por lo menos, una parte ya visible y considerable de él, responde formando comunidades eclesiales de base. Brasil constituye también aquí un caso ejemplar. Como es obvio, no todas esas comunidades llegan a los compromisos políticos, o no llegan a ellos a partir de la fe. Pero hay casos en que revoluciones importantes como las que han tenido o tienen lugar en Centroamérica echan parte de sus raíces (activas) en tales comunidades."

16. *The Community Called Church*, trans. John Drury (Maryknoll, N.Y.: Orbis Books, 1973), 3; henceforth *CCC*. The quotation from Porphyry appeared in the letter of Augustine to Deogratias, 102, question 2, *Letters*, trans. Sister Wilfrid Parsons, The Fathers of the Church, Vol. 18 (New York: Fathers of the Church, Inc., 1953), 153-9. Augustine quoted Porphyry: " 'If Christ says he is the way, the grace, and the truth and He places in Himself the approach of believing souls to Him, what did the men of so many centuries before Christ do?' "

Note also *The Hidden Motives of Pastoral Action*, trans. John Drury (Maryknoll, N.Y.: Orbis Books, 1978); henceforth *HM*. There two of the three principles of an alternative ecclesiology which the author proposed in the final chapter relate directly to the minority place of the church within the history of salvation: "The universality of the church is qualitative, not quantitative," (138), and "The church is not always the best place for salvation" (140).

17. "Y si suponemos que esos largos períodos anteriores representan precisamente aquellos en que la humanidad estuvo sujeta a las necesidades más urgentes de la supervivencia como hoy las clases más bajas de la sociedad, ¿no se deberá llamar a esa porción de humanidad acompañada por el cristianismo algo así como una 'clase media'? Debe haber algo intrínseco en él que lo destine a ese contexto espacio-temporal: ¿por qué, si no, el cristianismo no acompañó desde el comienzo el lento y penoso camino del 'proletariado' de la humanidad?" (*RC*, 162).

18. In *RC*, note particularly 139-48 and 203-12. In *The Liberation of Theology*, trans. John Drury (Maryknoll, N.Y.: Orbis Books, 1976), see Ch. VII, especially 192-105; henceforth *LT*.

19. The entire passage is a footnote expressing skepticism about the popular church. It follows the question, "When will they [who practice the Guadalupe devotion] be 'representatives' of that people and raise **their** voice?" ("¿Hasta cuándo serán 'representantes' de ese pueblo y llevarán su voz." [Footnote:] "A esta pregunta podrían seguir otras: ¿en qué medida esta Iglesia comunitaria que surge entre los pobres no constituirá, a corto o medio plazo, una 'Iglesia popular' (como la que SS. Juan Pablo II critica en su carta a los obispos de Nicaragua) separándose de la que 'usa' a la Virgen de Guadalupe para reunir, a bajo precio, las multitudes dentro de la Iglesia-institución?, o, ¿cuánto durará en estas comunidades populares el aprecio por una devoción que, desde el comienzo hasta hoy, ha estado actuando como un 'alivio' religioso no transformador de su miseria real?," *RC*, 208, text and note 13; cf. 142).

20. See Ch. Three above, "Two Orientations in the Medellín Documents" with accompanying notes.

21. "En una palabra, diferencias notorias separarían el caso de la sinagoga o de las autoridades religiosas de Israel en el tiempo de Jesús de lo que hoy ocurre con el pueblo 'cristiano' de América Latina. Aquí ya no estaríamos ante un pueblo alienado cuya religión lo lleva a la aceptación y a la pasividad. La Iglesia en este continente habría recobrado su potencialidad de convocar, y para cambios significativos, a un pueblo que actúa como sujeto. Si se trata de cambios propuestos por movimientos políticos populares, la Iglesia acompaña la movilización del pueblo. Si se trata de sus propias comunidades de base, la Iglesia parece ser, en buena parte, el detonante de la movilización" (*RC*, 143).

22. *CCC*, 60. In *La función de la Iglesia en la realidad rioplatense* (Montevideo: Barreiro y Ramos, 1962), see particularly 30-35, 38-40, 60-63, and 79-80. On the

final page, he summed up the role of the church in these words: "Our struggle is for the sake of creating a new, more Christian world, and we will create it. . . . Our duty, today as always, is to think of the complex, rich, heroic solutions which that Christianity which is our hope suggests to us."

("Nuestra lucha es por crear un mundo nuevo, más cristiano, y lo crearemos. . . . Nuestro deber, hoy como siempre, es pensar las soluciones complejas, ricas, heroicas, que nos sugiere ese Cristianismo que es nuestra certeza," 80).

Segundo did not provide a reference to Teilhard's expression. See, however, Teilhard's narrative of the ship's passengers who acquire an empowering vision (*The Activation of Energy*, trans. René Hague, New York: Harcourt, Brace, Jovanovich, Inc., 1970, 73-4). Segundo utilized this image in *Evolution and Guilt* (Maryknoll, N.Y.: Orbis Books, 1974, henceforth *EG*), 124, note 9. See also *An Evolutionary Approach to Jesus of Nazareth*, trans. John Drury (Maryknoll, N.Y.: Orbis Books, 1988), 21-29; henceforth *EA*.

23. *HM*, 136.

24. *The Historical Jesus of the Synoptics*, trans. John Drury (Maryknoll, N.Y.: Orbis Books, 1985), 149; emphasis Segundo's. Henceforth *HJS*. On Segundo's use of the expression "historical causality," see Ch. Four above, p. 102, note 4.

25. See *HCP*, 10; Ch. VIII, particularly 138-42.

26. "Excluido el supuesto monopolio de la gracia y de la salvación que tendrían los cristianos, no quedaba otra especificidad para la Iglesia y su misión en el mundo que la indicada por el Vaticano: la que pudiera surgir de un **servicio** que le estuviera reservado o en el que tuviera un aporte decisivo que hacer. . . . Traducir la fe a una humanización concreta del hombre, en circunstancias siempre nuevas y en diálogo con los demás. . . ." (*RC*, 18-19; emphasis Segundo's).

27. Refer to *La función de la Iglesia*, especially 27.

28. "Pero, ¿en qué consiste comprometerse en favor de los oprimidos? Sin duda en hacer todo lo posible para hacer cesar su opresión. Y ¿qué es hacer todo lo posible? Inmediatamente entramos en el problema de los medios. Todo lo posible no significa lo mismo para un marxista común y para un cristiano común" (*Masas y minorías en la dialéctica divina de la liberación*, Cuadernos de contestación polémica [Buenos Aires: Editorial La Aurora, 1973], 79; emphasis Segundo's).

29. *LT*, 94-5.

30. *LT*, 110; emphasis Segundo's.

31. *Grace and the Human Condition*, trans. John Drury (Maryknoll, N.Y.: Orbis Books, 1973), 39; henceforth *GHC*.

32. *Faith and Ideologies*, trans. John Drury (Maryknoll, N.Y.: Orbis Books, 1984), 285; emphasis Segundo's. Henceforth *FI*.

33. *LT*, 71. Cf. the same point made in *The Sacraments Today*, trans. John Drury (Maryknoll, N.Y.: Orbis Books, 1973), 107; henceforth *ST*.

34. *HJS*, 109-10; the author defined "religious" and "political" in relation to each other on 80. See also *RC*, 73.

35. Note *LT*, 90-95.

36. *ST*, 107; emphasis Segundo's.

37. *HCP*, 165; emphasis Segundo's.

38. *ST*, 9.

39. *ST*, 50.

40. See *ST*, 59. Sacrament as sign of the journey of love already taking place within history was important to the author; cf. 7.

41. Segundo discussed the magical approach to sacramental efficacy in *ST*, 53-67 and especially 63-67, and in *LT*, 40-43 (see above, note 19).

42. *LT*, 43.

43. See *RC*, 329.

44. "Hoy día encontramos, por un lado, a los que, sin prestar demasiada atención al contenido, se precipitan alegremente sobre la oportunidad [orig.: aportunidad] de practicar funciones cúlticas y sagradas hasta hace poco reservadas al clero. Se ha producido así una clericalización de parte del laicado — particularmente visible a nivel del **diaconado** — que no estaba, por cierto, en la intención del Vaticano II" (*RC*, 331).

45. "Por otro lado, una parte importante, cualitativamente por lo menos, ha comprendido lo que el latín le ocultaba: un vacío. Comprendió que la teología — la comprensión de la fe — transmitida por la liturgia databa de siglos atrás y no reflejaba la función del cristiano frente a las alegrías, las esperanzas, las quejas y las angustias de sus hermanos contemporáneos. De ahí que la crisis sacramental y litúrgica, la crisis de 'celebración' de Dios, de su gracia y de su reino, no haya sido en modo alguno superada por una revisón litúrgica que ha sido dada ya por concluida. Así, muchos de los cristianos más profundos y creadores se mantienen ajenos a algo tan íntimamente constitutivo de una comunidad cristiana: la celebración" (*RC*, 331).

46. See *RC*, 331-32.

47. *GHC*, 39.

48. *Evolution and Guilt*, trans. John Drury (Maryknoll, N.Y.: Orbis Books, 1974), 38; henceforth *EG*.

49. *EG*, 119.

50. *HCP*, 130-31.

51. *HCP*, 159.

52. *The Christ of the Ignatian Exercises*, trans. John Drury (Maryknoll, N.Y.: Orbis Books, 1987), 91; *IE*.

53. In *IE*, see particularly 98, 113.

6

CRITICAL REFLECTIONS

"Profound and enriching questions and suspicions about our real situation"[1] propelled Juan Luis Segundo into a theological enterprise which has spanned, to date, more than a quarter of a century. He has asked: What, really, is Christian faith when multitudes who have identified themselves as "Catholic" no longer observe the traditional practices? What does salvation mean to the thousands of people so weighed down by hunger, homelessness, illness, ignorance, and fear that they are scarcely human? What is the church's meaning in the face of these dilemmas?

Questions such as these have called forth all of Segundo's resources, all that he could offer as a Latin American, Uruguayan, postconciliar theologian. To address them he fashioned a theological method, joining contemporary understandings of interpretation to the conviction that religious questions are radically linked to political decisions.

This dissertation has posed a related question to Segundo's theology: What do the poor mean for the church? The preceding chapters, after surveying the historical context and method of his work, have explored two dimensions of the question. First, who are the poor in Segundo's thought and what is their role? Second, what is their significance for the church? On the basis of this exploration an assessment will now be made of his treatment of the question, followed by conclusions about its contribution to the church's mission with and for the poor.

KEY ELEMENTS OF SEGUNDO'S PROJECT

The evaluation of Segundo's thought on the significance of the poor for the church will look at eight prominent elements of the question. They are: (i) method in general; (ii) identity of the poor; (iii) popular religion; (iv) the political dimension; (v) interpretation of scripture; (vi) nature and mission of the church; (vii) response to the teaching authority of the church; and (viii) relationship of the poor to the church.

METHOD IN GENERAL

The fundamental strength of Segundo's theological and ecclesiological method is the source from which it originates and the end which it serves. His work is based on the lives of myriad poor and dehumanized people and is undertaken explicitly at their service. This strength is also his foundational contribution to the relationship of the poor and the church.

Further, Segundo's method, epitomized in the hermeneutic circle, refrains from imposing itself upon that experience. It begins with "questions rising out of the present . . . rich enough, general enough, and basic enough to force us to change our customary conceptions of life, death, knowledge, society, politics, and the world in general."[2] It then directs these questions to all levels of experience, especially the systemic and social, and generates new ways of understanding the human being, Jesus Christ, the church, God, and scripture.

Moreover, Segundo's method highlights the historical, dialectical character of God's action and human existence. Revelation and response, love and freedom, liberation and oppression work themselves out in the praxis of human choices and social interaction. He illuminates the course by which absolute values reveal their absoluteness through the often obscure concretizations of history: love is genuine love and an absolute value when it gives rise to action and becomes visibly effective.

In addition, Segundo has built a coherent framework, intelligible also to non-Christians, for his method and especially for his ethics of liberating action through the complementary notions of ideology and faith. In this way he has fashioned a tool to examine the systems which impede love and dehumanize people. He likewise provides an instrument to create systems which empower people and make visible the love for which the church exists. Through his faith-ideology analysis of Christianity and Marxism, and of capitalism and socialism, he has given his readers a method for posing critical questions in their own cultural, social, economic, and political settings.

Segundo seeks to counter attempts at a single definitive christology by exemplifying in his recent writings a plurality of christologies. In calling his christological project an "antichristology," he distinguishes it from "academic" christologies, as he terms them, which he views as attempts to formulate statements about Christ valid for all time. He encourages all Christians to multiply articulations of Christ's meaning, consistent with their historical character and constructed firmly on a base of praxis, namely love concretely and effectively expressed. To bring out the human significance of Christ, he advocates the incorporation of the more synthetic and intuitive "iconic" language as well as the more analytic, rational "digital" language.

Yet limitations as well as strengths are present in Segundo's general method. One concern is his mixed and at times ambiguous use of the word "ideology." Although he defined in *Faith and Ideologies* the primary sense in which he employed the term, he had not always used it clearly or consistently. In *The Liberation of Theology* (although written earlier than *FI*) for instance, he applied the word more than once to "false consciousness"; e.g., "A real, effective option on behalf of the oppressed can de-ideologize our minds and free our thinking for the gospel message."[3] This usage contradicted his basic meaning of "ideology" as a "system of means which actualizes values and meaning."[4] Since Segundo had formulated his own definition of "ideology" as a tool of critical analysis, such ambiguities impair its usefulness.

While the wide-ranging fields of knowledge from which Segundo drew added richness to his theological endeavor, it is difficult to know whether he has grasped the original context of these ideas. "Ontological and epistemological premises," "digital and iconic language," and "deutero-learning" were some of the concepts he drew from Gregory Bateson; "entropy and negentropy" from thermodynamics; "the Grand Inquisitor" from Dostoevsky and the figure of Caligula from Camus; and many others. A weakness of this diversity is his adoption of concepts extracted from their individual contexts in other systems of thought.

Segundo's protest against "academic" christologies and the claim that his alternative christological effort surmounts the tendency toward ideological neutrality and timelessness are not totally convincing. To the extent that his political key appears an absolute, it contradicts the inherent historical relativity of such an endeavor. Moreover, he uses a highly "digital" language despite his advocacy of a digital-iconic balance which respects both rational and nonrational elements of reality and language about it and his incorporation of artistic-literary insights.

The final points concerning methodology concern Segundo's practice of criticism toward his own work and toward that of others. His basic interpretative model, the hermeneutic circle, needs further self-criticism. On two counts Gregory Baum urged a closer look at the "shattering" experience of misery which engendered the first stage of the hermeneutic circle.[5] First, the discernment that this transformative experience is genuinely liberative requires the assistance of scripture and tradition. Second, other people have different "shattering" experiences, including experiences of poverty and oppression, that are necessary for a more complete liberative action. Segundo's harsh criticisms of other theologians, both his fellow Latin American theologians and those he categorized as "academic," seemed to stem at least partially from different foundational experiences and the resulting varied trajectories.[6] These polemical exchanges call for more careful listening and more extended dialogue with those he criticizes.

To summarize this review of Segundo's general method, his greatest strength is the following. Through the faith-ideology analysis he has provided a tool which can assist in the creation of systems that empower the poor and manifest the love for which the church exists. On the other hand, the major limitation of his method is the need for greater self-criticism in regard to the hermeneutical circle. In particular, the first stage of the circle requires further examination and elaboration. The limitations inherent in the author's foundational experience of poverty, the prior impact of scripture on this foundational experience, and the criticism which scripture offers to the experience and the subsequent critique based upon it need to be spelled out.

IDENTITY OF THE POOR

Throughout most of his writings, Segundo refers to those on whose behalf he developed his theology as the "dehumanized." By this term as well as his more recent usage of "the poor," he means primarily the socially and economically deprived. More particularly, he considers their deprivation to be theologically motivated, that is, based on a certain view of God and therefore a view of what is righteous and what is sinful. While this notion of the poor has been developed during his career, the clarity and theological focus of this primary meaning of "the poor" represents a decided strength.

It is particularly important to Segundo that, as shown in both Old and New Testaments, God singled out the poor to make known divine justice and compassion. Segundo is convincing in his argument, drawing upon the work of André Myre,[7] that this divine choice does not depend upon the moral or spiritual dispositions of the poor people themselves. While they utilized Jacques Dupont's excellent scholarship on the beatitudes, both Myre and Segundo went farther than Dupont on this point. They insisted that for God's own sake God acts to remedy the concretely inhuman situation of these persons. This emphasis on God's action points up the graced character of secular, socio-economic reality which is encompassed by God's intention. It also replies to the possible criticism that a love which produces concrete effects is "Pelagian."

While he maintained that the concept of "class struggle" was anachronistic when applied to universal history, Segundo makes the case that class differences have marked all ages. He points out that the Fathers of the church, among them John Chrysostom, Pseudo-Clement of Rome, and Ambrose, defined class inequalities according to wrongful appropriation by some of goods destined for the use of all.[8] Pope John Paul II himself has defended labor unions and treated the relationship of labor and capital in terms of the quest for justice. In *Laborem exercens* he noted that unions

> are indeed a mouthpiece for the struggle for social justice, for the just rights of working people in accordance with their individual professions. However, this struggle should be seen as a normal endeavor "for" the just good. . . .[9]

Thus when Segundo considered the poor in relation to class inequalities and in explicit response to the question of class struggle, he can be seen as well within the Catholic tradition.

While Segundo's identification of the poor has strong bases in scripture, church teaching, and social analysis, it manifests weaknesses as well. As noted earlier, his self-criticism regarding the first stage of the hermeneutic circle does not go far enough. The people with whom Segundo has worked most consistently have not been the extremely poor. Consequently his own foundational experience with the poor and the church has been different from that of Christians and theologians in, for example, Peru or Brazil. The different experiences do not invalidate each other, but neither does one become the criterion for the truth of the other.

Because of insufficient self-criticism, as Gregory Baum and Roger Haight have pointed out, Segundo too readily categorizes the poor as the "mass."[10] Although he insists that the passive, immediate, and simplifying "mass" characteristics tend to affect all natural and human existence, he is also inclined to identify the entire general population as "mass." He fails, in effect, to make adequate distinctions in regard to mass behavior and the poor as the "mass."

Related to this tendency to generalization is Segundo's almost exclusive definition of poor people as recipients or objects rather than agents or subjects.[11] The theological perspectives of other liberation thinkers are needed here. Gustavo Gutiérrez, for instance, stressed the roots of liberation theology in the spirituality of a people:

> The struggles of the poor for liberation represent an assertion of their right to life. . . . It is on the basis of this affirmation of life that the poor of Latin America are trying to live their faith, recognize the love of God, and proclaim their hope. . . . Latin American Christians will thus cease to be consumers of spiritualities that are doubtless valid but that nonetheless reflect other experiences and other goals, for they are carving out their own way of being faithful both to the Lord and to the experiences of the poorest.[12]

Leonardo and Clodovis Boff, who live and work in the midst of the poor, also emphasize the real agency of the poor in faith and theology. Describing three levels of liberation theology, the popular, the pastoral, and the professional, they say of popular theology:

> It is a theology in fact, just as folk remedies are real remedies.

> Is it a critical theology? Yes, it is critical because it is clear and prophetic; critical, not in the academic sense, but really so because it gives an account of causes and puts forward measures for dealing with them.[13]

To sum up, Segundo is most convincing in his designation of the poor when he presents the dehumanized persons of the world as those to whom God most wants to reveal the divine self. The author is least convincing when he depicts poor people as recipients of God's, and thus of Jesus' and of the church's action, to the nearly total exclusion of their capacity to be agents.

POPULAR RELIGION

Segundo's ability to delineate the shortcomings of popular religious expression in Latin America is one of his strengths. He considers as realistic and justified the dechristianization which has occurred throughout South America in this century to the extent that it served to challenge a religion practiced for primarily cultural motivations. In his writings on the church, grace, and the sacraments he has sought to highlight God's saving purpose for all people and at the same time to cleanse popular practices of superstitious instrumentality. He has made clear throughout his works that free, socially committed Christianity is not synonymous with cultural Catholicism.

Nonetheless, Segundo's assessment of popular religion represents too narrow a position, which is perhaps related to his national identity. Popular Catholicism and indigenous culture are much less prevalent in Uruguay than in other Latin American nations. Uruguayans do not celebrate the Marian feasts, for example, processing to famous shrines and fulfilling their *mandas* or promises as do many Catholics in Peru, Argentina, or Chile. Other theologians are also critical of the non-Christian dimensions of much popular religious practice. A number of alternatives are available, however, to Segundo's dismissal of this cultural phenomenon. By such a dismissal, he violates his own principle of the "mass"-"minority" tension present within every person and group, relegating the greater part of the population to the condition of "masses."

Two scholars who offer more positive critiques of popular religion than Segundo does are Aldo Büntig and Juan Carlos Scannone. At the same important 1973 conference on liberation theology held at the El Escorial, Spain, at which Segundo spoke, the Argentinian sociologist of religion Aldo Büntig lectured on the "Dimensions of Latin American Popular Catholicism and Its Insertion in the Process of Liberation."[14] Büntig described various pastoral attitudes toward popular Catholicism, and analyzed this form of religious practice according to the types of motivation observed in those who participate in it. In each case, he stressed the importance of a pastoral strategy directed toward transforming the ambiguous elements of a devotion:

> It is a matter of discovering and identifying those liberating values which apply in the oppressed sectors of our society, those same ones which are customarily expressed in ambiguous religious practices, to enrich them and make them grow in the critical light of the gospel, historically reinterpreted.[15]

Segundo discussed this paper of Büntig's in *The Liberation of Theology*. While he applauded many of the Argentinian's ideas, he attributed to him ambivalence and contradiction on several points. Segundo found Büntig's popular emphasis internally inconsistent. In addition, Büntig denied the necessity of minority structures to promote liberation values in contradiction to Segundo's own conviction.

Scannone, also Argentinian, has written extensively on popular culture. In his article in *Frontiers of Theology in Latin America*, he argued for "a liberation theology predominantly concerned with being a theology of popular pastoral activity. . . [which] implies an option for popular culture as the praxis of the People of God in all their dimensions."[16] He described the theologian's role as one of accompaniment, helping the people discern where the saving God is present and acting in the world.[17] To arbitrate the debate in which Segundo, Büntig, Scannone, and many others are engaged is beyond the scope of this thesis. It nevertheless points up unresolved issues in Segundo's thought on popular religion.

In brief then, Segundo's major strength in regard to popular religion is the distinction he makes between the practice of Catholicism as a cultural religion and the conscious, free commitment to Christianity according to the values of Jesus. His chief weakness lay in his nonacceptance of other ways to view the potential of cultural Catholicism for spiritual renewal.

POLITICAL DIMENSION

Out of all the social sciences, Segundo identifies politics as most helpful to theology in its efforts toward effective love in history. He sees politics as the realm where values become practical and love for the poor neighbor is enfleshed. The centrality which he grants to politics in theology has nevertheless given rise to much debate.

Even those who agree with his basic idea do so from differing points of view. Steven Schafer, for example, supports Segundo's concept by distinguishing his term "political key" from ordinary reference to partisan politics.[18] Arthur McGovern claims (inaccurately in view of Segundo's whole corpus) that liberation and not politics was the Uruguayan's all-inclusive category.[19] Roger Haight qualifies Segundo's christology and scriptural exegesis, describing Jesus as a "religio-political" figure, keeping both aspects carefully joined. He observes that "the religio-political framework, though **all-embracing, is not exclusive**."[20]

Segundo clearly makes a political option, as seen in his method, his treatment of the historical Jesus, and his ecclesiology in relation to the poor. He finds a political reading of the synoptic gospels most appropriate, since they highlighted the conflictive and therefore politcal character of Jesus' message and ministry. He acknowledges Paul's anthropological point of view in the composition of Romans, however, while recognizing its political significance for Christians today. Thus he demonstrates that the political dimension, even though it does not exhaust their meaning, pervades all historical realities. For this reason the most accurate formula for Segundo's political key is a slightly modified sense of Roger Haight's "all-embracing but not exclusive."

With the aid of the social critics, including Marxists, Segundo works to identify the hidden obstacles to visibly effective love in the world, especially for the poorest and most dehumanized. His foundational commitment to change means "that each new reality obliges us to interpret the word of God afresh, to change reality accordingly, and then to go back and reinterpret the word of God again, and so on."[21]

Matthew Lamb and Dermot Lane are particularly helpful in understanding and evaluating Segundo's use of social criticism. In *Solidarity with Victims*[22] Lamb schematizes five models of theory-praxis based on the praxis emphases in Karl Marx, the critical theorists, and Jürgen Habermas. Lane then relates these five models to praxis and contemporary theology in *Foundations for a Social Theology.* The following points from Lane's description of the fifth model of theory-praxis indicate that Segundo's theology and ecclesiology functioned within the critical praxis correlation:

> Put positively, praxis is always reflective, dialectical, and intentionally transformative; praxis is always constructively conflictual setting one over against the prevailing social and cultural consciousness; praxis is always liberating and therefore reconciliatory and emancipatory.
>
> Praxis arises out of some form of commitment to and solidarity with other human beings, a commitment and solidarity that demands social analysis of the human situation. To this extent praxis originates out of commitment and in theory.[23]

Segundo's active interchange with Marxist thinkers has been the target of sharp criticism. Yet on several counts, he justifiably listened to Marxist ideas and incorporated some of them into his own thought.

First, since he believes that the function of the church is to serve the world, he has logically engaged in serious dialogue with non-Christian thinkers, some of whom were socialists and Marxists. Serious dialogue implies treating the questions others as important and accepting their worthwhile ideas.

Secondly, Segundo professedly seeks not only to understand the reality in which he lives but also to change situations which dehumanize people. As Matthew Lamb and Dermot Lane have pointed out, Marx, the social critics, and Habermas have contributed significantly to knowledge about praxis and social change.

Thirdly, Segundo practices and articulates a theological method which employs ideological suspicion, drawing partially upon Marxism but in large measure upon the wider field of the sociology of knowledge. He applied his faith-ideology critique in detail to both Christianity and Marxism in *Faith and Ideologies.*

Fourthly, Segundo is heir to the cultural legacy of the twentieth century which Karl Marx and the other social critics have helped to shape, much in the way that Aristotle, or more recently, Sigmund Freud or Mahatma Ghandi has helped to shape Western thought. *Octogesima adveniens* of Pope Paul VI is one official document which has specifically addressed the contemporary influence of Marxism.

Octogesima adveniens is important in two ways that supported Segundo's thought in regard to the political dimension. First of all, *OA* together with the Medellín documents and the 1971 Synod statement *Justice in the World* marked a new recognition of the political implications of the Christian life. Pope Paul asserted that

> ... the need is felt to pass from economics to politics. It is true that in the term "politics" many confusions are possible and must be clarified, but each man feels that in the social and economic field, both national and international, the ultimate decision rests with political power.[24]

OA represented a significant turn also in respect to ideologies, that neuralgic point in the relationship of liberation theologians and the magisterium. For Segundo the relationship was particularly complex because of his unique definition of ideology. Official church teaching had characteristically denounced "false philosophical systems"[25] and "ideological systems,"[26] which ordinarily designated Marxism. In *OA*, however, Pope Paul distinguished four levels of expression in Marxism, very cautiously leaving open the possibility of limited critical use of Marxist thought. In addition, as Donal Dorr pointed out, the pope established in this apostolic letter the principle that concrete socio-political decisions depend to an important degree on the circumstances of place and time. Thus decisions about some forms of collaboration with socialism may be made differently in various places.[27]

Meanwhile, Marxism was not the only castigated ideology. Although official documents did not always use the term "ideology," church authorities from the time of Pope John XXIII and *Mater et Magistra*, especially, condemned the dehumanizing tendencies of capitalistic liberalism. The Latin American bishops spoke frankly at Medellín: "Both systems [of liberal capitalism and Marxism] militate against the dignity of the human person."[28] Eleven years later, they censured three distinct ideologies: capitalist liberalism, Marxist collectivism, and the "Doctrine of National Security."[29] In *Sollicitudo rei socialis* Pope John Paul II attributed to the opposition of Eastern and Western blocs, originating respectively in the ideologies of "liberal capitalism" and "Marxist collectivism," much responsibility for the underdevelopment of many nations today.[30] Thus the social teaching of the church has borne out insights which Segundo contributed through his faith — ideology critique and expressed in such writings as "Capitalism — Socialism: A Theological Crux."[31]

Nevertheless, while Segundo's political key to understanding Christian revelation and faith is basically convincing, certain shortcomings are also evident. He tends to present the political dimension too exclusively. Although he qualifies such definitiveness in other places, his assertion in *The Liberation of Theology* that in this world "politics is the fundamental human dimension"[32] downplays the importance of other crucial areas of human existence. For example, he at times inserts a political explicitness or emphasis into a commentary, as in *Reflexiones críticas* on the "political intention of God's mediating action so that God's will would be done on earth. . . ."[33]

In addition, to enter into the thoroughgoing political quality of Christian life as Segundo describes it is to undertake a highly risky endeavor in which one cannot determine before entering into the process what is a properly Christian contribution. The relativity of such discernment implies that Christian individuals and communities so politicized are highly vulnerable both to errors in their own judgments and to exploitation by partisan interests. Thus the unrelenting requirement for critical consciousness is clear.

Furthermore, Segundo frequently criticizes capitalism and international structures, such as trade and banking systems, which interfere with the

development of poor countries. He substantiates by examples these criticisms, shared by many others from underdeveloped countries. Nevertheless,
except for judging the passivity engendered by popular religion, he does not
give significant attention to the need for internal changes in these countries.
The Medellín document on "Justice," in contrast, included strong statements on behalf of agrarian reform and political transformation which is to
include popular participation. The conclusions on "Peace" denounced inter-
class tensions and internal colonialism manifest in various forms of mar-
gination, a high degree of social inequality, oppression by dominant social
and economic groups, and unjust uses of power which in some cases take the
form of violent repression.[34] While in today's interdependent society,
international influence is usually not totally absent in localized forms of
oppression, capitalistic excesses do not have to assume the blame for
conditions of poverty due to or exacerbated by such internal factors as the
corruption and greed of government officials.

Finally, a point that touches on the converse of *Pacem in terris'* and
Octogesima adveniens' qualified allowance for Christian uses of Marxist
thought. Pope Paul VI cautioned:

> While, through the concrete existing form of Marxism, one can
> distinguish these various aspects and the questions they pose for the
> reflection and activity of Christians, it would be illusory and danger-
> ous to reach a point of forgetting the intimate link which radically
> binds them together, to accept the elements of Marxist analysis
> without recognizing their relationships with ideology, and to enter
> into the practice of class struggle and its Marxist interpretation, while
> failing to note the kind of totalitarian and violent society to which this
> process leads.[35]

Here, Marxism appeared as one type of social analysis that some choose for
the sake of humanization. It is important to keep in mind the vulnerability of
any such social theory or method of analysis to claim loyalties to itself rather
than as a means to a more faithful liberating Christian praxis.

In short, Segundo's ability to explicitate the political quality of all
human activity, in particular understandings of God and ecclesial action in
God's name, is a major asset of his project. On the other hand, he tends to
delineate this quality so emphatically that he gives the impression that it is
the exclusive characteristic of authentic Christian faith.

BIBLICAL INTERPRETATION

Segundo's political hermeneutic extends to both social reality and to biblical understanding. His political interpretation of scripture, however, has been more pronounced since the early 1970's; in his earlier biblical work the political element was implicit rather than explicit. He not only sets in bold relief the principle that every theologian approaches scripture with a prejudice, but he declares clearly his own partiality for the poor, those dehumanized by world political structures. While he does not attribute to the poor themselves a privileged ability to grasp God's word, he makes commitment to their liberation a condition for understanding the bible.

Segundo's christological series, especially the volumes on the historical Jesus and the Christ of the *Spiritual Exercises*, manifests the centrality of the reign of God for his theology and ecclesiology. *Reflexiones críticas* continues the emphasis, elaborating on the reign of God as the "project" of love being carried out in history: ". . . In that historic plan of making a certain type or group of people happy, God's heart will be revealed."[36] Segundo asserts the truth of historical causality: because of the incarnation the act of shaping history participates causally in the coming of God's reign.

In *The Historical Jesus of the Synoptics* Segundo used historical criticism to interpret Jesus of Nazareth politically for people of today. Some critics, it is true, found his presentation of the historical Jesus too exclusively political.[37] Nonetheless, when one keeps in mind Segundo's qualification that "Jesus' revelation of God is simultaneously political and religious,"[38] his presentation appeared persuasive. Some scholars, as well, faulted him for too little cognizance of current historical critical research.[39] Even with its historical shortcomings, *The Historical Jesus* represented "a sustained theological and biblical reflection for liberation theology's preferential option for the poor."[40]

When he turned to Paul's writings, Segundo did not try to interpret the letter to the Romans in a directly political sense. He employed his key concepts of faith and ideology, and reflected on the pertinence of Paul's letter for the Latin American sociopolitical situation. He nonetheless respected the anthropological or existential character of Paul's interpretation of the gospel message.

An additional strength is that Segundo understands the scriptures as a process by which God teaches people how to learn. Through the analysis of faith and ideologies, he examines biblical history to identify the values operative at different stages. He elaborates evolving understandings of who God is, with their concomitant moral attitudes. He situates Jesus and the gospels within this evolution, highlighting the values of God's reign which Jesus proclaimed. In particular, he depicts Jesus revealing through his life, ministry, and death God's intention to transform the inhuman situation of the poor for the sake of God's own self. Just as Jesus needed to embody the values of the reign as effectively as possible, it falls to his disciples to fashion ideologies to actualize their faith and to create gospels which express for their time the meaning of Jesus Christ and of God's project which he undertook.

A consideration of the weaknesses in Segundo's biblical interpretation begins with another aspect of this same second-level, or deutero-learning, process. His typological presentation of salvation history as a learning process leading to Christ, although in harmony with patristic interpretations, does not correspond to contemporary Old Testament scholarship. Exegetes today more readily recognize the Hebrew texts as scriptures in their own right which incorporate a variety of theologies.[41]

Segundo's earlier scriptural work also employed extensive word studies, such as his exploration of the Pauline terms "flesh" and "spirit" and the Johannine notions of "world" and "hour" in his dissertation *La cristiandad ¿una utopía?*[42] While his political hermeneutic had not matured at that point, those studies showed an inclination to read his partiality into the text. In *Utopía* he tended to press the mass-minority tension into the Pauline and Johannine writings.

In this vein, Segundo's later exegesis at times overemphasizes the political interpretation of the synoptic gospels. It is true that he qualifies more than once his use of the "political key," as in *The Historical Jesus of the Synoptics*:

> I am not thereby suggesting that the religious should be relegated to a secondary plane, if there indeed is such a thing as an exclusively religious plane. . . . Still less am I suggesting that everything about Jesus can be explained by the political key. All I am saying here is that the political key is the best code for deciphering his destiny and teaching as a whole.[43]

Nevertheless, more than one critic has judged that Segundo's political interpretation of scripture has on occasion been too strongly stated.

Segundo leaves a number of historical issues unresolved in his exegesis of the synoptics, including the question of Jesus' expectation of an imminent coming of God's reign. The findings of recent scholarship need to be incorporated concerning the identities of "the poor" and "sinners," and the conflicts with authorities which led to Jesus' death. Neither does Segundo fully clarify the faith-ideology dynamic in regard to the historical Jesus. He shows distinctly the values by which Jesus lived: his total dedication to conveying the message of God's reign, that is, God's good news to the poor. He also portrays Jesus judging mistaken ideologies which marginalized people — that is, religious motivations for oppressive action. He does not, however, depict him creating ideologies which better actualized the message of God's reign than those which he denounced. Jesus appeared to leave this constructive work to his disciples.

The earlier section on Segundo's general methodology has already noted the necessity of further self-criticism. Elizabeth Schüssler Fiorenza pointed out in regard to the biblical dimension of the hermeneutic circle:

> this proposal does not consider that both the content of scripture and
> the second-level learning process can be distorted.... In other words,
> Segundo's model does not allow for a critical theological evaluation
> of biblical ideologies as "false consciousness."[44]

Likewise, Gregory Baum urged an evaluation by scripture and tradition of the initial level of experience in the hermeneutic circle, and further dialogue with critical thinkers in the process of applying ideological suspicion.[45] These imperatives indicate undeveloped areas within Segundo's hermeneutic circle; while he does not omit them totally in principle, he does not treat the contribution of scripture to the initial formative experience nor the critique it levels upon ideologies and social analysis in the course of the circle.

Concisely stated, Segundo's greatest contribution in regard to biblical interpretation is his openly stated partiality for the poor and dehumanized as the necessary condition for understanding the scriptures. Nevertheless, his christologies will be greatly strengthened through careful dialogue between contemporary scripture scholarship and his political perspective on poverty and human suffering.

NATURE AND MISSION OF THE CHURCH

Segundo carried out his theological reflection on an increasingly poor, violent, and dechristianized continent. Developing his theology of the church in a situation of faith in crisis, he laudably appeals not for the retrieval of the masses, but for a strengthened mission of evangelization. This priority, stated most explicitly in *Hidden Motives for Pastoral Action*,[46] anticipated by three years the theme of Pope Paul VI's 1975 Apostolic Exhortation, *Evangelii nuntiandi*.

Segundo also commendably locates the purpose of the church within its outward thrust to the world. He projects the vision of a church living out the mission received from Jesus — evolutionary, practical, and liberating. It exists as "an undreamed of possibility for love."[47] Integral to this love is its members' commitment to transform structures and create new ones that will effectively embody the values of God's reign which Jesus proclaimed and inaugurated. It is a church credible in an interdependent world which badly needs such a humanizing change of structures.

A particularly controversial point in Segundo's ecclesiology is his argument for the minority nature of Christianity in contrast to the mass character of Christendom or cultural Catholicism. While his position is problematic in certain respects, it has important arguments in its favor. In addition to explicitly theological reasons for it, several contextual factors help to clarify and situate his position.

First, as has already been seen, although by mid-twentieth century the majority of Latin Americans still identified themselves as Roman Catholic, traditional religious practice was disintegrating. Mass Catholicism, if it had ever really existed, was no more. Second, the majority of the people were poor, becoming poorer, often uprooted from centers of traditional values, and subject to increasing violence. Third, thinkers vigorously debated various aspects of the relationships between elites and masses in the development of their countries. Thus, to Segundo's credit, the mass-minority approach in his ecclesiology resulted from theological reflection on the Latin American experience in dialogue with believers and nonbelievers, many of whom were well versed in the social sciences.

Segundo also justifies theologically a model of church in which a minority of disciples place themselves at the service of the largely poor majority. Here "minority" essentially designates living the gospel message from personal conviction, while "majority" refers to depending for support upon institutions geared to mass acceptance. The contrast sums up the tension existing between an authentic Christianity and a Christendom which relied on civil structures for support. Yet along with this contrast, Segundo shows also how both mass tendencies toward the more simplified and immediate and minority tendencies toward the more complex and mediated operate in all areas of existence. He traces them at work in the four areas of church history, social change, the conservation of energy, and the biblical message.

The strength of the minority model lies in its principle of freely committed service to the world, to the neighbor in need, and especially to the poorest and most dehumanized. It implies the quality of Christian life described in the Introduction to the Rite of Christian Initiation of Adults:

> The rite of Christian initiation . . . is intended for adults. They hear the preaching of the mystery of Christ, the Holy Spirit opens their hearts, and they freely and knowingly seek the living God and enter the path of faith and conversion.[48]

It portrays the countercultural, prophetic way of living the gospel message that even many who disagree with Segundo's minority concept would seek or admire in Christian people, especially in leaders. Here also, Segundo's theology grew out of experience; he formulated it in collaboration with laypersons, and the reflection groups and seminars have served as means of lay formation. In these groups, a prerequisite for membership is commitment to service on behalf of the poor. The caliber of Christian commitment which Segundo outlined well described the quality of lay leadership needed by the church today and in the future.

Yet in the face of these strong, positive affirmations, it is necessary to consider certain less favorable sides to Segundo's view of the nature and mission of the church. As noted above in relation to popular religion, at the same time that Segundo acknowledges the necessity of the mass dimension in personal and social existence, he denies the capacity of the popular masses for full Christian awareness and commitment. Despite repeated statements that mass and minority elements intermingle in the individual and in the church, the impression was frequently given of separation rather than of distinction or interdependence. "Minority" tended to become identified with "real members," and "mass" with "inauthentic" or "non-members."

The danger of elitism is continually present whenever service to and liberation of the majority is not adequately emphasized and expressed. As Alfred Hennelly rightly noted:

> The dialectical interaction of masses and minorities is . . . utilized by Segundo to explain his understanding of the universal dimension of Christianity . . . . On the other hand, it cannot neglect its responsibility for the liberation of the majority, without becoming a "gnosis" for an aristocratic elite.[49]

While Segundo's overall approach strongly supports the proper and essential role of the laity in the ecclesial mission, traces of a clerical-hierarchical model occasionally appear. For example, while discussing in the final chapter of *Reflexiones críticas* the reign of God in motion, he commented on the importance of lay action as **helping** church authorities: ". . . In all parts of Latin America ecclesiastical authorites need for innumerable indispensable functions — even in what concerns the propagation of the faith — the creative help of the laity."[50] Although he sees the recognition of the laity as a victory for a transformed notion of church, he retains the hint of a hierarchical bias. At the same time, he refers only most briefly to the role of the hierarchy in the minority model of church.

Concerning the salvific effect of membership in the church, Segundo states

> membership in the ecclesial community saves people when it is
> shouldered as a new and more profound responsibility. And this fact
> is simply the ultimate consequence of something we already know:
> that the Church is an undreamed of possibility for love.[51]

In light of this orientation, it would be helpful to see articulated elements of the inner life of the church, a step which Segundo has not taken. Consistent with his chosen emphasis, neither does he treat *Lumen Gentium* or many other of the Vatican II documents.[52] Fuller theological development of the life of the Christian community, of prayer and contemplation, and of suffering accepted as the cost of following Jesus on behalf of the poor remain for a later time or another author. In addition, the value of healthy ritual and sacramental practice calls for much greater attention than they have yet received.

In summary, Segundo's conception of the nature and mission of the church is particularly strong in his recourse to a renewed evangelization as the solution to the crisis of faith in the Latin American church. His approach is weak particularly in that he has not shown strongly and consistently enough how the minority and the mass elements in Christianity depend upon each other. This lack results in the appearance of an exclusive "real" church membership contrasted with inauthentic or non-membership.

RESPONSE TO THE CHURCH'S TEACHING AUTHORITY

Segundo's response to church teaching authority was perhaps most evident in his appreciative use of *Gaudium et spes* as a source for his own theology. To the Second Vatican Council itself Segundo gave an ambivalent evaluation; he assessed it most positively when it turned to the role of the church in a suffering world. Only in *GS* did Segundo find expressed the church's mission of service to the world that had long dominated his own theology.

The episcopal conference in Medellín, Colombia, represented for Segundo a "geographically situated" Vatican II. There the Latin American church leaders occupied themselves with the questions and the cries which arose from their milieu. They searched scripture and church teaching, especially from the Council, in order to respond to what they heard with a view toward a transformed Latin America. Their conclusions strongly influenced Segundo's thought. At the same time, he treated the results of the conference critically, as his discussion of "Pastoral Care of the Elites" and "Pastoral Care of the Masses" showed.

Segundo's attitude toward church social teaching in general is, indeed, critical. As can be seen in the chapter up to this point, he often anticipated ideas expressed in official documents (e.g., *Gaudium et spes*, *Octogesima adveniens*, *Evangelii nuntiandi*). He has commented sharply, however, on church "social doctrine." "In reality," he charges, "the 'social doctrine of the Church' started out by trying to guide Christians to lead a societal life more in conformity with the gospel within the existing capitalist structures."[53] He says that "social doctrine" has given rise to nonviable "third way" political attempts between capitalism and socialism. In his view, such official teaching has offered ecclesiastical justification for failure to change inhuman structures. Thus, while affirming the basic values in church social teaching as essentially gospel values, he has rightly asked that this teaching be accountable for vested interests and ineffective action.

In place of a deductive, capitalistically oriented "social doctrine," Segundo advocates an inductive doctrinal and moral teaching, based on a concrete (political) commitment to change unjust structures. Recent magisterial statements have, in fact, approximated this model of teaching. The bishops at Medellín exemplified it, expressing each of their conclusions in three parts: the Latin American situation, doctrinal reflection, and pastoral guidelines.[54] The Bishops of the South Andean Region used this approach in their statement on land reform, "Peru: The Land, God's Gift, the People's Right"; the U.S. episcopate did so as well in their pastoral letter on the economy.[55] Similarly, Pope John Paul II in *Sollicitudo rei socialis*, after a synopsis of *Populorum progressio*, moved from a "Survey of the Contemporary World" through "A Theological Reading of Modern Problems" to "Some Particular Guidelines."

Finally to be mentioned here in regard to church teaching authority is Segundo's serious, detailed reply to the 1984 *Instruction on Certain Aspects of the "Theology of Liberation"* from the Congregation for the Doctrine of the Faith. Admittedly polemical, his book carefully examined both statements and underlying assumptions in the Instruction. His plausible final observation was that "the two parts [of the Instruction], despite their differences, are united by one point that affects the entire Church: **the negative evaluation of Vatican II and of the post-conciliar period.**"[56] He went on to assert his faith that the Spirit will continue the action of the council by assuring that the truth be spoken and service to humanity be implemented.[57]

The choices Segundo has made imply limitations alongside his accomplishments. As already noted, he has made very restricted use of Vatican II statements, and favored the Medellín documents. He has not used, for instance, the Declaration on the Relation of the Church to Non-Christian Religions, or the Decrees on the Apostolate of Lay People, the Means of Social Communication, or, until more recently, on Ecumenism, even though these dealt with areas of ecclesial outreach in which he has shown active concern.[58]

Moreover, he demands unduly from the social documents of the church results in the form of structural transformations. Such outcomes proceed more appropriately from pastoral and catechetical formation which supports the mature qualities of Christianity described above. At the same time, it must be admitted, with a renewal of such pastoral work and catechesis and a concomitant reflection on concrete commitments on behalf of the poor, official social teaching can and will change. When bishops and pope are more clearly in dialogue with vital Christian practice on the local level, the documents will better reflect the demands of this praxis. They will also more convincingly urge and support the prophetic action necessary for the transformation of structures.

Briefly stated, Segundo demonstrates a faithful but critical attitude toward official church teaching. He affirms the values it expresses, particularly in regard to its mission in the world. On the other hand, he criticizes what he considers to be inconsistency, vested interests, and words not translated into action. The major weakness of his view appears in his demand from official social teaching the means of effectiveness which catechetics and pastoral formation must provide within the church.

RELATIONSHIP OF THE POOR TO THE CHURCH

The partiality for the poor and dehumanized which Segundo articulates in his ecclesiology is a fundamental strength of his work. He views this partiality as a matter of commitment, not of joining the deprived physically or culturally in their situation of poverty. He states clearly the evil of poverty with its accompanying ignorance and oppressive patterns of thought and action.

Furthermore, he spells out another form of genuine Christian contribution to the poor. Committed persons engage in a circle of interpretation: they allow the experience surrounding action for liberation to raise questions, pose these questions to the structures of human and theological reality, reformulate theology in light of the questions, and reconceive God's word in scripture accordingly. The circle does not end, however. Christians are plunged into effective historical action at a new level and the process continues. Each turn of the circle represents a conversion, occasioned by the experience of human misery and expressing itself in further "profound and enriching questions." In this way Jesus' disciples collaborate in God's establishment of the reign of justice and joy promised to the poor.

Segundo has also addressed the issue of internal systems of oppression. Despite his emphasis on the poor as recipients, he envisions Christians striving in the name of the gospel to help people become aware of the forces of oppression operating within the mindsets of the poor themselves. Such efforts occur in the spirit of Jesus' own ministry:

> It is true from beginning to end that the kingdom of God has as its object the poor, marginalized masses of Israel. But that does not mean that Jesus would not take advantage of every available opportunity to turn them into conscious subjects insofar as that was possible, and insofar as people could or would like to be such.[59]

This principle of empowering people to assume a conscious, critical attitude toward their own situation is key to finding a balance in Segundo's thought concerning the poor. While he strongly emphasizes the initiative of God, of Jesus, of the church, and of individual Christians in serving the dehumanized, he adverts also to poor people's becoming the free human persons they were created to be.[60]

Segundo's metaphor of energy circuits adds another perspective on the potential of the poor to become subjects. In *An Evolutionary Approach to Jesus of Nazareth*, he described the violation which world poverty represents as a breakdown in the global circuit of energy. It is imperative that poor nations, the people on the periphery, be integrated into this world circuit. Yet the nature of the energy is such, as indicated in the paradoxical message of the beatitudes with "a set of woes addressed to the rich. In the circuit that

Jesus was seeking to establish in Israelite society, then, the rich could not be integrated in the same way as the poor — certainly not with the same richness and intensity."[61] The integration to which the author referred in numerous passages throughout this volume substantiated his explicit though brief treatment in *The Historical Jesus* of poor people's potential to be full subjects. To carry through his metaphor, there is a circuit only if the interconnected units are both receptors and conductors.

In view of the above, it is to Segundo's credit that he has made some enlightening distinctions in the continuing dialogue about evangelization and the poor. While, as suggested above, he has failed to make sufficient allowance for other theologians' experiences and reflections, he has pointed out certain internal contradictions in unnuanced understandings of the concept "being evangelized by the poor." Liberating action is for him not only action which brings about results, but action which emerges from discriminating perceptions of where the problem ultimately lies.

Segundo synthesizes the mission of the church in relation to the poor in the statement which formed the basis of the last three chapters, "The church, if it wants to be faithful to the gospel, can only be a prophetic community at the service of the poor, marginalized, and dehumanized of the earth."[62] From this perspective, the hermeneutical and political dimensions of his ecclesiology appear in a new, prophetic light. While the social sciences are essential auxiliaries to theology today, he maintains that its deideologizing stance and action orientation are rooted in the prophetic tradition of service to the reign of God.

Segundo configures the church's prophetic role quite specifically. Its shape is not that of church as institution. Nor is it the church as general populace of Catholic people. It is the church as small groups of energetic, committed followers of Jesus (incidentally, a very Jesuit sense of identity and mission) willing to assume the risk of being treated as prophets are customarily treated in order to collaborate with God in transforming the inhuman situation of the poor.

This portrayal of Christian faith in action contributes greatly to understanding the church in the world. What, on the other hand, are some of its drawbacks? Because some limitations of Segundo's theology related to this topic have been indicated already, two will be recapitulated here and a third added.

The first pertains to the assumptions underlying stage one of the hermeneutic circle. As Segundo has often reminded his reader, everything historical is by that fact relative. Yet he gives the impression at times of absolutizing the experience which founded the hermeneutic circle. His is a significant experience of the dehumanization suffered by multitudes. At the same time it bears the limitations of a theologian carrying on a primarily intellectual form of service to the poor. He has ministered in a country with the most advanced social welfare system in Latin America, with an educated and articulate population, and a highly secular cultural orientation. In addition, he has failed to make clear the ways that the scriptures and church tradition, themselves historically bounded, have shaped the questions arising out of that basic experience.

Secondly, as valuable as Segundo's insights have been on the prophetic service to the poor which the church is called to offer, they have suffered from the lack of appreciation for poor people's subjectivity. The overgeneralization of "the poor," with its stress on their massive characteristics, has rendered the consciousness-raising service of the church effectively one-sided.

Thirdly, the concentration on a small membership of Christians bent on challenging in the name of God's reign the systems which dehumanize has left undeveloped other dimensions of the church. Even in regard to small groups of committed, reflective Christians, Segundo did not speak extensively about basic ecclesial communities. He placed more emphasis in the groups he led (and leads) on critical consciousness, and on membership open to non-Christians who share the basic values of the group, than he found in many practicing basic communities.

Neither does Segundo draw out the broader pastoral implications of the option for a minority church. Should the general population who identify themselves as Catholics be essentially left to their own devices? To what extent can the appeal of a mature prophetic Christianity be made to them? In addition, what are the consequences for a minority church considered world wide? What might a world church look like when the vitality of faith in the service of human liberation has percolated upward? To ask one author who lives and works in a particular moment and space to speak to all the sides of a question is unfair. Nevertheless, these are some of the unresolved issues of Segundo's ecclesiology in relation to the poor.

To conclude, Segundo's chief insight concerning the poor and the church is his vision of the church as a prophetic community at the service of the dehumanized persons of the world. The primary limitation of his proposal is, however, seriously underrating the actual or potential subjectivity of poor people themselves both in human life and in the church.

CONCLUSION

Juan Luis Segundo remarked about Alfred Hennelly's book *Theologies in Conflict* in the preface which he wrote for it: "I think I have every right to expect that it will not join the ranks of the consumer theology that now overwhelms us . . . . [and] that Hennelly's thinking is directed toward other horizons and other problems that are even more his own."[63] It is the hope of the present writer that these words, which began the Introduction above, might be said also of this study and the work to which it will give rise.

For the originating question — What do the poor mean for the church? — was not solely an intellectual question. It was a query that arose from a concern for the growing situation of poverty not only in Latin America and other parts of the "Third World" but in the United States as well. It emerged from varied kinds of involvement in the church of the United States, often in sparsely populated regions, and from the conviction that the most isolated communities of Catholics and Christians are linked with the whole church.

Further, the guiding question sprang also from the belief that what is happening in the churches of Latin America — the death and the life there — is highly significant for the churches of the north. The latter, in fact, participate in the forces of death which threaten the former, and thus need conversion to life. This investigation has afforded an opportunity to probe these convictions through the carefully articulated theology of Juan Luis Segundo.

To what end has the investigation come? It has arrived at a critical but appreciative affirmation of the church which God's Spirit continually renews for its service in the world. As shown in Segundo's ecclesiology, **the church is sign** of effective love in history. Founded to serve humanity, especially the poor for whom God's reign is being established, it is called to employ the ideologies which will make concrete its faith in God's gratuitous love.

The church is community of committed disciples which expresses its universality in the freely chosen mission of service. They align themselves with Jesus who sided with those whom the religiously justified political structures of his day rendered effectively nonpersons.

The church is proclaimer of the good news that the poor are blessed because God is transforming their unhappy situation. Its commitment to a vital, concretized evangelization is the basis for its ability to understand God's word.

The church is prophet, willing to assume the risk of confronting uses of power that marginalize people. It utilizes the social sciences to uncover and change those systems in the world and within itself which oppress and dehumanize.

Yet this vision of the prophetic servant of the poor is far from realized. Through the insights of Juan Luis Segundo, may it be accomplished more effectively in the church of the United States, the church of Uruguay, and the church of the world.

NOTES

1. *The Liberation of Theology (LT)*, trans. John Drury (Maryknoll, N.Y.: Orbis Books, 1976), 9.

2. *LT*, 7.

3. *LT*, 87. See *Faith and Ideologies*, trans. John Drury (Maryknoll, N.Y.: Orbis Books, 1984; *FI*), 109-13, where Segundo offered distinctions between his usage of the term "ideology" and the "neutral" and "pejorative" meanings in common parlance. While these remarks gathered diverse conceptions and compared them, they did not totally dispel the ambiguities.

   Although written prior to *FI*, Anthony Tambasco's *The Bible for Ethics: Juan Luis Segundo and First-World Ethics* clarified various ways that Segundo used the word "ideology" according to "ideology$_n$" and "ideology$_p$" (Washington, D.C.: University of America Press, Inc., 1981), 91-106.

4. *FI*, 27; emphasis omitted from original. Even in *LT* Segundo had adopted this latter meaning as normative. Note: "By 'ideology' here I am simply referring to the system of goals and means that serves as the necessary backdrop for any human option or line of action," 102.

5. Baum, "The Theological Method of Segundo's *The Liberation of Theology*," *Catholic Theological Society of America: Proceedings* 32 (1977), 123.

6. Note Javier Jiménez Limón's comments in "Sobre la 'Cristología' de Juan Luis Segundo," *Christus* 49 (Agosto 1984), 57-61. See as well Hugo Assmann's in "Os Ardís do amor em busca de sua eficacia: As reflexões de Juan Luis Segundo sobre 'O Homem de Hoje Diante de Jesus de Nazaré," *Perspectiva Teologica* 15 (No. 36, 1983), 223-259.

7. " 'Heureux les pauvres': histoire passée et future d'une parole," *Cri de Dieu: espoir des pauvres*, Paul-André Giguère, Jean Martucci, and André Myre (Montreal: Éditions Paulines, 1977), 67-134.

8. *Theology and the Church*, trans. John W. Diercksmeier (Minneapolis, Winston Seabury; London, Geoffrey Chapman, 1985; *TC*), 108, 164.

9. *On Human Work* (*Laborem exercens*, 1981) (Washington, D.C.: United States Catholic Conference, 1981), art. 20, p. 46.

10. Refer to Baum, "The Theological Method," 123; Roger Haight, "A Political Interpretation: Review of *The Historical Jesus of the Synoptics*, Vol. II," *Cross Currents* 36 (Spring 1986), 89.

11. In this regard, Brazilian theologian Marcello Azevedo remarked in a private conversation April 27, 1984, that "if the poor become the determining factor in my

theology — with their history, culture, traditions, etc. — they become **subjects**, and I help them live their own evangelization." The dehumanized experience of the poor is a determining factor for Segundo's theology; from this perspective, then, the poor are subjects in his system.

12. *We Drink from Our Own Wells*, trans. Matthew J. O'Connell (Maryknoll, N.Y.: Orbis Books, 1984), 28.

13. *Introducing Liberation Theology*, trans. Paul Burns (Maryknoll, N.Y.: Orbis Books, 1986), 17.

14. Büntig, "Dimensiones del catolicismo popular latinoamericano y su inserción en el proceso de liberación. Diagnóstico y reflexiones pastorales," *Fe cristiana y cambio social en América latina*, ed. Alfonso Alvarez Bolado (Salamanca: Sígueme, 1973), 129-50.

15. "Se trata de descubrir e identificar aquellos valores liberadores que tienen vigencia en los sectores oprimidos de nuestra sociedad, esos mismos que suelen expresarse frecuentemente con gestos sacrales ambiguos, para enriquecerlos y hacerlos crecer a la luz crítica del evangelio, históricamente reinterpretado" (Büntig, 146; original emphasized in text).

16. "Theology, Popular Culture, and Discernment," *Frontiers of Theology in Latin America*, ed. Rosino Gibellini (Maryknoll, N.Y.: Orbis Books, 1975, 221; emphasis Scannone's.

17. *Ibid.*, especially 230-31.

18. "Book Notes: *The Historical Jesus of the Synoptics*," *Ecumenist* 25 (May-June 1987), 62.

19. *Marxism: An American Christian Perspective* (Maryknoll, N.Y.: Orbis Books, 1980, 467. Segundo's own work, however, especially *LT* and the series *Jesus of Nazareth Yesterday and Today*, 5 vols. (Maryknoll: Orbis Books, 1984-88) did not bear out McGovern's distinction.

20. "A Political Interpretation of Jesus," 86; emphasis added.

21. *LT*, 8.

22. Lamb, *Solidarity with Victims: Toward a Theology of Social Transformation* (New York: Crossroad, 1982). The five models of theory-praxis which he outlined in Ch. 3 are: the primacy of theory, the primacy of praxis, the primacy of faith-love, critical theoretic correlations, and critical praxis correlations. In the fifth, critical praxis correlations, he situated the method of Bernard Lonergan, the North Atlantic political theologies, and the liberation theologies.

23. Dermot A. Lane, *Foundations for a Social Theology: Praxis, Process and Salvation* (New York; Ramsey, N.J.: Paulist Press, 1984), 66.

24. Pope Paul VI, A *Call to Action: Letter on the Eightieth Anniversary of "Rerum Novarum" (Octogesima adveniens,* 1971), art. 46, in *Renewing the Earth,* ed. David J. O'Brien and Thomas A. Shannon (Garden City, N.Y.: Doubleday Image, 1977) 377.

25. Pope John XXIII, *Peace on Earth (Pacem in terris,* 1963), art. 159, in *Renewing the Earth,* 163.

26. *OA,* art. 26, *Renewing the Earth,* 366.

27. See Donal Dorr, *Option for the Poor: A Hundred Years of Vatican Social Teaching* (Dublin: Gill and Macmillan; Maryknoll, N.Y.: Orbis Books, 1983), 166-71.

28. "Justice," art. 10, Second General Conference, *The Church in the Present-Day Transformation of Latin America in the Light of the Council,* II, ed. Louis M. Colonnese (Washington, D.C.: United States Catholic Conference, 1968).

29. Third General Conference (Puebla, Mexico), *Evangelization in Latin America's Present and Future,* in *Puebla and Beyond: Documentation and Commentary,* ed. John Eagleson and Philip Scharper (Maryknoll, N.Y.: Orbis Books, 1979), arts. 542-9.

30. See *SRS,* art. 20, *Origins* 17 (March 3, 1988), 648.

31. In *Concilium* 96, *The Mystical and Political Dimension of the Christian Faith,* ed. Claude Geffré and Gustavo Gutiérrez (New York: Herder and Herder, 1974), 105-23.

32. *LT,* 71. This appearance of exclusivity leads some critics to conclude—mistakenly, in this writer's opinion — that Segundo forsakes a renewed theology for a critical social theory. One such critic is Marsha Aileen Hewitt, *From Theology to Social Theory: Juan Luis Segundo and the Theology of Liberation* (New York: Peter Lang, 1990); see particularly the Introduction and pp. 165-6.

33. "Tratándose de la intención — política — de Dios de intervenir a fin de que se hiciera su voluntad en la tierra. . . ." *(Teología abierta,* Vol. III, *Reflexiones críticas* [Madrid: Ediciones Cristiandad, 1984], 67; RC). See also the author's comment on the Medellín documents in *LT,* 84.

34. *Conclusions,* "Justice," arts. 14, 16; "Peace," arts. 2-7.

35. *OA,* art. 34.

36. ". . .En ese plan histórico de hacer felices a cierto tipo o grupo de hombres, Dios revelará su corazón" *(RC,* p. 70).

37. See, for example, Jiménez Limón, 57-61.

38. *The Historical Jesus of the Synoptics*, trans. John Drury (Maryknoll, N.Y.: Orbis Books, 1985; *HJS*), 118.

39. Here recall the criticisms, noted in Chapter Two above, by John P. Meier in "The Bible as a Source for Theology," *Proceedings* CTSAP 43 (1988), 1-14.

   Jon Nilson's "A Response to John P. Meier" in the same issue, 15-18, is critical yet more supportive of Segundo's christological project. Nilson maintains that the "methods and conclusions [of historical criticism] need to be brought into dialogue with the methods and conclusions of other mediations of the historical Jesus. The goal is a theology not less critical but more so" (17). While Nilson does not address Segundo's political approach *per se*, he affirms the knowledge of Christ derived from encounter with the poor and suffering. He advocates cooperation toward a theology enriched by both such encounter and historical critical research.

40. Schafer, 62.

41. Walter Brueggemann's two articles, "A Shape for Old Testament Theology, Vol. I: Structure and Legitimation," 28-46, and "A Shape for Old Testament Theology, Vol. II: Embrace of Pain," 395-415, in *Catholic Biblical Quarterly* (1985) surveyed several currents of Old Testament theology in the course of a contemporary proposal.

42. II, *Los principios* (Montevideo: Mimeográfica "Luz," 1964).

43. *HJS*, 160; see also 118.

44. "The Function of Scripture in the Liberation Struggle," in *Bread Not Stone: The Challenge of Feminist Biblical Interpretation* (Boston: Beacon Press, 1984), 51-2.

45. Baum, "The Theological Method," 122-3.

46. *Hidden Motives of Pastoral Action: Latin American Reflections*, trans. John Drury (Maryknoll, N.Y.: Orbis Books, 1978; henceforth *HM*); see also, for example, "Evangelización y humanización: ¿progreso del reino y progreso temporal?", *Perspectivas de diálogo* 5 (Marzo 1970), 9-17; "Derechos humanos, evangelización e ideología," *Christus* 43 (Noviembre 1978), 29-35.

47. *The Community Called Church*, trans. John Drury (Maryknoll, N.Y.: Orbis Books, 1973), 82-3; henceforth referred to as *CCC*.

48. *The Rites of the Catholic Church* (New York: Pueblo Publishing Company, 1983), 20.

49. *Theologies in Conflict: The Challenge of Juan Luis Segundo* (Maryknoll, N.Y.: Orbis Books, 1979, 77.

50. "Por otro lado, en todas partes de América Latina las autoridades eclesiásticas necesitan para innumerables funciones imprescindibles — aun en lo que toca a la propagación de la fe — de la ayuda creadora del laico" (*RC*, 332).

51. *CCC*, 83.

52. Martin Tripole strongly disagreed with Segundo's view of the church's contribution to the world as its primary purpose. See his argument for "its internal life of union with God in community" in "Segundo's Liberation Theology vs. an Eschatological Ecclesiology of the Kingdom," *Thomist* 45 (January 1981), 1-25.

53. *LT*, 91.

54. See, for example, "Peace," *Conclusions*, 46-57.

55. "Peru," *LADOC* 17 (No. 5, 1986), 29-45; *Economic Justice for All*, Pastoral Letter on Catholic Social Teaching and the U.S. Economy (Washington, D.C.: National Conference of Catholic Bishops, 1986.

56. *TC*, 155; emphasis Segundo's.

57. See *TC*, p. 156.

58. In "El legado de Colón y la jerarquía de verdades cristianas" (*Miscelánea Comillas* 46 [1988], 107-27), Segundo used the occasion of the approaching 500th anniversary of the "discovery of America" to reflect upon the Decree on Ecumenism. In light of the admonition to respect the relative importance of various doctrines in the dialogue with members of other churches, he reexamined the historical character of church teachings in relation to the core reality of evangelization.

59. *HJS*, 144; emphases Segundo's.

60. See the related discussion in Chapter Two, including a further reference to *RC*, 199, in the chapter on "The Poor, Subject of Their History."

61. *An Evolutionary Approach to Jesus of Nazareth*, trans. John Drury (Maryknoll, N.Y.: Orbis Books, 1988), 89; henceforth *EA*.

62. *RC*, 159.

63. In Hennelly, xviii.

BIBLIOGRAPHY

PRIMARY SOURCES

BOOKS WRITTEN BY JUAN L. SEGUNDO

Existencialismo, filosofía: ensayo de síntesis. Buenos Aires: Espasa-Calpe, 1948.

Etapas precristianas de la fe: Evolución de la idea de Dios en el Antiguo Testamento. Montevideo: Cursos de Complementación Cristiana, 1962.

Función de la Iglesia en la realidad rioplantense. Montevideo: Barreiro y Ramos, 1962.

Berdiaeff: Une réflexion chrétienne sur la personne. Paris: Éditions Montaigne, 1963.

Concepción cristiana del hombre. Montevideo: Mimeográfica "Luz," 1964.

La cristiandad, ¿Una utopía? I, *Los hechos.* Montevideo: Mimeográfica "Luz," 1964.

La cristiandad, ¿Una utopía? II, *Los principios.* Montevideo: Mimeográfica "Luz," 1964.

The Community Called Church. Translated by John Drury. *A Theology for Artisans of a New Humanity.* Vol. I. Maryknoll, N.Y.: Orbis Books, 1973. *Teología abierta para el laico adulto.* Vol. I, *Esa comunidad llamada Iglesia.* Buenos Aires: Ediciones Carlos Lohlé, 1968.

Grace and the Human Condition. Translated by John Drury. *A Theology for Artisans of a New Humanity.* Vol. II. Maryknoll, N.Y.: Orbis Books, 1973. *Teología abierta para el laico adulto.* Vol. II, *Gracia y condición humana.* Buenos Aires: Ediciones Carlos Lohlé, 1968.

De la Sociedad a la Teología. Buenos Aires: Ediciones Carlos Lohlé, 1970.

Our Idea of God. Translated by John Drury. *A Theology for Artisans of a New Humanity.* Vol. III. Maryknoll, N.Y.: Orbis Books, 1973. *Teología abierta para el laico adulto.* Vol. III, *Nuestra idea de Dios.* Buenos Aires: Ediciones Carlos Lohlé, 1970.

La Iglesia chilena ante el socialismo; una opinión desde Uruguay. Segundo aporte al documento de trabajo de los Obispos de Chile: "Evangelio, política y socialismo." Talca: Fundación Obispo Manuel Larraín Errázuriz, 1971.

¿Qué es un cristiano? Montevideo: Mosca Hnos. S.A. Editores, 1971.

The Sacraments Today. Translated by John Drury. *Theology for Artisans of a New Humanity.* Vol. IV. Maryknoll, N.Y.: Orbis Books, 1974. *Teología abierta para el laico adulto.* Vol. IV, *Los sacramentos hoy.* Buenos Aires: Ediciones Carlos Lohlé, 1971.

Visión cristiana: educación, comunicación social y liberación. Mexico: Centro Critico Universitario, 1971.

The Hidden Motives of Pastoral Action. Translated by John Drury. Maryknoll, N.Y.: Orbis Books, 1978. *Acción pastoral latinoamericana: sus motivos ocultos.* Buenos Aires: Búsqueda, 1972.

Evolution and Guilt. Translated by John Drury. *Theology for Artisans of a New Humanity.* Vol. V. Maryknoll, N.Y.: Orbis Books, 1974. *Teología abierta para el laico adulto.* Vol. V, *Evolución y culpa.* Buenos Aires: Ediciones Carlos Lohlé, 1972.

Masas y Minorías en la dialéctica divina de la liberación. Cuadernos de contestación polemica. Buenos Aires: Editorial La Aurora, 1973.

The Liberation of Theology. Translated by John Drury. Maryknoll, N.Y.: Orbis Books, 1976. *Liberación de la teología.* Buenos Aires: Ediciones Carlos Lohlé, 1975.

Faith and Ideologies. Translated by John Drury. *Jesus of Nazareth Yesterday and Today.* Vol. I. Maryknoll, N.Y.: Orbis Books, 1984. *El hombre de hoy ante Jesús de Nazaret.* Vol. I, *Fe e ideología.* Madrid: Ediciones Cristiandad, 1982.

The Historical Jesus of the Synoptics. Translated by John Drury. *Jesus of Nazareth Yesterday and Today.* Vol. II. Maryknoll, N.Y.: Orbis Books, 1985. *El hombre de hoy ante Jesús de Nazaret.* Vol. II/1, *Historia y actualidad: sinópticos y Pablo,* Primera Parte. Madrid: Ediciones Cristiandad, 1982.

The Humanist Christology of Paul. Translated by John Drury. *Jesus of Nazareth Yesterday and Today.* Vol. III. Maryknoll, N.Y.: Orbis Books, 1986. *El hombre de hoy ante Jesús de Nazaret* Vol. II/1, *Historia y actualidad: Sinópticos y Pablo,* Segunda Parte. Madrid: Ediciones Cristiandad, 1982.

The Christ of the Ignatian Exercises. Translated by John Drury. *Jesus of Nazareth Yesterday and Today.* Vol. IV. Maryknoll, N.Y.: Orbis Books, 1987. *El hombre de hoy ante Jesús de Nazaret.* Vol. II/2, *Historia y actualidad: Las cristologías en la espiritualidad,* Primera Parte. Madrid: Ediciones Cristiandad, 1982.

An Evolutionary Approach to Jesus of Nazareth. Translated by John Drury. *Jesus of Nazareth Yesterday and Today.* Vol. V. Maryknoll, N.Y.: Orbis Books, 1988. *El hombre de hoy ante Jesús de Nazaret.* Vol. II/2, *Historia y actualidad: Las cristologías en la espiritualidad,* Segunda Parte. Madrid: Ediciones Cristiandad, 1982.

Teología abierta, 3 vols. Vol. III, *Reflexiones críticas.* Madrid: Ediciones Cristiandad, 1984.

Theology and the Church: A Response to Cardinal Ratzinger and a Warning to the Whole Church. Translated by John W. Diercksmeier. Minneapolis: Winston Press, 1985. *Teología de la liberación: Respuesta al Cardenal Ratzinger.* Madrid: Ediciones Cristiandad, 1985.

Jésus devant la conscience moderne: L'histoire perdue. Théologie et sciences religieuses: Cogitatio fidei. Translated by Francis Guibal. Paris: Éditions du Cerf, 1988.

Dogma que libera: Fe y liberación y signos de los tiempos. Santander: Sal Terrae, 1990.

BOOKS WRITTEN IN COLLABORATION WITH OTHERS

With Pedro Olmos, Dionisio J. Garmendia and others. *Una Interpretación. Uruguay 67,* Vol. I. Montevideo: Alfa, 1967.

ARTICLES WRITTEN BY JUAN L. SEGUNDO

"The Future of Christianity in Latin America." *Cross Currents* 12 (1963): 273-81.

"Pastoral latinoamericana: hora de decisión." *Mensaje* 4 (Marzo-Abril 1964): 74-82.

"La función de la Iglesia." *Diálogo* (Centro Pedro Fabro, Montevideo) 1 (Dic. 1965): 4-7.

"La función de la Iglesia." *Diálogo* (Centro Pedro Fabro, Montevideo) 1 (Feb. 1966): 5-10.

"El diálogo, Iglesia, mundo, reflexión." *Diálogo* (Centro Pedro Fabro, Montevideo) 1 (Oct. 1966): 3-7.

"El diálogo, Iglesia-mundo." *Diálogo* (Centro Pedro Fabro, Montevideo) 1 (Nov. 1966): 8-12.

"Lo que el concilio dice." *Diálogo* (Centro Pedro Fabro, Montevideo) 1 (Dic. 1966): 3-13.

"¿Que nombre dar a la existencia cristiana?" *Perspectivas de Diálogo* 2 (Enero-Feb. 1967): 3-9.

"Intellecto y salvación." *Salvación y construcción del mundo.* Barcelona: Editorial Nova Terra, 1967, pp. 77-86.

"The Church: A New Direction in Latin America." *Catholic Mind* 65 (March 1967): 43-47.

"La condición humana." *Perspectivas de Diálogo* 2 (Marzo-Abril 1967): 30-35.

"La condición humana." *Perspectivas de Diálogo* 2 (Mayo 1967): 55-61.

"Camilo Torres, sacerdocio y violencia." *Víspera* 1 (Mayo 1967): 71-75.

"La vida eterna." *Perspectivas de Diálogo* 2 (Junio 1967): 83-89.

"La vida eterna." *Perspectivas de Diálogo* 2 (Julio 1967): 109-18.

"Un nuevo comienzo." *Víspera* 1 (Agosto 1967): 39-43.

"América hoy." *Víspera* 1 (Oct. 1967): 53-57.

"Profundidad de la gracia." *Perspectivas de Diálogo* 2 (Nov. 1967): 235-40.

"Profundidad de la gracia." *Perspectivas de Diálogo* 2 (Dic. 1967): 249-55.

"Hacia un exégesis dinámica." *Víspera* 1 (Oct. 1967): 77-84.

"¿Dios nos interesa o no?" *Perspectivas de Diálogo* 3 (Marzo 1968): 13-16.

"Del ateismo a la fe." *Perspectivas de Diálogo* 3 (Abril 1968): 44-47.

"Social Justice and Revolution." *America* 118 (April 27, 1968): 574-77.

"Padre, Hijo, Espiritu: una historia." Perspectivas de Diálogo 3 (Julio 1968): 71-76.

"El poder del habito." *Perspectivas de Diálogo* 3 (Julio 1968): 90-91.

"Padre, Hijo, Espiritu: una sociedad." *Perspectivas de Diálogo* 3 (Junio 1968): 103-9.

"Padre, Hijo, Espiritu: una libertad I." *Perspectivas de Diálogo* 3 (Julio 1968): 142-48.

"Padre, Hijo, Espiritu: una libertad II." *Perspectivas de Diálogo* 3 (Agosto 1968): 183-86.

"Has Latin America a Choice?" *America* 120 (Feb. 22, 1969): 213-16.

"¿Un Dios a nuestra imagen?" *Perspectivas de Diálogo* 4 (Marzo 1969): 14-18.

"¿Hacia una iglesia de izquierda?" *Perspectivas de Diálogo* 4 (Abril 1969): 35-39.

"Riqueza y pobreza como obstáculos al desarrollo." *Perspectivas de Diálogo* 4 (Abril 1969): 54-56.

"Ritmos de cambio y pastoral de conjunto." *Perspectivas de Diálogo* 4 (Julio 1969): 131-37.

"¿Autoridad o qué?" *Perspectivas de Diálogo* 4 (Dic. 1969): 270-72.

"Introduction." *Iglesia latinoamericana, ¿protesta o profecía?* Buenos Aires: Ediciones Búsqueda, 1969, 8-17.

"Evangelización y humanización: ¿progreso del reino y progreso temporal? *Perspectivas de Diálogo* 5 (Marzo 1970): 9-17.

"Desarrollo y subdesarrollo: polos teológicos." *Perspectivas de Diálogo* 5 (Mayo 1970): 76-80.

"La ideología de un diario católico." *Perspectivas de Diálogo* 5 (Junio-Julio 1970): 136-44.

"El possible aporte de la teología protestante para el cristianismo en el futuro." *Cristianismo y Sociedad* 8 (1970): 41-49.

"Wealth and Poverty as Obstacles to Development." Chap. in *Human Rights and the Liberation of Man in the Americas.* Edited by Louis Colonnese. Notre Dame: Notre Dame University Press, 1970.

"The Possible Contribution of Protestant Theology to Latin American Christianity in the Future." *Lutheran Quarterly* 22 (1970): 60-67.

"La Iglesia chilena ante el socialismo I." *Marcha* No. 1558 (27 Agosto 1971).

"La Iglesia chilena ante el socialismo II." *Marcha* No. 1559 (4 Set. 1971).

"La Iglesia chilena ante el socialismo III." *Marcha* No. 1560 (11 Set. 1971).

"Education, Communication and Liberation: A Christian Vision." *IDOC International.* North American Edition (Nov. 13, 1971): 63-96.

"Las Elites latinoamericanas: problemática humana y cristiana ante el cambio social." Chap. in *Fe cristiana y cambio social en América latina.* Encuentro de El Escorial, 1972. Instituto Fe y Secularidad. Edited by Alfonso Alvarez Bolado. Salamanca: Sígueme, 1973.

"Teología y ciencias sociales." Chap. in *Fe cristiana y cambio social en América latina.* Encuentro de El Escorial, 1972. Instituto Fe y Secularidad. Edited by Alfonso Alvarez Bolado. Salamanca: Sígueme, 1973.

"On a Missionary Awareness of One's Own Culture." *Jesuit Missions Newsletter*, No. 33 (May 1974): 1-6; *Studies in the International Apostolate of Jesuits* 3 (Sept. 1974): 33-47.

"Reconciliación y conflicto." *Perspectivas de Diálogo*, 9 (Set. 1974): 172-78.

"Fe y ideología." *Perspectivas de Diálogo* 9 (Dic. 1974): 79-82.

"Theological Response to a Talk on Evangelization and Development." *Studies in the International Apostolate of Jesuits* 3 (November 1974): 79-82.

"Teología: Mensaje y proceso." *Perspectivas de Diálogo* 9 (Dic. 1974): 259-70.

"Capitalism - Socialism: A Theological Crux." Chap. in *Concilium* 96: *The Mystical and Political Dimension of the Christian Faith.* Edited by Claude Geffré and Gustavo Gutiérrez. New York: Herder and Herder, 1974.

"Condicionamientos actuales de la reflexión teológica en latinoamérica." Chap. in *Liberación y cautiverio: debates en torno al método de la teología en América latina.* Edited by Enrique Ruiz Maldonado. Mexico City: Comité Organizador, 1975.

"Statement by Juan Luis Segundo." *Theology in the Americas*, 280-83. Edited by Sergio Torres and John Eagleson. Maryknoll, N.Y.: Orbis Books, 1976.

"Conversión y reconciliación en la perspectiva de la moderna teología de la liberación." *Cristianismo y sociedad* 13 (1975): 17-25.

"Conversión y reconciliación en la teología de la liberación." *Selecciones de Teología* 15 (No. 60, 1976): 263-75.

"Libération et Evangile (Interview exclusive avec Juan Luis Segundo)." *Relation* 36 (Mai 1976): 151-55.

"Libération et Evangile, II (Interview exclusive avec Juan Luis Segundo, suite)." *Relation* 36 (Juin 1976): 184-86.

"Libération et Evangile, III (Interview exclusive avec Juan Luis Segundo, suite)." *Relation* 36 (Juillet-Août 1976): 216-19.

"Perspectivas para una teologia latinoamericana." *Perspectiva Teologica* 19 (No. 17, 1977): 9-25.

"Comment l'Eglise est-elle universelle c'est-à-dire catholique?" *Eglise et Mission* 207 (1977): 24-30.

"Direitos Humanos, Evangelizaçäo e Ideologia," *Revista Eclesiástica Brasileira* 37 (Março 1977): 91-105.

"Derechos humanos, evangelización e ideología." *Christus* (Nov. 1978): 29-35.

"Ideas y orientaciones: Las teologías de la liberación," *Pastoral misionero* 18 (1982): 352-74.

"Las teologías de la liberación." *Pastoral Misionero* 18 (1982): 352-74.

"Nota sobre ironias e tristezas: Que aconteceu com a Teologia da Libertaçao em sua trajetória de mais de vinte anos (Resposta a Hugo Assmann)." *Perspectiva Teologica* 15 (No. 37, 1983): 385-400.

"Les deux tendances actuelles de la théologie de la libération." *Documentation Catholique* 81 (Oct. 7, 1984): 912-17.

"Les deux théologies de la libération en Amérique latine," *Études* 361 (Sept. 1984): 149-61.

"Two Theologies of Liberation." *Month* 17 (Oct. 1984): 321-27.

"El Cambio dentro de la Teología latinoaméricana (Dos etapas)." *Cuadernos de Teología* 6 (No. 4, 1985): 7-20.

"Disquisición sobre el misterio absoluto." *Revista Latinoamericana de Teología* (Sept.-Dic. 1985): 209-27.

"La opción por los pobres como clave hermenéutica para entender el Evangelio." *Sal Terrae* (Junio 1986).

"El legado de Colón y la jerarquía de verdades cristianas." *Miscelánea Comillas* 46 (1988): 107-27.

"Revelación, fe, signos de los tiempos." *Revista Latinoamericana de Teologia* 5 (1988): 125-144.

SECONDARY SOURCES

OFFICIAL DOCUMENTS
(Listed Chronologically)

Council Fathers. "Message to Humanity" (*Nuntius ad Universos Homines Summo Ponfifice Assentiente a Patribus Missus Ineunte Concilio Oecumenico Vaticano II*), *AAS* 54 (1962), 823-24. English translation in *The Gospel of Peace and Justice: Catholic Social Teaching since Pope John.* Edited by Joseph Gremillion. Maryknoll, N.Y.: Orbis Books, 1976.

John XXIII, Pope. *Peace on Earth* (*Pacem in terris*, 1963). In *Renewing the Earth.* Edited by David J. O'Brien and Thomas A. Shannon. Garden City, N.Y.: Doubleday Image, 1977.

Vatican II. *Pastoral Constitution on the Church in the Modern World* (*Gaudium et Spes*, 1965). In *Vatican Council II: The Conciliar and Post Conciliar Documents.* Edited by Austin Flannery. Northport, N.Y.: Costello Publishing Company, 1975.

Paul VI, Pope. *On the Development of Peoples (Populorum Progressio,* 1967). In *Renewing the Earth.* Edited by David J. O'Brien and Thomas A. Shannon. Garden City, N.Y.: Doubleday Image Books, 1977.

_____. A *Call to Action: Letter on the Eightieth Anniversary of "Rerum Novarum" (Octogesima adveniens,* 1971). In *Renewing the Earth.* Edited by David J. O'Brien and Thomas A. Shannon. Garden City, N.Y.: Doubleday Image, 1977.

Latin American Episcopate, Second General Conference (Medellín, Colombia, 1968). *The Church in the Present-Day Transformation of Latin America in the Light of the Council,* 2 vols. Edited by Louis M. Colonnese. Washington, D.C.: United States Catholic Conference, 1968. Vol. I: Position Papers; Vol. II: Conclusions.

Synod of Bishops. *Justice in the World (Convenientes ex universo,* 1971). In *Vatican Council II: More Post Conciliar Documents.* Edited by Austin Flannery. Northport, N.Y.: Costello Publishing Company, 1982.

Paul VI, Pope. *A Call to Action: Letter on the Eightieth Anniversary of "Rerum Novarum" (Octogesima Adveniens,* 1971). In *Renewing the Earth: Catholic Documents on Peace, Justice and Liberation.* Edited by David J. O'Brien and Thomas A. Shannon. Garden City, N.Y.: Doubleday, Image Books, 1977.

_____. *Evangelization in the Modern World (Evangelii Nuntiandi,* 1975). In *Vatican Council II: More Post Conciliar Documents.* Edited by Austin Flannery. Northport, N.Y.: Costello Publishing Company, 1982.

Latin American Episcopate, Third General Conference (Puebla, Mexico, 1979). *Evangelization in Latin America's Present and Future.* In *Puebla and Beyond: Documentation and Commentary,* pp. 122-285. Edited by John Eagleson and Philip Scharper. Maryknoll, NY: Orbis Books, 1979. *Puebla: La evangelización en el presente y en el futuro de América Latina.* CELAM, April 1979, and 2nd ed., June 1979.

John Paul II, Pope. *On Human Work* (Laborem exercens, 1981). Washington, D.C.: United States Catholic Conference, 1981.

_____. "Class Struggle and Identification with the Poor." Address to the African Bishops. *Origins* 14 (Sept. 6, 1984): 177-79.

_____. "Pope's Mandate to Brazilian Bishops." *Latinamerica Press* (May 1, 1986): 2.

_____. *On the Social Concern of the Church (Sollicitudo Rei Socialis,* 1987). *Origins* 17 (March 3, 1988): 641-60.

Congregation for the Doctrine of the Faith. *Instruction on Certain Aspects of the 'Theology of Liberation.'* *Origins* 14 (Sept. 13, 1984): 193-204.

_____. *Instruction on Christian Freedom and Liberation. Origins* 15 (April 17, 1986): 713-28.

United States Episcopate. *Economic Justice for All: Pastoral Letter on Catholic Social Teaching and the U.S. Economy.* Washington, D.C.: United States Catholic Conference, 1986.

BOOKS

Alvarez Bolado, Alfonso, ed. *Fe cristiana y cambio social en América latina.* Encuentro de El Escorial, 1972. Instituto Fe y Secularidad. Salamanca: Ediciones Sígueme, 1973.

Azevedo, Marcello de Carvalho. *Basic Ecclesial Communities in Brazil: The Challenge of a New Way of Being Church.* Translated by John Drury. Washington, D.C.: Georgetown University Press, 1987.

Barreiro, Alvaro. *Basic Ecclesial Communities: The Evangelization of the Poor.* Translated by Barbara Campbell. Maryknoll, N.Y.: Orbis Books, 1982. *Comunidades eclesiais de base e evangelização dos pobres.* São Paulo: Edições Loyola, 1977.

Bateson, Gregory. *Steps to an Ecology of Mind.* New York: Ballantine Books, 1972.

_____. *Mind and Nature.* New York: Bantam Books, 1980.

Baum, Gregory. *Religion and Alienation: A Sociological Reading of Theology.* New York: Paulist Press, 1975.

Berger, Peter, and Richard J. Neuhaus, eds. *Against the World, For the World.* New York: Seabury Press, 1976.

Bernhard, Virginia, ed. *Elites, Masses, and Modernization in Latin America, 1850-1930.* Austin: University of Texas Press, 1979.

Berryman, Philip. *Liberation Theology: Essential Facts about the Revolutionary Movement in Latin America and Beyond.* Oak Park, Illinois: Meyer Stone Books (Random House, Pantheon Books), 1987.

Boff, Leonardo. *Ecclesiogenesis: The Base Communities Reinvent the Church.* Translated by Robert R. Barr. Maryknoll, N.Y.: Orbis Books, 1986. *Eclesiogênese: As comunidades eclesiais de base reinventam a Igreja.* Petrópolis: Editora Vozes, 1977.

_____. *Passion of Christ, Passion of the World.* Maryknoll, N.Y.: Orbis Books, 1987. *Paixão de Cristo — Paixão do mundo.* Petrópolis, Brasil: Editora Vozes, 1978.

_____. *Church: Charism and Power: Liberation Theology and the Institutional Church.* Translated by John W. Diercksmeier. New York: Crossroad, 1985. *Igreja: Carisma e poder.* Petrópolis: Editora Vozes, 1981.

_____. *Desde el lugar del pobre*. Bogotá: Ediciones Paulinas, 1984.

Boff, Leonardo, and Clodovis Boff. *Introducing Liberation Theology*. Translated by Paul Burns. Maryknoll, N.Y.: Orbis Books, 1986. *Como fazer Teologia da Libertação*. Petrópolis, Brazil: Vozes Ltda., 1986.

Ching, Theresa Lowe. "The Meaning and Function of the Notion of 'Efficacious Love' in the Theology of Juan Luis Segundo." Ph.D. diss., University of St. Michael's College, Toronto, 1986.

Cleary, Edward A. *Crisis and Change: The Church in Latin America Today*. Maryknoll, NY: Orbis Books, 1985.

Comblin, Joseph. *The Church and the National Security State*. Maryknoll, N.Y.: Orbis Books, 1979.

Congar, Yves. *Power and Poverty in the Church*. Baltimore: Helicon, 1964.

Considine, John J., ed. *The Church in the New Latin America*. Notre Dame, Indiana: Fides Publishers, 1964.

Cranfield, C. E. B. *A Critical and Exegetical Commentary on the Epistle to the Romans*. 1975.

Davis, Charles. *Theology and Political Society*. Cambridge: Cambridge University Press, 1980.

Dorr, Donal. *Option for the Poor: A Hundred Years of Vatican Social Teaching*. Maryknoll, N.Y.: Orbis Books, 1983.

Dupont, Jacques. *Les Béatitudes. Le problème littéraire, le message doctrinal*. Bruges-Louvain, 1954. Revised edition: Vol. I, *Les Béatitudes, Le problème littéraire*. Paris: Études Bibliques, 1958. Vol. II, *Les Béatitudes, La Bonne Nouvelle*. Paris: Études Bibliques, 1969. Vol. III, *Les Béatitudes, Les Évangelistes*. Paris: J. Gabalda et Cie., 1973.

Dussel, Enrique. *A History of the Church in Latin America: Colonialism to Liberation (1492-1979)*. Translated and revised by Alan Neely. Grand Rapids, Michigan: William B. Eerdmans Publishing Company, 1981. *Historia de la Iglesia en América Latina*, 1974.

Eagleson, John, and Scharper, Philip, eds. *Puebla and Beyond: Documentation and Commentary*. Maryknoll, N.Y.: Orbis Books, 1979.

Evans, Alice Frazer; Robert A. Evans; and William Bean Kennedy. *Pedagogies for the Non-Poor*. Maryknoll, N.Y.: Orbis Books, 1987.

Fiorenza, Francis Schüssler. *Foundational Theology: Jesus and the Church*. New York: Crossroad, 1984.

Fitzmyer, Joseph A. *The Gospel According to Luke (I-IX).* The Anchor Bible. Garden City, N.Y.: Doubleday, 1981.

_____. *The Gospel According to Luke (X-XXIV).* The Anchor Bible. Garden City, N.Y.: Doubleday, 1985.

Galilea, Segundo. *El Mensaje de Puebla: Evangelizar en el presente y en el futuro de América Latina.* Santiago, Chile: Ediciones Paulinas, 1979.

Gibellini, Rosino, ed. *Frontiers of Theology in Latin America.* Translated by John Drury. Maryknoll, N.Y.: Orbis Books, 1975. *La nuova frontiera della teologia in America Latina.* Brescia, Italy: Editrice Queriniana, 1979.

Greinacher, Norbert, and Müller, Alois, eds. *The Poor and the Church. Concilium* 104. New York: Seabury (Crossroad Book), 1977.

Gutiérrez, Gustavo. *A Theology of Liberation: History, Politics and Salvation,* trans. and ed. Caridad Inda and John Eagleson. Maryknoll, N.Y.: Orbis Books, 1973. *Teología de la liberación, Perspectivas.* Lima: Centro de Educación y Publicación, 1971.

_____. *The Power of the Poor in History: Selected Writings.* Translated by Robert R. Barr. Maryknoll, N.Y.: Orbis Books, 1983. *La fuerza histórica de los pobres.* Lima: Centro de Estudios y Publicaciones, 1979.

_____. *We Drink from Our Own Wells.* Translated by Matthew J. O'Connell (Maryknoll, N.Y.: Orbis Books, 1986. *Beber en su propio pozo: En el itinerario espiritual de un pueblo,* second edition revised. Lima: Centro de Estudios y Publicaciones, 1983.

Haight, Roger. *An Alternative Vision: An Interpretation of Liberation Theology.* New York: Paulist, 1985.

Hennelly, Alfred T. *Theologies in Conflict: The Challenge of Juan Luis Segundo.* Maryknoll, N.Y.: Orbis Books, 1979.

Hewitt, Marsha Aileen. *From Theology to Social Theory: Juan Luis Segundo and the Theology of Liberation.* American University Studies: Theology and Religion 73. New York: Peter Lang, 1990.

Holland, Joe, and Peter Henriot. *Social Analysis: Linking Faith and Justice.* Revised and enlarged edition. In collaboration with the Center of Concern. Maryknoll, N.Y.: Orbis Books, 1983.

Jeremias, Joachim. *New Testament Theology: The Proclamation of Jesus.* Translated by John Bowden. New York: Charles Scribner's Sons, 1971.

Kloppenburg, Boaventura. *Temptations for the Theology of Liberation.* Translated by Matthew J. O'Connell. Chicago: Franciscan Herald Press, 1974.

_____. *The People's Church: A Defense of My Church*. Translated by Matthew J. O'Connell. Chicago: Franciscan Herald Press, 1978.

Lamb, Matthew. *Solidarity with Victims: Toward a Theology of Social Transformation*. New York: Crossroad, 1982.

Lane, Dermot A. *Foundations for a Social Theology: Praxis, Process and Salvation*. New York; Ramsey, N.J.: Paulist Press, 1984.

Lipset, Seymour Martin, and Solari, Aldo. *Elites in Latin America*. Papers presented at the Seminar on Elites and Development in Latin America, University of Montevideo, June 1965. New York: Oxford University Press, 1967.

Lúkacs, György. *Existentialisme ou Marxisme?* Translated by E. Kelemen. Paris: Nagel, 1948.

Machovec, Milan. *A Marxist Looks at Jesus*. Philadelphia: Fortress, 1976.

Mahan, Brian, and L. Dale Richesin, eds. *The Challenge of Liberation Theology: A First World Response*. Maryknoll, N.Y.: Orbis Books, 1981.

McCann, Dennis P. *Christian Realism and Liberation Theology: Practical Theologies in Creative Conflict*. Maryknoll, N.Y.: Orbis Books, 1981.

McGovern, Arthur F. *Marxism: An American Christian Perspective*. Maryknoll, N.Y.: Orbis Books.

Mecham, J. Lloyd. *The Church and State in Latin America*. Chapel Hill, NC: University of North Carolina Press, 1966.

Merkle, Judith. "The Fundamental Ethics of Juan Luis Segundo." Ph.D. diss., University of St. Michael's College, Toronto, 1985.

Muñoz, Ronaldo. *Nueva conciencia de la Iglesia en America Latina*. Materiales 1. Salamanca: Ediciones Sígueme, 1974.

_____. *La Iglesia en el pueblo: Hacia una eclesiología latinoamericana*. Lima: Centro de Estudios y Publicaciones, 1983.

Neal, Marie Augusta. *A Socio-Theology of Letting Go: The Role of a First World Church Facing Third World Peoples*. New York: Paulist Press, 1977.

Novak, Michael. *Will It Liberate? Questions About Liberation Theology*. New York: Paulist Press, 1986.

Oliveros Maqueo, Roberto. *Liberación y teología: Genesis y crecimiento de una reflexión 1966-1977*. Lima: Centro de Estudios y Publicaciones, 1977.

Persha, Gerald L. *Juan Luis Segundo: A Study Concerning the Relationship Between the Particularity of the Church and the Universality of Her Mission (1963-1977).* Maryknoll, N.Y.: Orbis Books, Probe Series, 1979.

Pike, Frederick B. *Spanish America 1900-1970: Tradition and Social Innovation.* New York: W. W. Norton and Company, 1973.

Pohier, Jacques, and Dietmar Mieth, eds. *The Dignity of the Despised of the Earth. Concilium* 130. New York: Seabury Press, 1979.

Porzecanski, Arturo C., *Uruguay's Tupamaros: The Urban Guerrilla.* New York, Washington, London: Praeger Publishers, 1973.

Quiroz Magaña, Alvaro. *Eclesiología en la teología de la liberación.* Verdad e Imágen 78. Salamanca: Ediciones Sígueme, 1983.

Rad, Gerhard von. *Old Testament Theology*, Vol. I. Translated by D. M. G. Stalker. New York: Harper & Brothers, 1962.

_____. *Old Testament Theology*, Vol. II. Translated by D. M. G. Stalker. New York: Harper and Row, 1965.

Ramos Regidor, José. *Jesús y el despertar de los oprimidos.* Translated by Alfonso Ortiz García. Verdad e Imágen 85. Salamanca: Ediciones Sígueme, 1984. *Gesú e il risveglio delli oppressi.* Milan: A. Mondadori Ed. S. p. A., 1981.

Ritt, Paul E. "The Concept of the Lordship of Jesus Christ in the Christologies of Hans Urs von Balthasar and Juan Luis Segundo." Ph.D. diss., Catholic University of America, Washington, D.C., 1988.

Sanders, E. P. *Jesus and Judaism.* Philadelphia: Fortress Press, 1985.

Schall, James V. *Liberation Theology in Latin America.* San Francisco: Ignatius Press, 1982.

Skidmore, Thomas E., and Peter H. Smith. *Modern Latin America.* New York: Oxford University Press, 1984.

Sobrino, Jon. *The True Church and the Poor.* Translated by Matthew J. O'Connell. Maryknoll, N.Y.: Orbis Books, 1981. *Resurrección de la verdadera Iglesia: Los pobres, lugar teológico de la eclesiología.* Santander: Editorial Sal Terrae, 1981.

_____. *Jesus in Latin America.* Maryknoll, N.Y.: Orbis Books, 1987. *Jesús en América Latina: Su significado para la fe y la cristología.* San Salvador: Universidad Centroamericana, and Santander: Editorial Sal Terrae, 1982.

The Social Teachings of Pope John Paul II. Social Thought 13 (Spring-Summer 1987).

Tambasco, Anthony. *The Bible for Ethics: Juan Luis Segundo and First-World Ethics.* Washington, D.C.: University Press of America, 1981.

Teilhard de Chardin, Pierre. *The Activation of Energy,* first American edition. Translated by René Hague. New York: Harcourt, Brace, Jovanovich, Inc., 1970. *L'activation de l'énergie.* Paris: Éd. du Seuil, 1963.

_____. *The Divine Milieu.* New York: Harper & Row; London: William Collins Sons & Co., Ltd., 1960. Edited by Bernard Wall from *Le Milieu Divin.* Paris: Éditions du Seuil, 1957.

_____. *The Phenomenon of Man,* revised English edition. New York: Harper and Row, 1965. *Le phénomène humaine.* Paris: Éd. du Seuil, 1955.

Vekemans, Roger. *Caesar and God: The Priesthood and Politics.* Translated by Aloysius Owen and Charles U. Quinn. Maryknoll, N.Y.: Orbis Books, 1972.

Vorgrimler, Herbert, ed. *Commentary on the Documents of Vatican II,* 5 vols. New York: Herder and Herder, 1967.

ARTICLES

Assmann, Hugo. "Os Ardís do amor em busca de sua eficacia: As reflexões de Juan Luis Segundo sobre 'O Homem de Hoje Diante de Jesus de Nazaré.' " *Perspectiva Teologica* 15 (No. 36, 1983): 223-259.

Baum, Gregory. "The Theological Method of Segundo's *The Liberation of Theology.*" *Catholic Theological Society of America: Proceedings* 32 (1977): 120-24.

_____. "Liberation Theology and Marxism." *Ecumenist* 25 (Jan.-Feb. 1987): 22-26.

Berten, Ignace. "The Poor in Roman Ecclesiology." *Theology Digest* 34 (Summer 1987): 154-58.

Boff, Leonardo. "Teologia a escuto do povo." *Revista Eclesiastica Brasileira* 41 (1981): 55-118.

Büntig, Aldo. "Dimensiones del catolicismo popular latinoamericano y su inserción en el proceso de liberación. Diagnóstico y reflexiones pastorales." Chap. in *Fe cristiana y cambio social en América latina.* Encuentro de El Escorial, 1972. Instituto Fe y Secularidad. Edited by Alfonso Alvarez Bolado. Salamanca: Ediciones Sígueme, 1973.

Comblin, Joseph. "La Conferencia episcopal de Puebla." *Mensaje* (Marzo-Abril 1979): 117-23.

Cormie, Lee. "The Hermeneutical Privilege of the Oppressed: Liberation Theologies, Biblical Faith, and Marxist Sociology of Knowledge." *Proceedings CTSA* 33 (1978): 155-81.

Dussel, Enrique. "Current Events in Latin America." Chap. in *The Challenge of Basic Christian Communities*. Papers from the International Congress of Theology, February-March 1980, São Paulo, Brazil. Edited by Sergio Torres and John Eagleson; translated by John Drury. Maryknoll, N.Y.: Orbis Books, 1981.

Ellacuría, Ignacio. "La Iglesia de los pobres sacramento histórico de liberación." *Estudios Centroamericanos* 32 (Oct.-Nov. 1977): 707-21.

Haight, Roger. "The Mission of the Church in the Theology of the Social Gospel." *Theological Studies* 49 (Sept. 1988): 477-97.

Harrington, Daniel J. "The Jewishness of Jesus: Facing Some Problems." *Catholic Biblical Quarterly* 49 (Jan. 1987): 1-13.

Hellwig, Monika K. "Good News to the Poor: Do They Understand It Better?" Chap. in *Tracing the Spirit: Communities, Social Action, and Theological Reflection*. Edited by James E. Hug. New York: Paulist Press, 1983.

Hennelly, Alfred T. "The Challenge of Juan Luis Segundo." *Theological Studies* 38 (March 1977): 125-35.

_____. "Theological Method: The Southern Exposure." *Theological Studies* 38 (December 1977): 709-35.

_____. "Steps to a Theology of Mind." *Newsletter*. American Academy of Religion. The Currents in Contemporary Christology Group: Papers for the Annual Meeting. Vol 8 (November 1988): 23-32.

Idigoras, José Luis. "¿La salvación al margen de la fe." *Revista Teológica Limense* 15 (No. 2, 1981): 181-201.

Jiménez Limón, Javier. "Sobre la `Cristología' de Juan Luis Segundo." *Christus* 49 (Agosto 1984): 57-61.

Johnson, Elizabeth. "Christology and Social Justice: John Paul II and the American Bishops." *Chicago Studies* 26 (Aug. 1987): 155-65.

Leech, Kenneth. "Liberating Theology: The Thought of Juan Luis Segundo." *Theology* 84 (July 1981): 258-66.

Lernoux, Penny. "The Long Path to Puebla." Chap. in *Puebla and Beyond: Documentation and Commentary*. Edited by John Eagleson and Philip Scharper. Maryknoll, N.Y.: Orbis Books, 1979.

Lord, Elizabeth. "Human History and the Kingdom of God: Past Perspectives and Those of J. L. Segundo." *Heythrop Journal* 30 (1989): 293-305.

Marx, Karl. "Theses on Feuerbach." Chap. in *On Religion*. By Karl Marx and Friedrich Engels. Introduction by Reinhold Niebuhr. *Classics in Religious Studies* 3. Chico, Calif.: Scholars Press, 1982.

Marx, Karl, and Friedrich Engels. "German Ideology," selection. Chap. in *On Religion*. By Karl Marx and Friedrich Engels. Introduction by Reinhold Niebuhr. *Classics in Religious Studies* 3. Chico, Calif.: Scholars Press, 1982.

_____. "The Holy Family, or Critique of Critical Criticism," selection. Chap. in *On Religion*. By Karl Marx and Friedrich Engels. Introduction by Reinhold Niebuhr. *Classics in Religious Studies* 3. Chico, Calif.: Scholars Press, 1982.

McCann, Dennis P. "Political Ideologies and Practical Theology: Is There a Difference?" *Union Seminary Quarterly Review* 36 (Summer 1981): 243-57.

McGovern, Arthur F. "The Bible in Latin American Liberation Theology." Chap. in *Marxism: An American Christian Perspective*. Maryknoll, N.Y.: Orbis Books, 1980.

McGovern, Arthur F., and Thomas L. Shubeck. "Updating Liberation Theology." *America* 159 (July 9-16, 1988): 32-35+.

McGrath, Marcos. "The Impact of *Gaudium et Spes*: Medellín, Puebla, and Pastoral Creativity." Chap. in *The Church and Culture Since Vatican II: The Experience of North and Latin America*. Edited by Joseph Gremillion. Notre Dame, IN: University of Notre Dame Press, 1985.

Meier, John. "The Bible as a Source for Theology [A Critique of the Use of Scripture by Jon Sobrino and Juan Luis Segundo]." *Proceedings CTSA* 43 (1988): 1-14.

Moltmann, Jürgen. "An Open Letter to José Míguez Bonino." *Christianity and Crisis* (March 29, 1976):

Myre, André. " 'Heureux les pauvres': histoire passée et future d'une parole." Chap. in *Cri de Dieu: Espoir des pauvres*. Edited by P.-A. Giguère, J. Martucci, and A. Myre. Montreal: Éditions Paulines, 1977.

Nealen, Mary Kaye. "The Poor in J. L. Segundo's Christology: the Synoptics and Paul." *Newsletter*. American Academy of Religion. The Currents in Contemporary Christology Group: Papers for the Annual Meeting. Vol. 8 (November 1988): 1-11.

O'Donnell, James G. "The Influence of Freud's Hermeneutic of Suspicion on the Writings of Juan Segundo." *Journal of Psychology and Theology* 10 (Spring 1982): 28-34.

Padilla, René. "Liberation Theology." Chap. in *The Challenge of Marxist and Neo-Marxist Ideologies for Christian Scholarship*. Third International Conference,

Institute of Christian Higher Education, 1981. Edited by J. Vander Stelt. Sioux Center, Iowa: Dordt College Press, 1982.

Peel, David R. "Juan Luis Segundo's *A Theology for Artisans of a New Humanity*: A Latin American Contribution to Contemporary Theological Understanding." *Perkins Journal of Theology* 30 (Spring 1977): 1-9.

Pike, Frederick B. "Catholicism in Latin America." Chap. in *The Church in a Secularized Society*. Vol. V, *The Christian Centuries*. By Roger Aubert et al. London: Darton, Longman, and Todd, 1978, and New York: Paulist Press, 1978.

Pottenger, John R. "Liberation Theology: Its Methodological Foundation for Violence." Chap. in *The Morality of Terrorism: Religious and Secular Justifications*. Edited by David C. Rapoport and Jonah Alexander. Pergamon Policy Studies on International Politics. N.Y.: Pergamon Press, 1982.

Richards, Glyn. "Faith and Praxis in Liberation Theology, Bonhoeffer and Gandhi." *Modern Theology* 3 (No. 4, 1987): 359-73.

Roberts, J. Deotis. "Hermeneutics: History and Providence." Chap. in *Hermeneutics and Horizons: The Shape of the Future*. Proceedings of Bahamas' Seminar on Hermeneutics and Divine Principle, 1980. Edited by Frank K. Flinn. New York: Rose of Sharon Press, 1982.

Sandoval, Moises. "Report from the Conference." Chap. in *Puebla and Beyond: Documentation and Commentary*. Edited by John Eagleson and Philip Scharper. Maryknoll, N.Y.: Orbis Books, 1979.

Scannone, Juan Carlos. "Theology, Popular Culture, and Discernment." Chap. in *Frontiers of Theology in Latin America*. Edited by Rosino Gibellini and translated by John Drury. Maryknoll, N.Y.: Orbis Books, 1975.

Schüssler Fiorenza, Elizabeth. "The Function of Scripture in the Liberation Struggle [article about Segundo]." Chap. in *Bread Not Stone: The Challenge of Feminist Biblical Interpretation*. Boston: Beacon Press, 1984.

Schweiker, William. "The Liberation of Theology and the Revolution of Love: an Engagement with Juan Luis Segundo's *Faith and Ideologies*." *Newsletter*. American Academy of Religion. The Currents in Contemporary Christology Group: Papers for the Annual Meeting. Vol. 8 (November 1988): 33-45.

Sobrino, Jon. "The Significance of Puebla for the Catholic Church in Latin America." Chap. in *Puebla and Beyond: Documentation and Commentary*. Edited by John Eagleson and Philip Scharper. Maryknoll, N.Y.: Orbis Books, 1979.

_____. "Instrucción sobre libertad cristiana y liberación." *Estudios Centroamericanos* 41 (Abril 1986): 335-41.

Starkloff, Carl. "The Church, Racism and North American Natives [about Segundo]." Chap. in *The Church and Racism. Concilium* 151. Edited by Gregory Baum and John Coleman. N.Y.: Seabury Press, 1982.

Stumme, John. "Biblioteca: Juan Luis Segundo, *El hombre de hoy ante Jesús de Nazaret.*" *Cuadernos de Teología* 7 (No. 3, 1986): 197-209).

Taborda, Francisco. "Métodos teológicos na América Latina." *Perspectiva teologica* 19 (1987): 293-319.

Tripole, Martin R. "Segundo's Liberation Theology vs. an Eschatological Ecclesiology of the Kingdom." *Thomist* 45 (Jan. 1981): 1-25.

Verkamp, Bernard J. "On Doing the Truth: Orthopraxis and the Theologian [about Segundo]." *Theological Studies* 49 (March 1988): 3-14.

Wells, Harold. "Segundo's Hermeneutical Circle." *Journal of Theology of South Africa* 34 (March 1981): 25-31.

_____. "The Question of Ideological Determination in Liberation Theology." *Toronto Journal of Theology* 3 (Fall 1987): 209-220.

Zimbelman, Joel. "Christology and Political Theology in the Thought of Juan Luis Segundo, S.J." *Newsletter.* American Academy of Religion. The Currents in Contemporary Christology Group: Papers for the Annual Meeting. Vol. 8 (November 1988): 12-23.

BOOK REVIEWS

Teología abierta/ A Theology for the Artisans of a New Humanity

Bracken, Joseph A. *Theological Studies* 36 (Dec. 1975): 791-5.

Davis, James J. (Vol. I and II). *Thomist* 38 (Oct. 1974): 978.

Neuhaus, Richard J. *Commonweal* 102 (July 4, 1975): 243-6.

Primavesi, Anne. *New Blackfriars* 62 (May 1981): 214-16.

Ribeiro Guimarães, Almir. *Revista Eclesiastica Brasileira* 37 (Set. 1977): 653.

Sell, Alan P. F. *Philosophical Studies* 28 (1981): 270-3.

Swanston, H. *New Blackfriars* 62 (Jan. 1981): 46-8.

Sweeney, John. "For the Builders of a New Ireland: The Theology of Juan Luis Segundo." *Furrow* 31 (Dec. 1980): 783-9.

Teología abierta, revised edition

Estudios eclesiasticos 61 (1986): 452-3.

Folgado Flórez, S. *La Ciudad de Dios* (Madrid) 199 (Enero-Abril 1986): 133-4.

The Community Called Church

Kilian, Sabbas. *Thought* 50 (Mar. 1975): 105-6.

Léonard, Gustave-Pierre. *Cross Currents* 25 (Spring 1975): 93-101.

The Sacraments Today

Budde, John. *Louvain Studies* 8 (Fall 1980): 211-12.

Hogan, John P. *The American Ecclesiastical Review* 169 (Dec. 1975): 712.

Kiesling, Christopher. *Cross and Crown* 27 (March 1975): 78-80.

Swift, Nancy. *The Living Light* 12 (Winter 1975): 620-21.

Evolution and Guilt

Silva, Sergio. *Mensaje* (Santiago) 23 (Nov. 1974): 587-9.

The Liberation of Theology

Burrell, David. *St. Luke's Journal of Theology* 21 (March 1978): 157-58.

Casey, Stephen J. *Best Sellers* 36 (Jan. 1977): 343.

Haight, Roger. *Emmanuel* 83 (No. 12, 1977): 605-10.

Hennelly, Alfred T. *Theological Studies* 38 (March 1977): 125-35.

Hollenweger, Walter J. *Expository Times* 88 (Summer 1977): 381.

Kress, Robert. *Horizons* (CTS) 4 (Spring 1977): 132-5.

McCann, Dennis P. *Religious Studies Review* 3 (April 1977): 98-105.

Ribeiro Guimarães, Almir. *Revista Eclesiastica Brasiliera* 39 (Mar. 1979): 171-2.

Russell, L. *Theology Today* 34 (July 1977): 222-24.

Sell, Alan. *Philosophical Studies* 26 (1977): 302-5.

Silva, Sergio. *Mensaje* 25 (Dic. 1976): 671-3.

Smith, S. E. *Missiology* 5 (April 1977): 245-48.

Song, Choan-Seng. *Occidental Bulletin of Missionary Research* 1 (Jan. 1977): 29.

Taborda, F. *Perspectiva Teologica* 19 (Nov.-Dez. 1987): 405.

Velasco Yañez, David. *Christus* 41 (March 1976): 61-2.

Hidden Motives for Pastoral Action

Hennelly, Alfred. *Theological Studies* 39 (Dec. 1978):   807-8.

MacEoin, Gary. *Cross Currents* 28 (Spring 1978): 106-8.

Mattern, Evelyn. *Journal of Ecumenical Studies* 16 (Spring 1979): 335-6.

Ribeiro Guimarães, Almir. *Revista Eclesiastica Brasileira* 38 (Dez. 1978): 770.

Snell, Priscilla. *Irish Theological Quarterly* 45 (No. 4, 1978): 288-91.

El hombre de hoy ante Jesús de Nazaret/ Jesus of Nazareth Yesterday and Today

Hennelly, Alfred T. "The Search for a Liberating Christology." *Religious Studies Review* 15 (January 1989): 45-7.

Hewitt, Marsha Aileen.   "The Search for a Liberating Christology." *Religious Studies Review* 15 (January 1989): 47-51.

Marlé, René. "Foi, idéologie, religion chez J.-L. Segundo." *Recherches de science religieuse* 76 (No. 2, 1988): 267-82.

Faith and Ideologies

Goizueta, Roberto S. *Horizons* (CTS) 12 (Fall 1985): 395-6.

Haight, Roger. *America* 151 (Sept. 29, 1984): 173.

_____. *Cross Currents* 34 (Spring 1984): 106-9.

Shinn, Roger L. *International Bulletin of Missionary Research* 10 (Jan. 1986): 10.

Stumme, Juan R. *Cuadernos de Teología* 7 (No. 3, 1986): 197-209.

Stumme, Juan R., and Juan C. Michel. *Cuadernos de Teología* 8 (No. 1, 1987): 87-101.

West, Cornel. *Commonweal* 111 (Jan. 27, 1984): 53-7.

Williams, T. S. M. *New Blackfriars* 66 (May 1985): 252-3.

The Historical Jesus of the Synoptics

Assmann, Hugo. *Perspectiva Teologica* 15 (No. 36, 1983): 223-59.

Dupuis, Jacques. *Gregorianum* 67 (1986): 551-3.

Haight, Roger. *Cross Currents* 36 (Spring 1986): 85-90.

Jiménez Limón, Javier. *Christus* 49 (Agosto 1984): 57-61.

Leonard, Ellen. *America* 155 (Aug. 9, 1986): 57-9.

Nevin, Michael. *Month* 19 (Mar. 1986): 106.

Schafer, Steven. *Ecumenist* 25 (May-June 1987), 62.

Williams, Trevor. *New Blackfriars* 67 (April 1987): 201-2.

The Humanist Christology of Paul

Deidun, T. *Month* 20 (June 1987): 242.

Dollen, Charles. *Priest* 43 (March 1987): 45.

Haight, Roger. *Cross Currents* 13 (Summer 1987): 99-104.

Hodgson, Peter E. *Month* 20 (June 1987): 242.

Turro, James C. *Catholic Biblical Quarterly* 50 (1988): 146-7.

The Christ of the Ignatian Exercises

Taborda, Francisco. "Métodos teológicos na América Latina." *Perspectiva teologica* 19 (1987): 293-319.

Theology and the Church

Dulles, Avery. *Theology Today* 43 (Oct. 1986): 427-30.

Hebblethwaite, Peter. *Tablet* 239 (Aug. 17, 1985).

Hennelly, Alfred. *Theological Studies* 47 (Summer 1986): 531-33.

_____. *America* 155 (Sept. 27, 1986): 152-5.

Kress, Robert. *Horizons* (CTS) 14 (Fall 1987): 391.

DATE DUE

HIGHSMITH 45-220